Evelyn Waugh and the
Forms of His Time

VOLUME I

Contexts and Literature

General Editor: Virgil Nemoianu

Robert Murray Davis

Evelyn Waugh and the Forms of His Time

The Catholic University of America Press
Washington, D.C.

Publication of this book has been funded in part by a
gift to the Associates of The Catholic University of
America Press by Dr. Mary Ann F. Rizzo.

**LIBRARY OF CONGRESS CATALOGING-IN-
PUBLICATION DATA**

Davis, Robert Murray.
   Evelyn Waugh and the forms of his time / Robert Murray
Davis.
      p. cm. —(Contexts and literature ; v. 1)
   Bibliography: p.
   Includes index.
   1. Waugh, Evelyn, 1903–1966—Criticism and
interpretation.
I. Title. II. Series.
PR6045.A97Z634 1989
823'.912—dc19   88–16161
ISBN 0–8132–0677–4

For Charles E. Linck, Jr.,
and Paul A. Doyle

Contents

Preface / ix
Acknowledgments / xiii
Works Cited Parenthetically / xv

Section I: Early Milieux

1. Imagining Defeat / 3
2. Shrinking Gardens: The Comic-Satiric Novel from Douglas to Waugh / 13
3. The Context of Waugh's Early Novels / 30

Section II: Formulating Theory

4. Waugh's Mind and Art / 51
5. Waugh on Fiction / 68
6. Waugh as Editor / 90

Section III: Applying Theory

7. Waugh's Juvenilia / 115
8. Context and Structure in *Vile Bodies* / 128
9. Toward a Mature Style: The Making of *Remote People* / 146
10. Waugh Edits Waugh: Author versus Reviser / 165
11. The Failure of Imagination: Waugh's School Stories / 178

Section IV: Later Milieux

12. The Rhetoric of Mexican Travel: Greene and Waugh / 191

13. <u>Recovering the Past</u>: Postwar First-Person Novels / 203

14. *Love Among the Ruins:* Text and Contexts / 220

Conclusion: Waugh and the Generation of Decline / 245

Works Cited / 255
Index / 261

Preface

Evelyn Waugh and the Forms of His Time is a complement rather than a sequel to my earlier study of the growth of Waugh's texts, *Evelyn Waugh, Writer* (Pilgrim Books, 1981), which focused almost exclusively on Waugh's attitudes as they affected the composition and revision of his novels. This study looks outward, at some of the literary contexts in which Waugh can be seen and in which he saw himself. It is consciously less definitive, or at any rate less definite, than its predecessor, but I think that it represents not merely a valid but an inevitable direction in the study of Waugh's work in the literary contexts of his time.

This study draws on essays published separately over the past twenty years, though all of the material has been revised and in some cases reconceived in light of material not available at the time of first publication—notably Waugh's *Diaries* and *Letters* and a large body of his nonfiction.

Moreover, in reconsidering this material, I have been able to see not only what I and others had done but what, though it might be implicit, we had failed to do. While there has been plenty of attention paid to Waugh's life and to individual works and even to recurring themes and techniques in his work, there has been almost no thorough discussion of the context in which he wrote. There have been casual comparisons between his novels and those of Aldous Huxley or broad historical generalizations about his place among Catholic novelists or novelists of the 1930's, but not since James Hall's *The Tragic Comedians* (Indiana University Press, 1963) has there been a serious attempt to place his work in even a social or thematic, let alone a generic, context except in the most casual and often the most tendentious way.

The reasons for this were fairly obvious. Twenty-five years ago, Waugh's critical reputation was so uncertain that those of us who thought his work valuable but who wished to be taken seriously as scholars and critics were forced to discover a context in which that might be possible. Most of us were not confident enough to place him in direct competition even with Graham Greene, let alone secular existentialists. Furthermore, though Waugh died in 1966, it was difficult to see him in a really historical perspective or to realize that he had not been a modernist, not because he could not write in modernist modes or with a modernist vision but because he wished to do quite other kinds of work for different purposes.

Northrop Frye and Wayne Booth offered critical and generic approaches by which to break out of post-Jamesian, New Critical, and Trillingesque novel-centered criticism and to consider Waugh as a serious artist working in a different form. In defining the genres in which he worked, other scholars and I were led to the work of predecessors such as Norman Douglas, Ronald Firbank, and Aldous Huxley and to that of successors such as Joseph Heller, Thomas Pynchon, John Barth, and other novelists now almost forgotten. At the same time, it seemed clear that Waugh's supposed nostalgia for the Edwardian age was not peculiar to his idiosyncratic Tory Catholicism but was shared by a number of writers whose opinions, or the critical perception of them, were quite different. If Waugh were to be understood rather than defended, it seemed clear and now seems even clearer, he would have to be seen in the historic contexts of his class, his generation, and his chosen genres. Furthermore, it has become increasingly obvious that the body of Waugh's work can best be understood not synchronically, as if his methods and themes were constant, but diachronically, as they developed and changed over the more than four decades of his career as an apprentice and a professional writer.

Evelyn Waugh and the Forms of His Time is organized with these concerns in mind. The first three essays deal with the imaginative and literary contexts in which Waugh developed. "Imagining Defeat" argues that he has more in common with his contemporaries than has been generally assumed. The two essays which follow place his work in specific generic contexts of writers from whose methods he could learn and of those whose formulas he could adapt and transcend.

The three essays of Section II deal more specifically with Waugh's habits of mind as man and writer and with the ways in which those habits were manifested in his fiction, in his theories, and in his editing of others' work.

The third section shows Waugh in the process of creating a voice, of changing that voice, and finally of attempting to combine early material with late style in a work which he could not bring to completion. The fourth section considers his work, major and minor, in the context of his major contemporaries, especially Graham Greene, a writer with whom he has been casually linked for forty years but with whom he has never been compared in detail. The final chapter suggests ways in which social and literary contexts can be established for his literary generation.

Other approaches are obviously valid, and I have learned a great deal from other students of Waugh. Jeffrey Heath, Jerome Meckier, and Martin Stannard have not always agreed with me, but they have caused me to reexamine some of my earlier positions. Leszek Kolek made me do so by adapting and extending one of my early arguments in directions where I might not have taken it. The late D. Paul Farr reminded me of some features of Waugh's Edwardian background, and the late Marston LaFrance showed me how important to the study of Waugh is a sense of humor. Donat Gallagher not only gave me copies of materials unavailable in the United States but strongly influenced my contextual approach to Waugh. Winnifred M. Bogaards is one of many friends here and abroad who have given me encouragement and support.

In practical terms, I am in the debt of innumerable librarians and journal editors, especially the late Nicholas Joost, the best copy editor with whom I have worked. Barbara Hillyer Davis and Jeanette Gregory Harris read early versions of most of the chapters and made valuable suggestions.

The dedication acknowledges special debts. My collaboration with Charles E. Linck, Jr., caused me to take a new approach to the study of Waugh. Paul A. Doyle, besides offering encouragement, support, and information for almost twenty years, is the only person who ever accused me of being too nice.

Acknowledgments

This book draws on material previously published, though all of that material has been revised, cut, and augmented. Chapter by chapter, material has been adapted from the following: Chapter 1: "Introduction," *Modern British Short Novels* (Scott, Foresman, 1972). Chapter 2: "The Shrinking Garden and New Exits: The Comic-Satiric Novel in the Twentieth Century," *Kansas Quarterly*, 1 (Summer 1969). Chapter 4: "The Mind and Art of Evelyn Waugh," *Papers on Language and Literature*, 3 (Summer 1967). Chapter 5: "Evelyn Waugh and the Art of Fiction," *Papers on Language and Literature*, 2 (Summer 1966) in an early version; "Waugh on Fiction," *Les Années 30* (February 1987), in a later version. Chapter 6: "How Waugh Cut Merton," *Month*, NS 6 (April 1973), and "Grace Beyond the Reach of Sullen Art: Waugh Edits Merton," *Journal of Modern Literature*, 13 (March 1986). Chapter 7: "Introduction," *Evelyn Waugh, Apprentice* (Pilgrim Books, 1985) and *Evelyn Waugh Newsletter*, 10 (Winter 1976). Chapter 8: "The Bright Young People in *Vile Bodies*," *Papers on Language and Literature*, 5 (Winter 1969), written in collaboration with Charles E. Linck, Jr., and "Title, Theme, and Structure in *Vile Bodies*," *Southern Humanities Review*, 11 (Winter 1977). Chapter 9: "Towards a Mature Style: The Manuscript of Waugh's *Remote People*," *Analytical & Enumerative Bibliography*, 7 (1983). Chapter 10: Review of Hershel Parker, *Flawed Texts and Verbal Icons*, *Genre*, 18 (Summer 1985). Chapter 11: "The Failure of Imagination: Waugh's School Stories," *London Magazine*, 25 (April/May 1985). Chapter 12: "The Rhetoric of Mexican Travel," *Renascence*, 38 (Spring 1986). Chapter 13: "*Brideshead Revisited* and *All the King's Men*: Towards a Definition of For-

ties Sensibility," *Evelyn Waugh Newsletter*, 14 (Autumn 1980), and
"The Struggle with Genre in *The End of the Affair*," *Genre*, 18 (Winter 1985). Chapter 14: *Modern British Short Novels* (Scott, Foresman, 1972), and "Shaping a World: The Textual History of *Love Among the Ruins*," *Analytical and Enumerative Bibliography*, 1 (April 1977), and "Waugh and the Generation of Decline": "Bloomsbury—And After?" *South Central Review*, 3 (Summer 1986).

Works Cited Parenthetically

Diaries *The Diaries of Evelyn Waugh*, ed. Michael Davie. Boston: Little, Brown, 1976.

EAR   *The Essays, Articles and Reviews of Evelyn Waugh*, ed. Donat Gallagher. Boston: Little, Brown, 1984.

Letters *The Letters of Evelyn Waugh*, ed. Mark Amory. New Haven and New York: Ticknor & Fields, 1980.

Catalogue Davis, Robert Murray. *A Catalogue of the Evelyn Waugh Collection at the Humanities Research Center, The University of Texas at Austin*. Troy: Whitson, 1981.

Early Milieux

CHAPTER I

Imagining Defeat

For at least the past thirty years, discussions of modern British fiction have tended to be as much lament as analysis: a recent article titled "Why Is the English Novel So Boring?" is unusual only for its drama.[1] Critics have deplored or bewailed the decline in experiment, scope, and energy; publishers fear that rising costs will destroy the market for new writers;[2] and until very recently literary historians have been reluctant to cross the magic border of 1930 (D. H. Lawrence's death) or 1939 (*Finnegan's Wake*) to explore the terra incognita of the modern novel.[3] The difficulties are obvious: once past the peaks of Conrad, Joyce, Lawrence, and Woolf, the student encounters ranges of writers more or less equal in talent whose similarity makes them seem smaller than they really are.

Although Evelyn Waugh is not usually regarded—and never regarded himself—as a literary historian, he was a wide and astute

1. Brian McHale, "Why Is the English Novel So Boring? Or Who Killed Bryan Johnson?" *American Book Review*, 8 (January-February 1986), 1, 7–8. McHale blames the dominance of "a realism that has succeeded in assimilating the most readily domesticated scraps of modernist practice, in particular modernism's focus on The Inner Life." Waugh, of course, tries to break that dominance in his early fiction. Further, if unwitting, confirmation of the judgment in the title is provided in David Leon Higdon's *Shadows of the Past in Contemporary British Fiction* (Athens: University of Georgia Press, 1985), which makes the best possible case for a number of writers who, in quotation, seem worthy but undistinguished.

2. See J. A. Sutherland, *Fiction and the Fiction Industry* (London: University of London/Athlone Press, 1978).

3. Two major exceptions, neither quite satisfactory in discussing the novel, are Samuel Hynes, *The Auden Generation: Literature and Politics in England in the 1930's* (New York: Viking, 1976) and Bernard Bergonzi, *Reading the Thirties: Texts and Contexts* (Pittsburgh: University of Pittsburgh Press, 1978). James Hall's *The Tragic Comedians* (Bloomington: Indiana University Press, 1963) is in many ways still the best discussion of the English novel after modernism.

3

reader and, torn between pride in his craft and distaste for any products of the modern world, put the case for his contemporaries in positive terms:

It may happen in the next hundred years that the English novelists of the present day [1957] will come to be valued as we now value the artists and craftsmen of the late eighteenth century. The originators, the exuberant men, are extinct and in their place subsists and modestly flourishes a generation notable for elegance and variety of contrivance. It may well happen that there are lean years ahead in which our posterity will look back hungrily to this period, when there was so much will and so much ability to please.[4]

"Elegance and variety of contrivance" have not been popular in recent years and with the rise of poststructuralism have come to be discounted almost entirely. Furthermore, serious readers tend to regard a "desire to please" as obsequious courting of the audience or as mere entertainment.[5]

For these and for a variety of historical and broadly cultural reasons, critics of the modern British novel and nonspecialist critics of Waugh's novels in particular have focused less on what they have done than on what they do not do. But only when we begin to understand those limits can we begin to assess the artistic achievement within them.

In order to do so, it is necessary to invoke generalizations about the culture in which these novels were written. Scholars argue that the classic English novel was the product of bourgeois society,[6] that its theme "is essentially that of formation, of education,"[7] or that it dealt with "learning how to dispense with fantasy."[8] These statements all presuppose a confidence in the coherence of the society and its continuation into an indefinite future, and even tragic novels

4. Evelyn Waugh, *The Ordeal of Gilbert Pinfold* (Boston: Little, Brown, 1957), p. 3.

5. For example, Steven Marcus, "Evelyn Waugh and the Art of Entertainment," *Partisan Review*, 23 (Summer 1956), 348–357.

6. See especially Ian Watt, *The Rise of the Novel* (Berkeley: University of California Press, 1957).

7. Maurice Z. Shroder, "The Novel as a Genre," *Massachusetts Review*, 4 (Winter 1963), 254.

8. Barbara Hardy, "Towards a Poetics of Fiction: 3) An Approach through Narrative," *Novel*, 2 (Fall 1968), 12.

such as *Wuthering Heights* or *The Mayor of Casterbridge* invoke at the end a peaceful world which the survivors, lesser but more stable people than the protagonists—and surrogates for the middle-class reader—can gracefully inhabit. The basic optimism about the possibilities of human character and human society for change and development within and without led critics such as Lionel Trilling and W. J. Harvey to identify the novel as the characteristic form of liberalism, essentially a melioristic, humanistic philosophy.[9]

Most English novelists of the twentieth century have had bourgeois origins—if one is willing to use the considerable elasticity of that term to cover people like Elizabeth Bowen and Ronald Firbank—and many of them came from a class which was at the same time the result and the source of liberal thought, called by Waugh "the moneyless, landless, educated gentry who managed the country,"[10] oriented toward Oxford and Cambridge and toward the Oxbridge-Bloomsbury-London West End world. Obviously, exceptions abound—Joyce, Lawrence, Conrad, and all artists can be regarded as aliens in some fashion—but all found major sources of support and encouragement among the higher bourgeoisie. Perhaps the outsiders were first to detect the malaise of English society, so that Michael Arlen's *The Green Hat* is a more obvious critique of English society than Aldous Huxley's *Antic Hay*. But those immersed in the culture also recognized the unavoidable and unmistakable signs of decay and helped to shift the novel from its traditional orientation toward a new subject, a subject characteristic of the British novel in the twentieth century: the undermining and destruction of the middle class, or, what may amount to the same thing, of that group's conception of itself and therefore of the civilization which gave rise to it.

Inevitably, this meant a shift in the traditional treatment of the individual in relation to society. Novelists of the previous two centuries conveyed the sense that the individual could pursue his own life parallel to if not entirely independent of society as mechanism.

---

9. Lionel Trilling, *The Liberal Imagination* (New York: Viking, 1950) and W. J. Harvey, *Character and the Novel* (Ithaca: Cornell University Press, 1965).

10. Evelyn Waugh, "Work Suspended," *Tactical Exercise* (Boston: Little, Brown, 1954), p. 135. The fragment was written in 1939 and first published in 1942.

Vanity Fair can continue; the major characters need not stay in it. Becky Sharp goes on being Becky Sharp while the Dobbin ménage retire to placid domesticity; Lady Booby returns to London and the consolations of a half-pay captain while Joseph Andrews lives the good life in the country. Waugh knew this pattern well enough to adapt it for *Decline and Fall*, in which Paul Pennyfeather is told that "life" need not be defined as motion on an amusement park wheel, that he has been thrown off that wheel because he is "static" rather than "dynamic," and that in effect it is all right to immure himself in Anglican orthodoxy.

But Waugh's ending, and his conception of society, differ profoundly from those of Fielding, Thackeray, and most of their contemporaries which made not only possible but inevitable the happy ending with its "distribution at the last of prizes, pensions, husbands, wives, babies, millions, appended paragraphs, and cheerful remarks"[11]—though James' last element does not adequately reflect the irony or melancholy of many endings otherwise covered by the description. Paul Pennyfeather knows what he is rejecting, and he has learned how to lie in order to protect a way of life which he values but in which he does not necessarily believe.

In fact, modern novelists have been much more aware than their precursors of the ways in which characters are immersed in and shaped by society, all the way from Conrad's Kurtz, to whose making "All Europe contributed," to Waugh's Miles Plastic in *Love Among the Ruins*: "No clean-living, God-fearing, Victorian gentleman . . . no complete man of the Renaissance; no gentil knight nor dutiful pagan nor, even, noble savage. . . . He was the Modern Man." Like Waugh, many novelists shifted their focus to society, using character in order to illustrate its effects and constructing plots which led to the characters' acquiescence or rebellion rather than to triumph or self-knowledge. (In many ways, John Fowles' *The French Lieutenant's Woman* is paradigmatic because it deals with all of these issues and manages to embrace all of the contradictions.) In part, the shift results from a loss of confidence in society, in part from a loss of a sense of immunity. The loss is treated in many

11. Henry James, "The Art of Fiction," reprinted widely.

ways, but pathos underlies the attitude of most authors. Even—perhaps especially—the comedians are touched by melancholy.

Like any historical process, the erosion of confidence and its portrayal in fiction were confused in their beginnings, intermittent in their workings, and uncertain in their results, but the theme of preparation for defeat can be traced through several stages. At first, authors sought to undercut late Victorian and Edwardian optimism by attacking its basic assumptions. Usually regarded as the spokesman for British imperialism, Rudyard Kipling ridiculed, in prose and verse, homegrown pieties and social certainties by testing them against the oppressive climate and moral ambiguities of India and against the struggles of the people who tried to govern the empire and themselves. In *Heart of Darkness*, Joseph Conrad denied that society is a civilizing force, though it can be a controlling force. In his vision, social forms, even laws, become nonsense in Africa, in fact serve to insulate human beings from reality. Or, what is better or worse, depending on the point of view, social restrictions can fall away completely, placing the individual in isolation in which he can appeal to nothing outside himself. Marlow compromises his principles and lies to Kurtz's Intended because he comes to see that only the strong can bear reality and that the weak, ignorant, and flabby (and, in *Nostromo*, even the ironic) need the old concept of society and value. Of course, he lets the secret out, and in a way the knowledge is exhilarating: man is not determined by society; he can confront the depths within himself.

But what if there is nothing beneath the surface; what if the primitive consciousness within man leads to minor confusion rather than to unspeakable rites; what if instead of horror there is merely nothing? Marlow's tale turns London into an immense darkness for one listener; for Saki and other writers of social satire, it becomes a tidy chessboard on which a class gone fat and soft maneuvers for illusory advantages within confines the characters do not even begin to realize. Comus Bassington, *The Unbearable Bassington* of Saki's novel, is taken like Kurtz and Marlow to central Africa, and he too begins to see that English society is only an excrescence, that not everyone necessarily has a soul, and—a step further than Marlow—that time is the nemesis of the way of life that he knows he can never escape. Kurtz at least has something to say and an audience to hear it; Comus is silent and alone.

Both Conrad and Saki predicted defeat for those strong enough or flawed enough to recognize it, but neither doubted that society would remain as a refuge for all the others. World War I moved Englishmen beyond doubt that society was coherent to near certainty that it was not. Figuratively, the war finished off those who had attacked Edwardian complacency from a sense of liberal optimism: E. M. Forster, John Galsworthy, Bernard Shaw, and others who continued to write but who had no real contact with the new world. Those with a taste for drama can date exactly the death of British innocence and confidence and of the European dream of progress through reason: 1, July 1916, the beginning of the Battle of the Somme, in which the British Army had nineteen thousand killed and fifty-seven thousand wounded on the first day alone. The battle lasted until November, with no gain on either side and over a million casualties.[12] One of them was Saki.

Some of the survivors later wrote fictional accounts, but disillusion with the war, with society, and indirectly with the novel as a liberal form found more enduring expression in the work of noncombatants such as Aldous Huxley and Ronald Firbank. In extreme formulations, all human societies were seen as bound to a cycle, whether Vico's, Spengler's, or Yeats', doomed to decline and fall as surely as they rose. From this prospect artists turned to various refuges: to an unillusioned and ironic nostalgia for a past in which dreams and confidence were possible, like the world which could allow Sir Christopher Wren at least to plan for if not to build a new London, described in Huxley's *Antic Hay*, or like the decorative and decadent quasi-Edwardian societies of Ronald Firbank's novels. Without a belief in society as a force, seeing it merely as a weight, Firbank, Huxley, and even Lawrence turned toward the individual who sought in isolation to preserve a sense of the self. Firbank was content to portray the problem; Huxley and Lawrence proposed solutions which ended in mysticism or extreme forms of personalism in such works as *Those Barren Leaves* and *The Man Who Died*.

12. A. J. P. Taylor, *English History 1914–1945*, vol. 9 of The Oxford History of England (New York: Oxford University Press, 1965), pp. 60–61.

In their most characteristic work, however, the endings are problematic, with more questions than answers, and a sense of unresolved, necessarily incomplete action which, if not defeat, is certainly not victory.[13]

Younger men, less able or willing to turn away from society and
the possibility of action in it, were ambivalent in a different way.
Acutely conscious of the identity of their generation, writers such
as Evelyn Waugh and Anthony Powell seemed to believe that to act
is to live, but they had a strong sense that action was not possible,
that for them there would be nothing to *do*. In novels like *A Handful
of Dust* and *Afternoon Men* the young hang about the fringes of conventional society, waiting for calls that never come or going
through meaningless and boring social rituals because they can
imagine no other way of life. Like their predecessors, though on a
less obviously humanistic-religious basis, the younger novelists
turned inward to find meaning. Individual aberrance and vitality
become proof of the individual's capacity for survival, especially
survival of boredom, and characters such as Waugh's Basil Seal (in
Black Mischief and *Put Out More Flags*) and Christopher Isherwood's
Mr. Norris (in *Mr. Norris Changes Trains*) enjoy flux and chaos as
escapes from society. But in *Black Mischief* Basil must return to an
England in which everyone has grown much poorer and duller and
in *Put Out More Flags* must ultimately profess a kind of patriotism
because the war gives him something to do and because he or at
least his creator realizes that up to this point he could indulge his
private whims only because society provided a context for them.
And Mr. Norris is finally caught by his own machinations.

Before the Second World War, novelists like Waugh portrayed the
individual in retreat from a decaying, boring society—Basil's escape to Africa and William Boot's to Boot Magna, the picturesque,
moribund country house of his family in *Scoop*, represent opposite
extremes—but the war cut off both of these escapes and delivered
the individual into the hands of the state. "You used to know what
you were like," Elizabeth Bowen said, "from the things you liked,
and chose. Now there was not what you liked, and you did not

13. For a discussion of the changing conventions in novel endings, see Alan Friedman, *The Turn of the Novel* (New York: Oxford University Press, 1966).

choose." [14] Reacting against the physical and emotional privations of wartime, authors such as Bowen and Waugh turned toward a past projected as dream, an "unconscious, instinctive, saving resort on the part of the characters" in *The Demon Lover* or as contained within and judged by the structure of an unchanging religious faith in Waugh's *Brideshead Revisited*, or even, as Waugh later parodied himself in Ludovic's *The Death Wish*, as "the odorous gardens of a recent past transformed and illuminated by disordered memory and imagination." [15] With defeat imminent, the imagination counterattacks or marks off new territories of the spirit which the world cannot invade—and thus acknowledges defeat as a norm in the old realms.

The war did not destroy the English class system, though education acts and changes in tax laws modified somewhat its external marks. Everyone did get rather poorer and, from a prewar point of view, duller. Still, having accepted limitation, authors seemed disposed to agree with Angela Lyne in *Put Out More Flags*: "one can't expect anything to be perfect now. In the old days if there was one thing wrong it spoiled everything; from now on for all our lives, if there's one thing right the day is made." [16] Some authors like Alan Sillitoe (and a number of Americans) not only accept the idea of limits but use them to outline, as in a life mask, the dimensions of man defined by his inherent resistance to the pressures of society and cosmos. These writers may seem to disprove the generalization that English fiction of the twentieth century explores the ways in which defeat is rendered, but in fact they either accept defeat as inevitable or acknowledge their incapacity to define victory and then go on to explore the ways in which life remains bearable.

If valid experiment arises from new, expansive concepts of reality or of the human psyche, and certainly the experiments of the modernist novel did so, then writers who accept the idea of defeat are

14. Elizabeth Bowen, "Preface to *The Demon Lover*," *Collected Impressions* (New York: Alfred A. Knopf, 1950), p. 49. See also George Orwell's *Coming Up for Air* (1939), in which the narrator predicts the end of "anything you care a curse about" before relapsing into domestic misery.

15. Evelyn Waugh, *Sword of Honour* (London: Chapman & Hall, 1965), p. 737.

16. Evelyn Waugh, *Put Out More Flags*, new and corrected uniform edition (London: Chapman & Hall, 1967), p. 49.

unlikely to be experimental. Portraying a tradition, a culture, and a class in decline, they have found traditional means adequate.

For the most part, the novelists of whom I speak have, unlike their modernist predecessors, used traditional techniques because the world had come to seem chaotic rather than delightfully confusing. To be able to see coherence and order enough for art to survive, they had to retreat. They and much of their audience are fully aware of confusion, which for them no longer seems vital or promising. Similarly, questioning linear time no longer offers release from the burden of history, since the oppressive weight has been shifted to present or future. With metaphysical and social structures tottering, order remains possible as a product of the imagination—but of an imagination which arranges rather than transmutes. These writers know that lead will not change to gold, that they will not create uncreated consciences. They seek to understand what can be done with lead.

This tendency—and it is a tendency rather than a universal—may seem to be fatal to art, which must have energy, vitality, interest in order to thrive. However, there are different ways of achieving energy, a fact overlooked by critics for whom technical experiment is paramount and by the literary mountebanks who proclaim that their lead is gold. One kind of energy results from the struggle with limitations imposed or accepted, as in the sonnet or the miniature. In fact, most of the novelists of whom Waugh spoke looked for energy not to broad and sweeping subjects or to extensions into new psychic and moral areas, but to methods which harmonize style and subject so carefully that art supports vision. Thus when Evelyn Waugh praises Christopher Isherwood's writing not simply for eschewing clichés but for never seeming to avoid clichés,[17] he commends not merely craft but a habit of mind exercised in art. And when, as in the novels of Firbank, Waugh, and Bowen, art calls attention to itself, it does so intentionally and meaningfully.

As John Dowell says in *The Good Soldier*, "the death of a mouse

17. "Mr. Isherwood and Friend," *The Essays, Articles, and Reviews of Evelyn Waugh*, ed. Donat Gallagher (London: Methuen, 1983), p. 252. Waugh was reviewing Auden and Isherwood's *Journey to a War*.

by cancer is the whole sack of Rome by the Goths. . . ."[18] To go even further, one could argue that the decline of a class and a culture can be presented by the fall of a trained mouse from a low wire— or the death of a little boy inadvertently shot by a starter's pistol or the crash of a racing car into a market cross or a shift from hunting to raising foxes or in any of the disasters, increasingly more painful and more serious, in Waugh's novels. In his last novel, *Unconditional Surrender* (titled *The End of the Battle* in the United States), Guy Crouchback has accepted legal paternity of another man's child. This means that an ancient name will continue, and thus the forms will be preserved. Furthermore, the child will have a home. But Waugh did not intend the ending to be happy.[19] Yet Guy cannot, on the evidence of the ending, be called unhappy. He has accepted his situation, living not in the manor but in the "Lesser House," and apparently he is content to live rather than to question or strive. This final novel in Waugh's long career has the babies (two were cut for the subsequent English editions) and a husband and a wife and even some minor prizes, but socially and novelistically, everyone has lost.

18. Ford Madox Ford, *The Good Soldier* (New York: Vintage, 1958), p. 5. The novel was published in 1915.

19. See his letters to Nancy Mitford and to Anthony Powell, *Letters*, pp. 577, 579.

CHAPTER 2

Shrinking Gardens: The Comic-Satiric Novel from Douglas to Waugh

One of the problems in generalizing about Evelyn Waugh's themes is that he was not always writing about Guy Crouchback, he was not always fifty-eight years old, and he was not always exclusively or even primarily concerned with theme. Sometimes he reacted as a man affected by social and political events in the twentieth century; sometimes he reacted as a writer responding to the work of other writers. And just as there is a context for the major themes in his novels, so there is a formal context which he knew as a reader if not as a theorist, in which he participated, and in which he served as an influence in his turn.

I

That context is not easy to establish because relatively few historians of the twentieth-century English novel have dealt with comic and satiric fiction.[1] Scholars trained in the novel-centered tradition seem to have the impression that these books are peripheral to the tradition of the novel; more recently trained theorists are not interested in what seems to many narrowly defined issues of mode or genre. Moreover, comic and satiric writers may seem less closely tied to history, including literary history, for they seize and dissect events in a fashion less subservient to the tyranny of time than pure novelists such as Conrad, who, approaching the moment in "tenderness and faith," seek to reproduce or recreate its vitality.

---

1. A notable exception is James Hall's *The Tragic Comedians: Seven Modern British Novelists* (Bloomington: Indiana University Press, 1963).

Nevertheless, the modern comic-satiric novel has a history, it is related to an era, and like other forms it is subject to change.

One way to exemplify this change is to isolate the ways in which comic and satiric works deal with the saving remnant among the story's characters. At the end of Greek New Comedy and of much comedy since, a new society is formed, and because it is "one that the audience has recognized all along to be the proper and desirable state of affairs, an act of communion with the audience is in order." Although a scapegoat is sometimes expelled, comedy tends "to include as many people as possible in its final society."[2] In satire, on the other hand, the characters who inhabit the good society are a minority, sometimes a minority of one: the lonely poet at the end of the *Dunciad* is a notable but not a unique example.

It is tempting, in fact, to simplify the difficult distinction between comedy and satire by measuring the relative sizes of good and bad societies. In the novel, however, the two modes are usually, and increasingly, mixed. More important are the existence and the nature of the good society that conquers or provides a refuge from the grotesque or chaotic world, whether it is Mr. Wilson's idyllic farm, Mr. Allworthy's estate, Rasselas' Happy Valley, or Candide's garden. The size and nature of that refuge can help to underscore the considerable changes that have occurred in the method, form, and temper of the modern comic-satiric novel in English—changes that reflect a modification in the sensibility that produces and the audience that enjoys it.

Despite the shift in method between Norman Douglas' *South Wind* and Evelyn Waugh's early fiction, these narratives have more in common with each other than with books generally regarded as their ancestors. Although Thomas Love Peacock is obviously the literary ancestor of Douglas and of Aldous Huxley, only the framework of the country house filled with enthusiasts, projectors, and obsessed philosophers is really similar. Whereas Peacock's characters are essentially mouthpieces for ideas, almost humors, who persist in their madness or, in the case of his heroes, are suddenly con-

2. Northrop Frye, *Anatomy of Criticism* (Princeton: Princeton University Press, 1957), pp. 164, 165.

verted to common sense, Huxley's characters struggle, suffer, and realize in their minds and in their actions the incapacity of their ideas to deal with an almost overwhelmingly complex social, moral, and physical universe. And whereas Voltaire, an obvious predecessor of Waugh, presents in *Candide* two-dimensional puppets who lose virtue, blood, and backside but are able to translate their losses into resigned and competitive anecdotes, Waugh uses the epigraph of *Vile Bodies*—"If I wasn't real . . . I shouldn't be able to cry" and the response, "I hope you don't suppose those are real tears"—both to deny and to affirm the reality of his characters' suffering in a way that Voltaire explicitly refuses to do.

These changes are symptomatic of the impulse toward internalization observable in Western culture and specifically in its literary methods over the past two centuries. If we view behavior, good and bad, aberrant and conformist, as to a considerable extent conditioned and to an even greater extent mixed, then praise and blame, though they may not be impossible, can be less readily assessed than in the past.

Accompanying and to some extent preparing the way for the psychological revolution is the humanistic-romantic placing of value on the individual as an individual, with the corollary that to understand is to mitigate blame if not to forgive. This makes it more difficult for author or audience to reject any character because of race, class, or sexual preference. The well-known shift in attitudes toward Shylock is evidence enough of this change. Then, too, the increase in both tolerance for behavior and sympathy for misfortune makes us less likely, except in the so-called sick joke or in momentary revulsion, to band the normal majority together in attacking minorities, even by ridicule. Alexander Pope said that a cripple was not ridiculous unless he called himself a dancer. We are not the worse for sponsoring Special Olympics (in which Pope might be invited to participate), but we are certainly different. Last, but by no means finally, the breakdown of specifically religious and social standards of good and evil, done and not done, has forced the individual to look, often rather uncertainly, into himself for values.

All of these generalizations are commonplaces, but they describe real cultural changes, and these changes make the creator of and the audience for comedy and satire considerably less confident about norms and about their own superiority than were their predecessors. As Casimir Lypiatt, the genius manqué, observes in Huxley's *Antic Hay*,

every man is ludicrous if you look at him from outside, without taking into account what's going on in his heart and mind. . . . It's a question of the point of view. Everyone's a walking farce and a walking tragedy at the same time. The man who slips on a banana-skin and fractures his skull describes against the sky, as he falls, the most richly comical arabesques. (Chapter 19)

Whether as cause or result—probably both—the rise and dominance of the novel have on the whole tended to ensure that the point of view will be internal rather than external. As Ian Watt has pointed out, the novel takes seriously everyday material—including everyday people—and the central traditions of high comedy and satire are essentially aristocratic and exclusive. Furthermore, from Richardson on, both the spirit and the technique of the novel have tended to allow for a greater degree of reader identification with characters. It is obvious that most of the novels with which I am concerned share this approach to some degree, and thus one cannot, without some wrenching of definitions and of books, apply without heavy qualification Northrop Frye's distinction between the novel and the anatomy or Menippean satire because this dominance of the form and vision of the novel has affected writers of comic-satiric fiction even more strongly than have broader cultural conditions. When they write fiction they either partly succumb to the influence of the novel or engage in an active and generally losing struggle to resist these influences.

Nevertheless, the impulse toward mockery and ridicule seems ineradicable in human nature, and a number of writers have attempted to blend these qualities into books that, while recognizably novels, are special kinds of novel. Although several stages are discernible in the process of change from Douglas to the late 1960's, I am particularly interested in the shift from the novel of ideas, represented by Douglas and Huxley, to the externalist novel, represented by Ronald Firbank and Evelyn Waugh, which supplanted the novel of ideas.

II

Although the novel of ideas is, or was, "a narrative form peculiar to an 'unstable' age—one in which standards are not fixed beyond removal or alteration,"[3] it is also an essentially optimistic form, since it implies a conception of man as rational, or at least as ratiocinative, of society as offering wide possibilities for self-determination and self-expression; and of reality as being structured and continuous, giving the characters at least the hope of meeting new situations by means of principles formulated from precept and experience. Typical of characters in these novels are Denis in *South Wind* and his namesake in Huxley's *Crome Yellow*. Before they can enter life, they must realize themselves, and the process of realization involves a conscious attempt to expand and integrate their personalities, to free themselves from the weight of useless strictures and conceptions of reality, and, as their name indicates—it derives from *Dionysius*—begin a new era of freedom for the whole self. In fact, these two novels are very compact versions of the *Bildungsroman*, except that the characters enter an intellectual community rather than break through into solitary illumination.

South Wind is especially notable for its sense of freedom and expansiveness. Both the mental and physical atmospheres of the Mediterranean island of Nepenthe bring Bishop Thomas Heard to a new sanity and health in which he can abandon his career in the Anglican Church, approve of a murder, and face the world disencumbered of former prejudice. Near the end of the book, the bishop reflects that

There was something bright and diabolical in the tone of the place, something kaleidoscopic—a frolicsome perversity. Purifying, at the same time. It swept away the cobwebs. It gave you a measure, a standard, whereby to compute earthly affairs. Another landmark passed; another mile-stone in the road to enlightenment. That period of doubt was over. His values had

3. Frederick J. Hoffman, "Aldous Huxley and the Novel of Ideas," in *Forms of Modern Fiction*, ed. William Van O'Connor (Bloomington: Indiana University Press, 1959), p. 193.

righted themselves. He had carved out new and sound ones; a workable, up-to-date theory of life. He was in fine trim. . . . (Chapter 49)

And he prepares to leave Nepenthe, with its kindly hedonists and admirable murderess, the world all before him, where to choose his sphere of action and content.

For Heard, Denis Phipps, and most of the other characters, Nepenthe is a retreat in the religious sense—a place for meditation on the mountain heights and of vital renewal in the caves where one can prepare to confront and transform oneself and the world. One need only compare the caves of Douglas and of E. M. Forster's *A Passage to India* to see the effect of World War I on the English intellectual classes. Douglas could still advance the classical ideal of balance, poise, and beauty, wherein behavior was harmonious or ugly rather than good or bad. But *South Wind* must have been almost the last straightforward and sane expression of the Greek ideal formulated and beloved by Victorian dons and pederasts. Forster's postwar universe tries to make room for these qualities, but in the depths of the psyche and of the Marabar Caves, they carry no authority. And though Douglas and Forster continued to publish, they were finished as imaginative writers.

But at least they had lived in a period when escape was imaginatively possible and had located a place—Italy—to which to escape. For Aldous Huxley, who began his career as a writer during a war more permanently disastrous to the European imagination than to the landscape and population and haunted by the readily foreseeable triumph of a mass society, the possibilities of escape were more limited. When his characters went to Italy, in *Those Barren Leaves*, they kept on being themselves; passion and independence were no easier in Mrs. Aldwinkle's villa than in a London rooming house. And although he could conceive of and portray places of refuge, they had boundaries which had been imposed upon rather than selected by the inhabitants. In his first novel, Mr. Scogan defends an aristocracy rather like the one Douglas imagined on the grounds that

The eccentricities of the artist and the new-fangled thinker don't inspire it with that fear, loathing, and disgust which the burgess instinctively feel towards them. It is a sort of Red Indian Reservation planted in the midst of a vast horde of Poor Whites—colonials at that. Within its boundaries wild men disport themselves—often, it must be admitted, a little grossly, a little too flamboyantly, and when kindred spirits are born outside the pale it offers them some sort of refuge from the hatred which the Poor Whites, *en bon bourgeois*, lavish on anything that is wild or out of the ordinary. After the social revolution there will be no Reservations; the Redskins will be drowned in the great sea of Poor Whites. What then? (Chapter 11)

Such reservations seemed—and continued to seem—to Huxley to offer the prospect at least of social salvation: the literal Reservation and the islands for disaffected Alphas in *Brave New World*; the tiny Jeffersonian colony of Mr. Propter in *After Many a Summer Dies the Swan*; and the rational-religious society of *Island*—all were conceived as solutions to the problem of mass society for all who could and would listen.

In *South Wind*, however, the Poor Whites could be ignored or shoved off a convenient cliff. Huxley knew that they surrounded and could destroy any refuge that he could imagine. In response, perhaps, he conceived the ultimate refuge, "the silence beyond the futile noise and bustle . . . the mental silence that lies beyond the body . . ." (*Those Barren Leaves*, Chapter 13). This refuge is difficult to attain, and in fear of the difficulty or in a perverse desire to lose themselves in the bustle and to "glory in the name of earwig," characters in most of his novels from *Antic Hay* to *Time Must Have a Stop* turned from this freedom into a bondage in phenomena. Yet these characters have a choice, and if they choose damnation it is quite a lively damnation.

III

Writing of *Antic Hay* two decades after it was published, Evelyn Waugh felt that the novel had "the lilt of Old Vienna," that the city portrayed was "Henry James' London possessed by carnival," inhabited by "A chain of brilliant young people linked and inter-laced [which] winds past the burnished front-doors in pursuit of happiness"—a happiness that is within easy grasp—and that the climate is "warm and airy and brilliant." As he says, "We certainly do not find it in modern fiction" (*EAR*, 470–472).

In part, of course, Waugh's viewpoint was colored by his vantage point in postblitz London and by his sense of a race of Bright Young People who had vanished into death or middle age. But it is also clear from Waugh's work at the end of the twenties that Huxley's world, attractive to young readers like Waugh or Angus Wilson[4] though sordid and insecure to Huxley, was no longer imaginatively viable. For older writers like Ronald Firbank as well as newer ones like Waugh, the sense that a civilized reserve was possible had given way to a still further diminished vista, a more constricted refuge, and a definition of humanity by negation rather than by inclusion. Moreover, this newer kind of fiction countered the tendency toward internalization observable in Douglas and Huxley and often refused not only to analyze motive but even to present it.

The types of fiction represented by Douglas and Huxley on the one hand and by Firbank and Waugh on the other differ not only in spirit but in every typical structural unit from the word to the plot. In the typical novel of ideas, the word is abstract; the sentence is a generalization or an illustration; the scene is a discourse or argument wherein the sequence is rhetorical or logical; and the plot involves the presentation of theories, their modification by experience, and the final recognition by the characters of change, failure, or stasis. In the externalist novel, the word is concrete; the sentence—often a fragment selected by an undramatized narrator—is gossip about specific behavior; the scene a party wherein sequence is established only by juxtaposition and by confinement to a formalized situation; and the plot a movement through a variety of episodes toward an external change in the characters' circumstances. Obviously these distinctions are frequently blurred, but in the main they account for the obvious differences in method and tone between Huxley and Waugh, between, say, the musicale at Tantamount House in Chapters 2 through 5 of *Point Counter Point* and Lady Metroland's party in honor of Mrs. Melrose Ape in Chapter 6 of *Vile Bodies*.

Furthermore, novels of ideas by Douglas and Huxley contain a

4. Angus Wilson, "The House Party Novels," *London Magazine*, 2 (August 1955), 53–55.

good deal of internalization in which characters pause to consider states of soul or courses of action. The externalist novel, as the term implies, remains on the surface of behavior, flattening and diminishing character. Significantly, both Firbank and Waugh used visual analogies in describing the roles of characters in their novels. Firbank told his publisher that in *Vainglory* "He had attempted to do something like Beardsley had done in the illustrations to *The Rape of the Lock*,"[5] and in the novel itself he described the books of a novelist much like Ronald Firbank as recalling "a frieze with figures of varying heights trotting all the same way" (Chapter 21). In an essay on Firbank praising his discovery of "a new, balanced interrelationship of subject and form," Waugh was even more explicit about the analogy between fiction and painting: "Just as in painting until the last generation the aesthetically significant activity of the artist had always to be occasioned by anecdote and representation, so the novelist was fettered by the chain of cause and effect." Firbank's innovation was superior to other types, Waugh argued, because in them "the author has been forced into a subjective attitude towards his material; Firbank remains objective . . ." (*EAR*, 57, 59). In other words, escape from older forms, which Waugh seemed here to regard as a matter of choice rather than psychic or artistic necessity, involved either going beneath the surface or remaining rigorously on it. As I shall argue in Chapter 4, Waugh chose the latter course as a result of temperament as much as technical choice. The analogies from painting in Firbank and Waugh attempt to fix character, to view it from the outside, to emphasize external rather than internal movement, and to make character an element in a composition which is kept firmly under authorial control. In short, this is an aesthetic rather than a psychological conception of character.

Both Firbank and Waugh simplified character in order to emphasize the impersonality and hostility of the world in ways that the novelists of ideas did not. At the end of *Antic Hay*, Theodore Gumbril glumly prepares for a trip to Europe to forget the girl he has lost through his own folly. Waugh saw him as a cad rather like his

5. Grant Richards, *Author Hunting*, 2nd ed. (London: Unicorn, 1960), p. 200.

own Basil Seal, viewed his world as essentially open, and predicted that "He will be all right" (*EAR*, 533). But in *Vile Bodies*, Adam Fenwick-Symes loses his girl through a series of accidents and leaves England for "the biggest battlefield in the history of the world" in a war totally without explanation or overt cause, and the novel ends with the sound of battle returning. Less dramatic but no less pointed is the contrast between Calamy of *Those Barren Leaves*, who retires to a mountain top with at least the possibility of finding himself and making his soul after an unsatisfying love affair, and Laura de Nazianzi in Firbank's *The Flower Beneath the Foot*, who immures herself in a convent only to pound her hands on the glass-strewn wall in agonized frustration as the novel ends.

Characters in the externalist novel for the most part lack volition or ability to make their wills effective. Instead, they are pushed along by what might be called the pressure of events: not exactly determinism in the mechanistic sense but a set of circumstances produced by whim, coincidence, or manipulations by remote and impersonal forces which the characters cannot control and often cannot perceive. Firbank seemed to be getting at something like this notion when he wrote of Sally Sinquier in *Caprice*: "Subjective. On a rack in the loom. Powerless oneself to grasp the design. Operated on by others. At the mercy of chance fingers, unskilled fingers, tender fingers; nails of all sorts. Unable to progress alone. Finding fulfilment through friction and because of friction" (Chapter 7). Sally may find fulfilment—*Caprice* is the lightest and gayest of Firbank's novels—but most characters in this type of novel are bewildered and frustrated. In *The Flower Beneath the Foot*, Laura's desire to marry Prince Yousef is not actively opposed, but it is nevertheless thwarted. Waugh's novels depend heavily on this kind of process: Paul Pennyfeather is pushed through *Decline and Fall* by a series of odd accidents; the characters in *Vile Bodies* are often thwarted by circumstance; William Boot's journalistic triumph in *Scoop* is the result of a wild series of coincidences in names and in situations.

A particularly important example, since it demonstrates that the implications of the externalist method are not grounded solely in the desire of the farceur for rapid and surprising action, is *A Hand-*

ful of Dust, notably the episode in which John Andrew Last is killed. Waugh carefully establishes the peculiarities of the setting and the huntsmen that result in the fatal accident. Afterward, huntsmen and author repeat, like a refrain, "It wasn't anyone's fault." Here reasonable expectation can be misleading, for several times in the course of the novel this kind of insistent repetition is ironic. On this occasion, however, the sense of the words is literal, if limited: no one can be directly blamed for the accident; the whole situation is the cause. Yet it leads directly to the final breach between his parents and to his father's departure for and lifelong imprisonment in the wilds of Brazil.

The eponymous hero of Firbank's last novel, *Concerning the Eccentricities of Cardinal Pirelli*, is similarly defined but not fulfilled by friction, and in comparison with Bishop Heard of *South Wind* illustrates the fundamental differences in plot between the novel of ideas and the externalist novel. Neither cleric is tiresomely orthodox: the bishop, though moral and at first conventional, has "a sneaking fondness for the natives—they were such fine, healthy animals," and he consorts, in increasing contentment, with gilded sinners, though he and Douglas draw the line at publicans. The cardinal has quite overt interests in actresses, dancers, and choir boys, and he officiates urbanely at the baptism—in white crème de menthe—of a blue-eyed police dog puppy.

Less important than differences in character are their different functions in the plots. The bishop seeks out theories, encounters people and events with an open but questioning mind, and arrives, by the end of the novel, at a new set of values. His personal conduct has not been affected. In contrast to this optimistic, expansive character in charge of his destiny is Cardinal Pirelli, caught inescapably between the demands of flesh and spirit and between attraction toward and repulsion from a social and physical milieu which he cannot really escape:

Morality. Poise! For without temperance and equilibrium—the Cardinal halted.
But in the shifting underlight about him the flushed camellias and the sweet night-jasmines suggested none: neither did the shape of a garden-Eros pointing radiantly at the dusk.

"For unless we have balance—" the Cardinal murmured, distraught, admiring against the elusive nuances of the afterglow the cupid's voluptuous hams. (Chapter 2)

Unlike Heard, he is not capable of the detachment necessary to analyze and learn from experience. In fact, he never questions his position in the Church or in society, and in the novel's terms he is not to be criticized for this limitation. Society, as shown in a series of parties, is undeniably corrupt; the institutional Church, revealed by scenes in the cathedral booking office, has become trivial, fashionable, and irrelevant to any spiritual purpose. But there is no sense that any of this can be changed; the characters must exist, suffer, and aspire to vaguely conceived ideals of beatitude. Until the end of the novel, Pirelli's plight, like that of most of the characters in Firbank and Waugh, is comic, but the end introduces a new mood and a further dimension of character by a process of simplification and retreat. Naked in his cathedral, Pirelli says, to "some phantom image in the air," "As you can perfectly see, I have nothing but myself to declare. . . ." Only in death, when "the ache of life, with its fevers, passions, doubts, its routine, vulgarity, and boredom" has ended, is integrity possible (Chapter 9).

The process of simplification and of retreat from complexity involves for most of Firbank's and Waugh's characters a considerable cost. In most cases, that cost is death or retreat into a limbo that, pleasant or not, is free from good and evil and from the process that gives rise to both—and that is a living death. Paul Pennyfeather has removed himself from the Luna Park wheel of the modern world and the spurious glamour of Margot Metroland's London, but he has cut himself off from sex and friendship. Tony Last, seeking a sham Gothic refuge from the modern world, is reduced to mere existence in the timeless vacuum of Mr. Todd's compound. William Boot retreats from the chaotic world of modern journalism to a literal garden, but that garden is decaying, and as he writes the nature column that is his last contact with the outside world, Waugh emphasizes his blindness and sentimentality by contrasting his phrases with the ominous context of the novel's closing words: "Outside the owls hunted maternal rodents and their furry broods."

Even though these characters have been driven into empty corners, they have escaped from a threatening world—if not into a garden, at least into a place where the chaos outside cannot touch them. In Firbank, this place is presented as a kind of picturesque ironic fantasy; in Waugh, it is a denial of responsibility for and relationship to a "world of wild aberration without theological significance."[6] Yet Firbank knew that fantasy, however qualified, offered no real escape, and the events of the thirties and forties showed Waugh that "the little independent systems of order of his own" which the artist creates in—and out of—an age and a society which can provide none (*EAR*, 304) were also a fantasy and that the world could not finally be abjured.

This recognition forced Waugh to change his method and stance as a novelist, as the example of *Put Out More Flags* illustrates. As he said in the dedicatory letter to that novel, he had sought to resurrect "a race of ghosts, the survivors of the world . . . [of] ten years ago. . . ." Yet the ghosts would not assume the same forms. Instead of submitting to the indignities and misadventures prepared for them by the author, they began to assume proportions remarkably like those of real people, and when they cried, their tears, unlike those of Lewis Carroll's Alice in the epigraph to *Vile Bodies*, were obviously getting on toward real. Although Waugh used most of his old narrative devices, the new complexity of the characters strained the externalist method, forcing him to analyze them more and more thoroughly.

The old methods could not, for example, deal with the complications and ambiguities of the relationship between Basil Seal and his sister, partly narcissistic, partly—though latently—incestuous. Other characters, such as Cedric Lyne, musing on individualism as he moves toward his death in battle, clearly matter more to author and reader than had Paul Pennyfeather. Waugh's testimony indicates a change in the kind of character he was creating. In 1946, he said that his characters assumed a life of their own, citing Angela Lyne, whose secret drinking came as a great surprise to him and forced him to change earlier episodes to prepare for it. While he does not

6. *Monsignor Ronald Knox* (Boston: Little, Brown, 1959), p. 314.

say that Angela was the first of his characters to surprise him, it is difficult to believe that William Boot, Paul Pennyfeather, or even Tony Last exhibited anything like her independence.

In addition to character types, the narrative methods and authorial stance suited to the externalist novel mix uneasily with more traditional methods in Waugh's later work. Indeed, Marston LaFrance argued that the weakness of *Brideshead Revisited* results not from Waugh's abandonment of his earlier method but from the use of that method to make an overtly serious point, with the result that "both dramatic motivation and characters are forced to give way in the direction of the pasteboard puppets of the earlier tradition."[7] Certainly in the war trilogy, *Sword of Honour*, farce and seriousness, even pathos, are uneasily yoked. For example, in the first two books, the comic secret service man amasses misinformation about other characters in the belief, "Somewhere in the ultimate curlicues of his mind," that everyone in the war will prove to be on the same side. In the last volume, he is replaced by his brother who, indifferent to the Jews that Guy Crouchback is trying to save, busily though ignorantly sends royalist officers to certain death at the hands of the Yugoslav communists. And at the end, having failed to save the Jews he most cared about and having lost to a rocket bomb the wife who has come to represent the glamour of the twenties, Guy retires to a diminished family estate and a new wife. Neither defeated nor triumphant, he has lost the illusions of chivalric romance and of the just cause with which he began and has accepted his lot.[8]

If the novel of ideas was irrevocably altered by the First World War, the climate that produced the externalist novel was beginning to disappear in the 1930's as the concentration camp or the limbo

---

7. "Context and Structure of Evelyn Waugh's *Brideshead Revisited*," *Twentieth Century Literature*, 10 (April 1964), 16.

8. It is difficult to determine whether the closing line of the novel, "Things have turned out very conveniently for Guy," is straightforward or ironic in tone, and if ironic, toward whom—character, author, reader, or speaker—the irony is directed. Waugh insisted that only the obnoxious speaker "thought the ending happy," but he had to explain his intention to Nancy Mitford and Anthony Powell (*Letters*, 577, 579), and since the last view of Guy shows him enjoying himself thoroughly, Waugh's solution, to deny him legitimate offspring, does not really solve the dramatic, let alone the dynastic, issue.

of a neutral and irrelevant country began to obsess the imaginations of writers such as Waugh's fictional Ambrose Seal. If the novel of ideas offered, however tenuously, the possibility that society might be redeemed or leavened by the intelligent few, the externalist novel offered the possibility that one or two might not be crushed by the outer world. Even after the war, Waugh could outline a plan for putting the upper classes on reservations, but here they, more than the artists and eccentrics they patronized, were to be protected from the drab modern world (*EAR*, 312–316). When he wrote *Love Among the Ruins*, his antiutopia, he created a refuge only to have it destroyed.

More recent English comic-satiric novelists have tended not even to consider the possibility of a refuge. In the early novels of Kingsley Amis, the central characters enter or reenter conventional society, and in the novels of Anthony Burgess, even in *A Clockwork Orange*, the impulse to be a normal, social human being cannot really be escaped.[9] The characters of David Lodge's and Malcolm Bradbury's novels can never really escape the pressures of the everyday world or the conventions of realism. In Huxley's terms, the Poor Whites have swallowed up the Redskins.

Other novelists, more energetic or less complacent thematically and technically, have moved actively to close the refuges provided in earlier work. Antiutopias have denied us the future as an escape: the garden is mechanized, whether by the helicopters and news cameras that invade John Savage's retreat in *Brave New World* or by the recorded hum that fills the bee-loud glade of the faked Isle of Innisfree in *The Loved One*. And the nightmares of technology have cut us off equally from the planned urban socialist paradise of Edward Bellamy's *Looking Backward* and from the almost anarchic medieval decentralism of William Morris' *News from Nowhere*. For the modern satiric novelist, there is no exit in time. The growth of cities and of electronically transmitted stimuli forbids these writers, in imagination if not in fact, the refuge of solitude or of vacuum.

9. This generalization applies only to the English edition, the last chapter of which was cut for American publication. See my "On Editing Modern Texts: Who Should Do What and to Whom," *Journal of Modern Literature*, 3 (April 1974), 1012–1020.

Huck Finn's territory ahead has turned into Oklahoma, and there is no exit in space. Increased awareness denies us the refuges of detachment, irresponsibility, contempt. In fact, in *Our Man in Havana* Graham Greene alludes to Paul Pennyfeather and demonstrates that no fiction can be morally neutral and that survival depends on a commitment, even though a limited commitment, to those one loves—and that commitment leaves one vulnerable. Paul Pennyfeather's ironic salvation lies in his imperviousness to experience. Guy Crouchback's literal salvation lies in the exercise of humility and charity. Like the novel of ideas, the externalist novel as a form ended with an era.

Recognizing the historical limitations of a form does not necessarily work to its disadvantage. We have now reached a point where we no longer have to try to regard Evelyn Waugh as a contemporary, and this allows us to see his work more clearly and more accurately than it was possible to do in his last years—partly because he could not see us very clearly. For example, he thought that *Catch-22* had "many passages quite unsuitable to a lady's reading" and suffered

not only from indelicacy but from prolixity. It should be cut by about a half. In particular the activities of "Milo" should be eliminated or greatly reduced.

You are mistaken in calling it a novel. It is a collection of sketches—often repetitious—totally without structure.

Much of the dialogue is funny.

You may quote me as saying: "This exposure of corruption, cowardice and incivility of American officers will outrage all friends of your country (such as myself) and greatly comfort your enemies." (*Letters*, 571–572)

There is a structure in the novel, the very kind that Waugh had praised in 1930 (see Chapter 5), the kind, indeed, that Heller had probably learned from reading Waugh as he worked on revisions of his own novel.[10]

Waugh's misunderstanding of Heller was matched by Heller's of Waugh. Features of *Unconditional Surrender* were bound to be su-

10. The information comes from a conversation with Heller, spring 1969. See also his comments about specific technical debts and about his response to Waugh's letter in Nathan Cohen, "A Profile of Evelyn Waugh," CBC Radio, 28 October 1969. Unpublished.

perficially repellent to him. Crouchback he thought a bore; the style he described as having "an emotionless precision that borders on indifference." In fact, he longed for the early Waugh.[11]

Now Joseph Heller is older than the Waugh who wrote *Unconditional Surrender* and, as the reviews of *God Knows* indicate, losing the struggle to be contemporary. Waugh, Douglas, Huxley, and Firbank no longer have to struggle, and their accomplishments can be identified and appreciated.

11. Review of *The End of the Battle* in *Nation*, 20 January 1962, 62–63; reprinted in *Evelyn Waugh: The Critical Heritage*, ed. Martin Stannard (London: Routledge & Kegan Paul, 1984), pp. 442–444.

CHAPTER 3

The Context of Waugh's Early Novels

As the previous chapter demonstrates, one can place Waugh's early novels in a fairly broad formal context of novels drawn from the first quarter of the century and show, as I shall in Chapter 5, that he was aware of the developments in technique which preceded his own work.[1] But he was also reading his contemporaries with a competitive eye, and his early fiction was written in a clearly identifiable context of novels of the 1920's which deal with the fashionable and disillusioned younger generation. When we begin to see what elements those novels have in common, what generic conventions and body of allusion the audience could be expected to recognize, what Waugh adapted, undercut, or took for granted from the work of his predecessors, then it is possible to understand the place of his first two novels in the fictional context of the late 1920's.

This immediate context can be described from novelists well known to Waugh: Aldous Huxley, Michael Arlen, Carl Van Vechten, Ernest Hemingway, and Beverley Nichols. He read *Antic Hay* not long after it was published in 1923,[2] and he referred sardonically to Michael Arlen in *Decline and Fall*. Carl Van Vechten and Ernest Hemingway were, he thought, among the writers "developing the technical discoveries upon which Ronald Firbank so neg-

1. For an example of another kind of influence study, see Stewart H. Benedict, "The Candide Figure in the Novels of Evelyn Waugh," *Papers of the Michigan Academy of Science, Arts, and Letters*, 48 (1963), 685–690.
2. *EAR*, p. 470. Twenty-three years later he told Nancy Mitford that Huxley "never wrote a good novel after *Antic Hay*." *Letters*, p. 237.

ligently stumbled."[3] While there is no direct evidence that he read Beverley Nichols' *Crazy Pavements*, later references to Nichols imply that Waugh knew him and his work, and this novel and Waugh's first two have similarities which indicate, if not direct influence, a literary climate in which form and theme had become common property.

Although I have spoken of the 1920's and Waugh and Van Vechten wrote this kind of novel in modified form as late as 1930, the basic pattern was established within a span of four years. All of these novelists had produced fiction on other themes and in other modes, but all were regarded as daring moralists if not technical innovators. While I shall not discuss all of them, the following were most readily identifiable to the contemporary audience:[4]

August 1923   Van Vechten, *The Blind Bow-Boy: A Cartoon for a Stained Glass Window*

November 1923   Huxley, *Antic Hay*

June 1924   Arlen, *The Green Hat*

August 1925   Van Vechten, *Firecrackers*

October 1926   Hemingway, *The Sun Also Rises*

February 1927   Nichols, *Crazy Pavements*

August 1928   Van Vechten, *Spider Boy*

September 1928   Waugh, *Decline and Fall*

January 1930   Waugh, *Vile Bodies*

September 1930   Van Vechten, *Parties*

All of these novels are set in London or Paris or New York; all present highly sophisticated characters whose major occupation is amusing themselves; all not only reflect disillusion with conventional morals but indicate that new styles of behavior are not en-

---

3. *EAR*, 56. The other writers mentioned were Osbert Sitwell, Harold Acton, and William Gerhardi. Except for the tone of Gerhardi's early novels, the connection between these writers and either Firbank and Waugh seems rather tenuous.

4. The editions cited are as follows: Carl Van Vechten: *The Blind Bow-Boy* (New York: Alfred A. Knopf, 1925), Pocket Book Edition; *Firecrackers* (New York: Alfred A. Knopf, 1925); *Parties* (New York: Alfred A. Knopf, 1930). Aldous Huxley, *Antic Hay* (London: Panther, 1984). Michael Arlen, *The Green Hat* (New York: George H. Doran, 1924). Ernest Hemingway, *The Sun Also Rises* (New York: Charles Scrib-

tirely satisfactory. All demonstrate an overt awareness not only of new modes of behaving but of new forms in which to describe them. All of them describe worlds in which, to use Dr. Fagan's words, "taste and dignity . . . go unhampered" (*Decline and Fall*, 59). Most have for central character, or at least focal character, an ingenu being exposed to the sophisticated world. All have female characters, variously portrayed as magnets of desire or as catalysts of action or as just plain fatal, who are almost interchangeable. All consciously embody a new approach to fiction as well as to life.

Perhaps because Van Vechten was aware of breaking ground in a country not known for light and sophisticated fiction, he developed in *The Blind Bow-Boy* an extensive apologia for his kind of fiction. Throwing aside a (real) novel by Waldo Frank, Campaspe Lorillard, Van Vechten's most sophisticated character, rejects the whole realist-naturalist movement because "it was only behind laughter that true tragedy could lie concealed," because, tragedies being "ridiculous or sordid," they can be captured by withdrawing from "reality." Instead, a book

should have the swiftness of melodrama, the lightness of farce, to be a real contribution to thought. . . . Plot was certainly unimportant in the novel; character drawing a silly device. . . . Justification? Preparation? In life we never know anything about the families and early lives of the people we meet; why should we have to learn all about them in books? Growth of character in a novel was nonsense. People never change. Psychology: the supreme imbecility. . . . in the best work of Nicolas Poussin [she paraphrases Clive Bell] the human figure is treated as a shape cut out of coloured paper to be pinned on as the composition directs. That was the right way to treat the human figure; the mistake lay in making these shapes retain the characteristic gestures of classical rhetoric. (160, 163, 164)

Campaspe's aesthetic sounds rather like that attributed to the imaginary Knockespotch in Huxley's *Crome Yellow* (1922) who is "tired of seeing the human mind bogged in a social plenum; I prefer

ner's Sons, 1926), Scribner Library Contemporary Classics Edition. Beverley Nichols, *Crazy Pavements* (London: Jonathan Cape, 1927). Evelyn Waugh, *Decline and Fall* (Boston: Little, Brown, [1928]); *Vile Bodies* (Boston: Little, Brown, [1930]). The American editions of Waugh's novels have not changed since their first publication.

to paint it in a vacuum, freely and sportively bombinating." In his tales,

Fabulous characters shoot across his pages like gaily dressed performers on the trapeze. . . . Intelligences and emotions, relieved of all the imbecile preoccupations of civilized life, move in intricate and subtle dances, crossing and recrossing, advancing, retreating, impinging. An immense erudition and an immense fancy go hand in hand. . . . The verbal surface of his writing is rich and fantastically diversified. The wit is incessant. (Chapter 14)

Antic Hay has nothing this lighthearted in practice or this developed in theory, but Casimir Lypiatt, the failed artist, sees, like Campaspe, a relationship between tragedy and farce in the contrast between exterior and interior views because "every man is ludicrous if you look at him from outside, without taking into account what's going on in his heart and mind" (Chapter 19).

Later novelists make less overt pronouncements of theory, but both Arlen and Nichols contrast the behavior of their characters with that found in other novels and imply that their own ways of telling a story are more original than and superior to conventional methods. In Hemingway, Jake's comments on other books establish an implied standard for all fiction: W. H. Hudson's *The Purple Land* is a poor guide to perception and conduct; Turgenev's *A Sportsman's Sketches* not only gives Jake something he will always have but is a good specific against dizziness (9, 147, 194). Here, however, the standards are implicit, the general aesthetic not announced.

These later novelists reject conventional, commodity fiction. Van Vechten and Huxley are much more radical, attacking the very ontological and psychological premises of fiction as art. But in all of these novels comedy seems more important than tragedy, surface behavior than psychological analysis, style than sincerity. These writers sought a new manner not merely because it was new but because they were dealing with new modes of behavior which lacked justification in either the fictional or the theological sense and were attempting to give narrative form to experiences whose outcome they could not foresee.

At first, some of these novelists seemed almost complacent about what they seemed to see as not just a change in but the disappearance of moral and social forms. Van Vechten, the most vocal about changes in narrative form, was also the most radical in rejecting conventional styles of behavior. In *The Blind Bow-Boy*, people defined as normal are considered stuffy and boring, and radical, detached individualism is presented as the only sane way to live. At the end of the novel, one character has married for money, a solution which no one condemns; one has fled from a conventional and stifling love match with a materialistic socialite to a purely physical heterosexual affair and then to a homosexual liaison; and one takes a trip, leaving behind her husband and sons at Christmas because, apparently, both she and the boys need independence and the husband, who keeps succumbing to conventional uxorious emotion, does not matter. At the end, the coterie on which the novel has focused has been dissipated, but Van Vechten gives the impression that it does not much matter, that each member will follow his or her bent unimpeded and uninvolved with society at large or with any specific person.

Huxley's characters do not seem to have the option of being conventional, but they worry about it a good deal more than do Van Vechten's. At the end of *Antic Hay*, the only connections are fortuitous or potentially (if not very seriously) destructive. The central coterie has dispersed, each too frightened or busy or embittered to join Theodore Gumbril and Myra Viveash, who have lost their only chances at love and who drive back and forth across London without finding consolation in each other. Once again, the action is not resolved: the central woman character will not get the man she wants, and no man who wants her will have her for long. But even the characters who are able to imagine another way of living cannot put it into practice, and those who can move are made to seem no better off than those who have reached various psychological or artistic dead ends.

In Hemingway, only Jake Barnes even tries to imagine another way of living. Aside from his peculiar limitations, he is, like all the other members of his group, set apart by temperament and experience from the midwesterners who share the train compartment and even from his married colleagues who rather wistfully think of visiting the Left Bank some time. Unlike his friends, he attempts to give some internal structure to his life, but because he cannot isolate himself emotionally, he is drawn back into Brett's circle.

Arlen and Nichols, who vulgarize and domesticate the form, present much fuller views of conventional life. The narrow world of English county society judges and ultimately destroys the generous and passionate heroine of Arlen's novel, and that world survives unchanged at the end. Nichols offers normality as a refuge, but for him normal is defined as rough-tender, lower-middle-class male bonding with a dimly and sentimentally perceived marriage in the distance.

Nichols is the only one of these novelists who can posit, even vaguely, marriage as a possibility. Perhaps as a result, the women in these novels are more interesting than the other characters because they embody both the confusions and the potential strengths of the postwar world. All of them are free of usual economic and social constraints. Some are married, but even they are not domestic. In fact, their divorce from traditional female roles accounts for much of their fascination. Campaspe Lorillard is unusual in the degree to which she values her physical and intellectual autonomy, but she differs in degree, not in kind. Though Myra Viveash and Iris Storm might be satisfied by the right kind of male, it is clear that they are not going to get the right kind of male, and therefore they cannot live in the forms and by the standards of the past. Only Iris and Brett are really sexual creatures, and only Brett is described as sexy.

These women are by no means ingenues, and most are not even technically eligible for the role. Campaspe is "about thirty"; Waugh guessed that Myra was twenty-five (*EAR*, 471); Iris is twenty-nine; Brett must be pushing thirty-five; Margot Beste-Chetwynde just might, Paul Pennyfeather thinks, be no older than thirty-three. All except Lady Julia Cressy have been wed, or at least bedded, before the end of the First World War. All have aristocratic connections. Because of their ages and their social standing, they are shown as connected to an older, more stable society which no longer exists, and while all but Campaspe occasionally feel displaced, they represent to their lovers and to society at large a kind of mystery which is fascinating but finally not comprehensible. Only Campaspe has children (two, off-stage, from whom she feels detached), though Iris feels the lack of them; only Campaspe and Lady Julia have a living (female) parent.

They also have distinct physical resemblances. Campaspe has gray eyes; a *retroussé* nose; a square jaw; a clear, soft, and sympathetic voice with a tinge of mockery; an "intensely feline" aura (57, 58). Myra has eyes with "a formidable capacity for looking and expressing nothing; they were like the pale blue eyes which peer out of the Siamese cat's black-velvet mask"; a voice which "seemed always on the point of expiring, as though each word were the last, uttered faintly and breakingly from a death-bed"; and a way of "placing her feet with a meticulous precision one after the other in the same straight line, as though she were treading a knife edge between goodness only knew what invisible gulfs. Floating she seemed to go, with a little spring at every step . . ." (58, 59, 72). Iris has eyes "blazing blue," "set very wide apart . . . cool, impersonal, sensible," which "glowed like an animal's"; hair "dancing a tawny, formal dance about small white cheeks"; a manner grave and sad (20–21, 42). Her "slightly husky voice expired" on one occasion (39).[5] Brett's eyes "had different depths, sometimes they seemed perfectly flat" and sometimes "you could see all the way into them" (26); her hair is "brushed back like a boy's" in a fashion she originated (22). All have rejected the conventional feminine look, or created a new one, just as all have abandoned traditional female roles, and the fact that they are set apart from other women helps to create the fascination they exercise over young men.

The ingenus in these novels are somewhat more diverse than the fatally attractive women, and only Harold Prewett (*The Blind Bow-Boy*), Brian Elme (*Crazy Pavements*), and Paul Pennyfeather (*Decline and Fall*) are pure examples of the type: the young man with good looks, latent vitality, and innocence cast into a society with stronger drinks than principles in which he discovers that his previous system of belief and code of behavior are inadequate and that

5. See Jacqueline A. McDonnell, *Waugh on Women* (New York: St. Martin's Press, 1985), for an inventory of characteristics of these and other heroines. Her evidence is often sound; her interpretations are often, shall we say, open to question.

he must invent new ones. In *The Blind Bow-Boy*, Harold, raised in the country by a maiden aunt, is pushed by his father into New York society, with a rake for tutor, in order to learn about life. Although fascinated by Campaspe, he marries the first conventional girl he meets, discovers that he has been led to do so by his father's plot, and rebels. After being taken up by a movie star (almost entirely animal, as Campaspe is almost entirely mind), he leaves the country with Ronald, Duke of Middlebottom, his reactions rendered inscrutable by a shift in narrative point of view.

In *Crazy Pavements*, Brian Elme is a twenty-year-old gossip writer for *The Lady's Mail* with "the most delicious hair" (39), "a single dress-shirt," "a crying hunger to get out of the whole thing" (14), and Walter, a bosom friend (the cliché is here inevitable) who has a taste for pubs and other quintessentially British institutions and two passions, one "for freedom" and the other "an almost absurd hero-worship of Brian" (23). Brian's overt attractions are his charm and his courage in keeping alive his dreams. Other reasons for the bond may be hidden from the author's consciousness or at least from his audience. Drawn into the circle of corrupt aristocrats, Brian breaks with Walter and falls in love with Lady Julia until she tires of her caprice and attempts to drive him into the bed of an aging, much-tucked nymphomaniac who is blackmailing her by threatening to reveal the discreditable news that she was once capable of genuine feeling for Brian. Disillusioned, Brian seeks as an antidote the vulgarity, color, and movement of Great Charlotte Street on the night of 4 August, anniversary of the Great War's beginning. He finds it: "This was England. This would go on, triumphant, coarse, obscene, vital, long after [the aristocratic degenerates] had retired to their futile tombs" (315–316). Bucked up and a bit drunk, he accidentally sits on Walter's knee. They clasp hands and one says, "I want you—awfully." The next morning, Brian has forgotten all about his adventures: "He was, in fact, exactly as we first met him" (318).

The focal characters in Huxley and Arlen are less naive—Arlen's reeks with sophistication—but they are no more effectual than those in Van Vechten and Nichols, and they lack the freshness of Harold and Brian in Van Vechten and Nichols. Although Huxley emphasizes the diffidence, mildness, and melancholy of Theodore Gumbril, Jr., the character shows ineradicable signs of worldliness, and he is or has been at least temporarily successful with all three women he encounters. His problem is not that he knows too little but that he knows too much—and that he is unable to reconcile the claims of flesh and spirit, time and eternity, worldly and heavenly cities. By the end of the novel, unlike Brian, he has been changed, in that he knows that he is incapable of choosing the highest good. Like Harold, he leaves the country at the end of the novel, but his departure is an acknowledgment of defeat rather than a gesture of rebellion or movement into new experience. Arlen's narrator tries to absent himself from responsibility for anything but the narration of the story, but he would like to help his friends, caught between personal desire and social pressure, and at the end takes refuge in sentimental stoicism.

The Sun Also Rises incorporates and modifies elements from all four of these novels. Robert Cohn can be seen as the ingenu, but his innocence is in fact ignorance and his idealism shallow and conventional. Rather than moving outward, enlightened, or moving backward, unchanged, he is presumably destroyed by his encounter with experience. Like Gumbril and the narrator of *The Green Hat*—for different reasons—Jake Barnes cannot change, though unlike Gumbril he can draw minimal conclusions from his experience and unlike Arlen's narrator can detach himself from the material enough to comment on it. And unlike Gumbril and Harold, he has, having already been everywhere, literally no place to go.

The movement from Harold to Jake recapitulates in a shorter span the process described in Chapter 2. In fact, those changes are evident in the novels—*The Blind Bow-Boy, Firecrackers*, and *Parties*—which Carl Van Vechten set in New York.[6] At first, the world is full of a number of things, and if not quite all are in exquisite taste, one can have a comfortable sense of superiority to those which are not. Even Paul Moody, a likable ne'er-do-well, has,

---

6. The best discussion of Van Vechten's life and fiction is Bruce Kellner's *Carl Van Vechten and the Irreverent Decades* (Norman: University of Oklahoma Press, 1968).

a charming room with orange and gold lacquer screens, escritoires and tables of a severe Directoire pattern, needle-point chairs, and a chaste marble fireplace. Stalks of indigo larkspurs and salmon snapdragons emerged from tall crystal vases. A few books bound in gaily coloured boards lay on one of the tables, and the others were cluttered, hugger-mugger, with a variety of picturesque and valuable objects. A bright Manila shawl, embroidered in vermilion and lemon flowers, was thrown over the piano, and was held in place by a blue Canton china pitcher full of magenta roses. A copper bowl, heaped with ripe figs, stood on a console-table. Sanguines by Boucher and Fragonard, with indelicate subjects, hung on the walls. (*The Blind Bow-Boy*, 56)

The *Blind Bow-Boy* is filled with similar descriptions or mere inventories of fashionable objects, books, people, and ideas. No one has to worry about money; there is plenty to eat and just enough to drink and enough orgasms for anyone who wants them. Love may be unrequited, but there are no hangovers, physical or moral, and Campaspe has even arranged her life so that "If I can prevent it, things never do happen to me, and *I can prevent it*. I have even arranged it so that I do not suffer physical pain when it is inconvenient for me" (157).

In *Firecrackers*, objects, people, and one's emotions are less easy to arrange. Although Van Vechten still uses catalogues and descriptions, they are less pervasive and less striking than in *The Blind Bow-Boy*. And his characters are more subdued. Even Campaspe has greater difficulty in preventing things from happening to her. The emblem which represents her mental state in *The Blind Bow-Boy* is a fertile garden with "a marble Eros" and a weeping nymph surrounded by narcissi; in *Firecrackers*, the key image is of a Penitente chapel with "a little wagon with wooden wheels on which was seated a life-sized skeleton, laughing, bearing bow and arrow, the arrow poised, the bow drawn" (231). Death, not Love, is the archer. Even the formerly insouciant Paul Moody can perceive that Campaspe "was tired of inventing means for making the days and nights pleasant and capriciously variable for others" (2). The focal character is another ingenu, but Gunnar O'Grady is the antithesis of Harold in his desire for "complete freedom" and his striving for "perfection, so far as [is] humanly possible" (228) in every field of endeavor.

Gunnar (brother of the splendidly animalistic Zimbule of *The Blind Bow-Boy*) sets the other characters in motion by his physical magnetism and the example of his energy. Paul Moody, married to a fat, rich wife, has lost the élan and the taste he nonchalantly revealed in the earlier novel and goes to work on Wall Street, where he discovers that making money is both easy and amusing. Campaspe herself is so attracted to Gunnar that "she half-belonged to someone else, a state of affairs which she did not condone—rather, she loathed it—but over which, in the circumstances, she held no sway . . ." (198). However, she is given the example of the Countess Ella Nattatorini, a grisly specimen of "forlorn and ungratified lust," who on her deathbed dangles between fear of divine punishment and hope that the priest will be her great love. Campaspe is finally able to free herself from her desire because, as she tells Gunnar, "I have given it up of my own accord" (229), but since the Penitente image controls the last view of her mind given in the novel, it seems unlikely that Van Vechten regards her as successful. Gunnar, who has tried to stamp out his sexual impulses, fails because the whole thrust of his philosophy is expansive, inclusive, and he is devastated by the conflict.

Firecrackers illustrates Campaspe's idea that "Life based on disenchantment was comparatively sane; life based on ideals, actually dangerous" (103). Gareth Johns, a novelist-character who has a physical as well as a philosophical resemblance to Van Vechten, goes even further:

It doesn't seem to occur to the crowd that it is possible for an author to believe that life is largely without excuse, that if there is a God he conducts the show aimlessly, if not, indeed, maliciously, that men and women run around automatically seeking escapes from their troubles and outlets for their lusts. The crowd is still more incensed when an author who believes these things refuses to write about them seriously. (164–165)

This theory asserts not form but "The incoherence of life . . . the appalling disconnection" (167). While *The Blind Bow-Boy* did not have much dramatic development beyond the fulfillment of Campaspe's expectation that Harold might assert himself, the setting of the scene and the various revelations of mental states gave the novel a kind of progression. In *Firecrackers*, Gareth Johns outlines a form adequate to his theory of inconsequence:

abruptly, quite unreasonably, one individual unconsciously—it's always unconsciously—produces an effect, a chemical change, let us call it, in another person with whom he comes in contact. This phenomenon in itself creates enough energy so that presently still others are affected. Wider and wider sweep the circles created by the tossing of a pebble into a lake, until at last they dissipate, and the lake becomes placid again. . . .

Or, to put it figuratively, in another fashion—you must think of a group of people in terms of a packet of firecrackers. You ignite the first cracker and the flash fires the second, and so on, until, after a series of crackling detonations, the whole bunch has exploded, and nothing survives but a few torn and scattered bits of paper, blackened with powder. (167)

In fact, the two figures describe quite different kinds of book—*The Blind Bow-Boy* and *Firecrackers*, for example—because the first assumes a natural state which, disturbed, is self-renewing, while the second posits a world which consumes itself or explodes and cannot be restored.

Moreover, the first trope assumes that no character can remain completely uninvolved, while the second posits an initiator who observes and survives the string of explosions. In *Parties*, no one theorizes about narrative method, Campaspe and her circle do not appear, and the characters cannot prevent anything from happening to them. And more things are happening. In *The Blind Bow-Boy*, the duke is able to dismiss as old-fashioned the things "called modern a year or two ago" (128), and none of these things has any connection with politics or economics or anything but cultural history. In *Parties*, though the mutability of New York is part of its charm (137–142), the atmosphere seems quite separate from the moods of its inhabitants, the list of events during the winter of 1930 (170) given by the omniscient author is recorded without being denigrated or dismissed, and the central character remarks casually near the end of the novel, "I plunged and lost all. I'm no longer in the market" (259).

The characters are screened from the perception of most of these events by an alcoholic haze which is both cause and result of their confusion. David and Rilda Westlake (based on Scott and Zelda

Fitzgerald) cannot live together or apart; their friend Hamish Wilding loves them both; Simone Fly, a colorful and dissolute companion who is often literally upside down or sideways, has no goals and no interior life. Except at the end of *Parties*, when she appears in black and white, even her dress is startling rather than stylish like that of Campaspe. There is plenty to drink—"A man with an extensive acquaintance . . . could drink steadily in New York from the beginning of cocktail time until eleven in the evening without any more expense than that entailed by car- or cab-fare" (172)—but for the first time in a Van Vechten novel, there are blackouts and hangovers. Campaspe could withdraw into her garden to indulge in reverie and to order her life, but in this novel the title passage, spoken by David, encapsulates the action and the mood:

We're swine, filthy swine, and we are Japanese mice, and we are polar bears walking from one end of our cage to the other, to and fro, to and fro, all day, all week, all month, for ever to eternity. We'll be drunk pretty soon and then I'll be off to Donald's to get drunker and you'll be off with Siegfried and get drunker and we'll go to a lot of cocktail parties and then we'll all turn up for dinner at Rosalie's where we are never invited. She won't want you, and I shall hate you, but Siegfried will want you. And we'll get drunker and drunker and drift about night clubs so drunk that we won't know where we are, and then we'll go to Harlem and stay up all night and go to bed late tomorrow morning, and wake up and begin it all over again.
  Parties, sighed Rilda. Parties! (87)

In the middle of the novel—rather than, as in *The Blind Bow-Boy* and *Antic Hay*, at the end—David leaves New York to search for something he cannot define, but in London and elsewhere he discovers only the senseless round of drinking and promiscuity. In Hamish's view, David "requires nothing. He only yields now and then to the requirements of others" (159). This freedom from desire makes him no happier than his friends. Campaspe could regain her inner serenity in *Firecrackers* by giving up her desire for Gunnar. David has neither desire nor serenity.

  The only character not caught up in the confusion is the Gräfin Adele von Pulmernl und Stilzernl, an elderly rebel against the dull conformity of the post-Armistice German nobility who finds in New York people "who could actually cope with her superb vitality" (12). She represents an earlier generation exhilarated by the new freedom from conventional propriety, a freedom which has lost its meaning for David and his circle. In 1930, she is almost a decade behind the real spirit of the times. At the end of the novel, David outlines another evening's drunken activity and adds:

This is the life of our times. . . . I am not bitter about it. I accept it as the best we can do. . . . We're here because we're here and we should be extremely silly not to make the worst of it.

His resignation is capped by the Gräfin's straightforward amusement: "It is so funny, David, so very funny, and I love your country" (260). Real pain is reduced to farce; people are reduced to roles.

Even for Van Vechten, fashion and sophistication no longer seemed adequate. The self-conscious revision of narrative theory had given way to an immersion in events. The women in *Parties*, unlike Campaspe, are confused or inconscient or both. Objects have ceased, in themselves, to have the power to charm, and ideas, either as amusements or as guides, simply do not exist in *Parties*. The coterie of insiders still exists, but it has become fixed rather than organic, and unlike those of earlier novels in the subgenre, it cannot be escaped. As in *The Sun Also Rises*, the old, boring, solid, conventional world has ceased to exist either as a refuge or as a structure against which to define rebellion. In fact, the characters of this stage do not really have places in which to live. Campaspe had her house and the garden at its core which contained and defined her. The Westlakes have a luxurious apartment, but it is not home: they may sleep and have their first drink of the day there, but they dine and spend their nights elsewhere. Jake Barnes has a flat where he sleeps, perforce, alone, and balances his checkbook, but he does not really live there. What in the early novels was a quest to realize the full possibilities of the self has in the later ones become a flight to escape the self. Campaspe glories in her isolation; Jake endures his; David cannot even get free. And none of them can go back to the old world.

Evelyn Waugh not only knew these novels individually, he also had fairly clear ideas about their methods (see Chapter 5) and, a decade later at any rate, a strong sense of particular patterns in character and form. His views of the paradigmatic heroine are particularly interesting. Reviewing Kenneth Allott and Stephen Tait's *The Rhubarb Tree*, he commented that

The heroine is straight from the 1920's—elusive, irresponsible, promiscuous, a little wistful, avaricious, delectable, ruthless—how often we have all read or written about such people. Well, the type wears well. . . .[7]

Almost twenty years later he commented that the power of Myra Viveash "has never much impressed me." He thought her, at twenty, twenty-five and "appallingly mature"; he classed her, at fifty, with "moody children" (*EAR*, 472). Yet Myra's ghost walks through his last novel, *Unconditional Surrender*, for when Virginia Troy is killed by a buzz bomb, Huxley's description of Myra serves as a not entirely absurd epitaph.[8] The speaker's assistants, rather jealous of Virginia, compare the description to that in Ludovic's awful novel, *The Death Wish*, but they are shown to be far less interesting than Virginia or Myra and not fascinating at all.

Waugh had some ambivalence about the heroine,[9] but he had nothing but praise for the kind of pattern he found in Peter Chamberlain's novel, *Sing Holiday*:

a prosaic hero sets out for a brief holiday, falls accidentally into strange company and finds himself transported far beyond his normal horizons and translated into a new character; finally he returns to his humdrum habits. It is one of the basic stories of the world; in recent times it was the plot of *The Wheels of Chance*, *Faraway*, and a thousand others; it has been treated romantically, farcically, sentimentally, satirically, melodramatically; it never fails if it is well treated.[10]

He does not mention *Crazy Pavements* or *Decline and Fall*, but both fit the pattern.

7. "Love Among the Underdogs," *Night and Day*, 1 (7 October 1937), 29.

8. See *Sword of Honour* (London: Chapman & Hall, 1965), p. 752. Everard Spruce misdates Huxley's novel as 1922, and his printed speech spells Hemingway's Brett with one *t*. It is difficult to decide whether Waugh is having sly fun at the expense of Cyril Connolly (despite his explicit denials the model for Spruce) or was simply mistaken.

9. Jacqueline McDonnell and others trace most of Waugh's leading women to Evelyn Gardner and see in his broken first marriage the pattern developed in every novel after *Decline and Fall*. While the separation and divorce were traumatic, the theory is frequently overenforced.

10. "Bonhomie in the Saloon Bar," *Night and Day*, 1 (22 July 1937), 24.

In fact, if *Crazy Pavements* is a vulgarization and partly unconscious parody of the novel of fashionable rebellion, *Decline and Fall*
and *Vile Bodies* can be seen as playing with the conventions of the
form and as recapitulating in two years its development or decay.
Decline and Fall has numerous and obvious connections with the
novels I have mentioned. In one of the few London scenes, "All
Mayfair seemed to throb with the heart of Mr. Arlen" (196); the
architecture and interior decor of Margot's country house, King's
Thursday, outdo even the tastes of Van Vechten's characters; Paul
Pennyfeather, an ingenu like Harold Prewett, is like Brian Elme at
the end of the novel exactly as he was at the beginning; and Margot
Beste-Chetwynde resembles, in many respects, her fictional predecessors.

Despite the similarities in content, however, the tone of *Decline
and Fall* is quite different from that of its predecessors. The description of Margot is particularly instructive:

Margot Beste-Chetwynde—two lizard-skin feet, silk legs, chinchilla
body, a tight little black hat pinned with platinum and diamonds, and the
high invariable voice that may be heard in any Ritz Hotel from New York
to Buda-Pesth. (95)

In this passage and elsewhere Margot has no individual qualities of
mind or body and seems to be almost the platonic idea of a desirable woman and is in fact equated with, or reduced to, the sum of
her accessories. Later the accessories include her house, her office,
and her life. Unlike Campaspe, she cannot live alone, indifferent to
society.

Yet Waugh does not, like Beverley Nichols, recoil in Dissenting
horror at the waste and frivolity of the decadent aristocracy. Paul
explicitly refuses to judge Margot, and he thoroughly enjoys the
good things with which Margot showers him as prospective bride-
groom or as prisoner. Left to his own devices, he purchases "two
new ties, three pairs of shoes, an umbrella and a set of Proust"
(200). That is one of his few overt choices, for he is reduced in the
novel to the shadow of

the solid figure of an intelligent, well-educated, well-conducted young
man, a man who could be trusted to use his vote at a general election with

discretion and proper detachment, whose opinion on a *ballet* or a critical essay was rather better than most people's, who could order a dinner without embarrassment and in a creditable French accent, who could be trusted to see to luggage at foreign railway stations, and might be expected to acquit himself with decision and decorum in all the emergencies of civilized life. This was the Paul Pennyfeather who had been developing in the placid years which precede this story. (162–163)

The novel, according to the omniscient narrator, "is really an account of the mysterious disappearance of Paul Pennyfeather," the creation of the English Establishment: middle-class, honorable, solid, socialized, and, Waugh implies, boring. Campaspe theorizes that the best fiction reduces character to outline and places it in a design; John Plant's theorizes (see Chapter 5) that characters should be reduced to elements in a design; *Decline and Fall* reduces and stylizes without generalizing overtly.

In thematic terms, Paul learns, like Harold Prewett, that there is another kind of world. Unlike Harold, he chooses not to join it. Like Brian Elme, he returns to his point of origin. Unlike Brian, he has in fact learned something—don't go outdoors when the Bollinger Club is raging about—and has made a conscious decision to resume, in a very different spirit and kind of knowledge, his old way of life.

At the beginning of the novel, Paul's vocation is conventional. At the end, it is orthodox. The process can be traced in his choice of reading matter. In the Prelude he looks forward to reading some chapters of *The Forsyte Saga* (rather than the borrowed copy of Dean Stanley's *Eastern Church*) before going to bed. In the middle of the novel he buys Proust and reads the new Virginia Woolf (spelled *Wolf*; the book is probably *Orlando*), ignoring his Bible and *Prayers on Various Occasions of Illness, Uncertainty and Loss, by the Rev. Septimus Bead, M.A., Edinburgh*, 1863, because he is no longer uncertain and is about to decide that he has not lost anything. At the end, he owns a copy of Stanley, beside which he places Dr. Fagan's heart-felt exposé, *Mother Wales*, as an equally valuable way of looking at the world, and Von Hügel. In the last paragraph, reading an ecclesiastical history, he notes that "the ascetic Ebionites used to turn towards Jerusalem when they prayed" and concludes that it was "Quite right to suppress them" (293) before going peacefully to bed. His conclusion is not just the result of neoorthodoxy but the end of the process by which he learns that contentment depends not on physical location or orientation but on inner stability based on personal preference.

In fact, Waugh manages to have things both ways because (see Chapter 4) he is able to posit an individual refuge without condemning the external world. Paul's choice happens to be orthodox, but Waugh does not condemn the "dynamic" characters who disport themselves in frantic activity. By the time he finished *Vile Bodies*, however, he was less confident in the possibility either of a personal retreat or of an amusing outer world. Paul does not repine in his cell or in his rooms at Scone College, Oxford, because he has inner resources which Waugh is careful not to specify.[11] In contrast, Adam Fenwick-Symes can only afford to live in a sordid hotel room, and in the novel there is no refuge from the frenetic world around him.

Decline and Fall laughs at this world at least as lovingly as tolerantly; *Vile Bodies* strips it of glamour and undercuts the conventions of the novels which created it. Like Brian Elme, Adam invents gossip-column items, but unlike him he is already an insider in a world which is not fascinatingly decadent but rather dull and which he is trying to make more interesting. None of the characters weeps, but in the epigraph from Lewis Carroll Alice insists that she is real because she can weep, only to have her claim rejected because "I hope you don't suppose those are real tears?" The pursuit of fashion and sensation is undercut by the other epigraph passage, which announces that "it takes all the running you can do, to keep in the same place. If you want to get somewhere else, you must run at least twice as fast as that!"

At the end of the novel, Adam has, like several of his predecessors, left the country, his coterie dispersed or dead, but though he has not, like Gumbril, lost emotional contact with the woman he

11. See my *Evelyn Waugh, Writer*, pp. 47–48, for a passage titled "Paul's Meditations" and concerned with self-definition which Waugh canceled in manuscript.

loves, he does not have Gumbril's hope of continued movement, having taken exhausted refuge in a derelict and mud-bound car in a desolate landscape as the sounds of an apocalyptic battle return.

Unlike Arlen, Waugh was able to maintain relative popular and critical favor not merely because he was a better writer but because he could adapt to changing conditions even though, as Sonia Trumpington says in *Black Mischief*, "Every one's got very poor and it makes them duller." [12] Unlike Huxley, whose expatriation Waugh regarded as one reason for his decline as a novelist (*Letters*, 237), he stayed in or on the fringes of the world he created or described. And unlike Van Vechten, he did not inherit a trust fund which enabled him to cease writing for money (Kellner, 232). His material and some of his techniques may have been exhausted by the time he completed *Vile Bodies*, but his inventive and adaptive talents had not.

12. *Black Mischief* (Boston: Little, Brown, 1977 [1932]), p. 303.

Formulating Theory

CHAPTER 4

Waugh's Mind and Art

Except for Hemingway and to a lesser extent Huxley, the novelists discussed in the previous section now have few readers and even less critical support. Only Waugh's reputation as a literary artist continues to increase. However, as a result of the controversy over his opinions during his lifetime and the attention given to his eccentric personality thereafter, surprisingly little attention has been paid to what kind of artist he was and to what his strengths and limitations were.

It could be argued that Waugh himself did not have a clear or at least a consistent view of these issues. There is ample evidence that he did not want to be a literary artist at all and that he consistently disparaged his talent. He turned to writing only after he had gone down from Oxford without taking a degree, abandoned art school, and failed as a schoolmaster. Early in his career, he adopted a half-deprecating, half-defensive irony toward his work. In his first travel book, *A Bachelor Abroad*, he dwelt on the mechanics of publicizing oneself as an author and lamented the difficulty of finding "any aspect of social organization about which one can get down one's seventy thousand words without obvious plagiarism."[1] By 1934, he had reduced the travel book to a formula, and one can see from his comments in *Ninety-Two Days* and from his parody of that book in *Scoop* as John Boot's *Waste of Time* that the routine had become irksome to him. Before he turned to *Scoop* in order to raise money for his second marriage, he was searching for a new method

1. *A Bachelor Abroad* (New York: J. Cape/H. Smith, 1930), p. 14. The English title, *Labels*, was somewhat less ironic than the American for a book based on Waugh's belated honeymoon.

and a new subject, and once established at Piers Court, his first country house, he began work on what he regarded as his first serious novel, *Work Suspended*, which the outbreak of World War II caused him to abandon.

Toward the end of the war, planning and writing *Brideshead Revisited*, he had a renewed sense of his vocation as a writer. This wavered somewhat: after the war came conflicting pronouncements on the writer as a sort of superior bootmaker, elegantly stitching together material in order to exchange the product for money, and, conversely, on the writer as artist and seer, creating, unlike the politician, "a few objects of permanent value that were not there before him and would not have been there but for him."[2] The first mood tended to dominate when Waugh had finished a creative task, the second in periods of relative sterility. During the ten years he worked on the three novels which became *Sword of Honor*, he had, according to Fr. Martin D'Arcy, S.J., a sense that this was work for which he had been chosen by God. In his public pronouncements, he was more modest. Summing up his education—in which he did not include Oxford—he asserted that it had prepared him to become a writer of English prose—not a novelist or an artist, but a writer. It is tempting to apply to him the analysis of Lactantius in *Helena*, that he "delighted in writing, in the joinery and embellishment of his sentences, in the consciousness of high rare virtue when every word had been used in its purest and most precise sense, in the kitten games of syntax and rhetoric. Words could do anything except generate their own meaning."[3]

Except generate their own meaning: This must come from the working of the artist's mind and imagination, not merely the craftsman's joinery, on the world that he experiences. It has been widely argued that Waugh did not have the mind of a complete artist and that his weaknesses and perhaps his self-chosen limitations as a novelist are the result. Readers with expectations formed by modernist or realistic fiction are almost certain to be disappointed by his novels, largely because the cast of his mind was exclusive rather

2. *Tourist in Africa* (Boston: Little, Brown, 1960), p. 187.
3. *Helena* (London: Chapman & Hall, 1950), p. 120.

than inclusive, more inclined to judgment than to sympathy, and more likely to illuminate strikingly a series of details than to shape and order those details into an epiphanic whole. These characteristics—weaknesses in the view of many critics—are obvious enough. But in the wake of modernism, perhaps there are other qualities to value.

One of the traits of Waugh's character obvious to him as well as to everyone who ever knew him or read his work was the inability to sympathize with or even to attempt to understand those who did not share his tastes. Acknowledging a desire to be a man of the world in *They Were Still Dancing*, he admitted that he was scarcely fitted for the role on the grounds that "I shall always be ill at ease with nine out of every ten people I meet, that I shall always find something startling and rather abhorrent in the things most other people think worth doing and something puzzling in their standards of importance, that I shall probably be increasingly rather than decreasingly vulnerable to the inevitable minor disasters and injustices of life . . ."[4]—that, in sum, twenty-five years later he would become the model for Gilbert Pinfold. Even when he was moved to sympathy and interest—for English settlers in the highlands of Kenya, for Mexican landowners and peasants deprived of property and religion, and for the Masai and Arab cultures of East Africa—he seemed to be moved by preconceived principles of class and racial solidarity, by financial and religious sympathies, or by an interest in coherent, picturesque social survivals that could pose no threat to institutions and ideals he valued more directly, and in each case he spent at least as much energy in denouncing their opponents as in advancing their case.[5]

Even when he liked people, he could keep them at the point of his barbed style and regard them as specimens. Rebuked by Cyril Connolly, who replied stiffly to a request for current gossip by say-

4. *Remote People* (London: Duckworth, 1931), p. 143. The American title is *They Were Still Dancing*.

5. Anthony Powell, Waugh's friend for many years, notes Waugh's tendency to think in "stylized concepts" and argues that this is "by no means a disadvantage to a novelist, clearing the air automatically of extraneous detail that can clog a narrative." *Messengers of Day* (New York: Holt, Rinehart and Winston, 1978), pp. 20–21.

ing that he "did not regard the sufferings of his fellow men as the subject for humor," Waugh replied that he could not see "how you can bear to go so much into society if you feel this" (*Letters*, 688, 689).

Whether cause, effect, or condition, Waugh's inability to identify with other people or groups was accompanied by his tendency to classify, analyze, separate, and judge. These habits of mind can be seen in his biographies, where aspects of the subject's life are sorted into discrete compartments and presented as a series of activities rather than as a complex whole, contradictory and confusing, but vital. This tendency is as marked in his first book, *Rossetti*,[6] as in his last, *A Little Learning*.[7] Presenting a phase of Rossetti's life, Waugh composed a series of essays, first on his relations with Ruskin, then with Morris and Burne-Jones, then with Elizabeth Siddal—and then, as if it were a wholly separate matter, he discussed Rossetti's career as a painter (67–91). *A Little Learning* contains even more striking illustrations of this tendency: "Under 'environment' I have included all the memories of childhood and some of my boyhood as it was lived at home. School . . . was for the following eight years a different world, sometimes agreeable, more often not, inhabited by a quite different and rather nastier little boy who had no share in the real life of the third of a year he spent at home" (62). It is not strange that as a schoolboy Waugh should accept his brother Alec's view that "he keep his life in 'watertight' compartments" (*Diaries*, 19), but for a man of sixty, it is more remarkable.

As a mental operation, classification involves both abstraction and distinction; distinction necessitates qualification (the addition of characteristics to differentiate one type from another); and the more complex but related operation, discrimination, involves judgment. From these basic habits of mind stem Waugh's choice of subject, his attitude toward it, and at least some features of the style and technique in which he embodied it. Leaving aside for the moment larger questions of subject matter, one can see clearly enough the effect of his way of thinking on his means of creating characters. In the first edition of *Work Suspended*, he spoke of them as "man-

6. *Rossetti: His Life and Works* (London: Duckworth, 1928).
7. *A Little Learning* (Boston: Little, Brown, 1964).

ageable abstractions."[8] Paul Pennyfeather is not a hero but, says the omniscient author, a shadow of himself in most of *Decline and Fall*; Adam Fenwick-Symes in *Vile Bodies* looks "exactly as young men like him do look" and speaks, on one occasion, "in no particular manner."[9]

Almost as obvious as this minimalism is Waugh's tendency to portray character by use of stereotype and caricature. In theory, and certainly in Waugh's practice, caricature involves the reduction of personality to near-abstraction, then presentation by means of a few qualifying characteristics that give the figure the only individuality it has. Accidents (in the Thomistic sense) are as important as, in fact become, substance. Consciously or not, Waugh filled his early novels, especially the first three, with people who rush about in search of characteristics with which they can construct identity: questionnaire and interrogation, in which the external marks of individuality and motive are recorded, recur again and again in *Decline and Fall*; smart people and places and fashions, including green bowler hats and suede evening shoes, are eagerly grasped at by the socially insecure in *Vile Bodies*; in *Black Mischief* the Emperor Seth seeks to define himself as modern by frantic, eclectic rummaging through catalogues of objects and compendiums of ideas.

Waugh's style also bears some marks of the classifier's attitude. Unlike Hemingway, for whom nouns and verbs, things and actions, are of primary importance, Waugh achieved some of his most telling effects by using striking adjectives and adverbs to modify relatively abstract terms. The categorization of the members of the Bollinger Club in *Decline and Fall* is one example: "epileptic royalty from their villas of exile; uncouth peers from crumbling country seats; smooth young men of uncertain tastes from the embassies and legations; illiterate lairds from wet granite hovels in the Highlands; ambitious young barristers and Conservative candidates torn from the London season and the indelicate advances of

8. *Work Suspended* (London: Chapman & Hall, 1942), pp. 82–83. The revised version was published initially in *Work Suspended and Other Stories Written before the Second World War* (London: Chapman and Hall, 1949).

9. *Vile Bodies* (London: Chapman & Hall, 1965), p. 15. This, from the Uniform Edition, has a Preface by Waugh.

debutantes." [10] Here the adjectives establish the tone of humorous detachment, but on occasion Waugh used the same pattern to attack by frontal assault or to ambush with concealed pitfalls. For example, it is easy to pass over casually the effect of adjectives like the one in Gilbert Pinfold's comparative estimate of his own books: "he thought them well made, better than many reputed works of genius." [11]

In this last quotation, we are moving from caricature to discrimination. The former is primarily a matter of perception, a way of seeing the world in physical outline. The latter performs something of the same function in the moral sphere; it recognizes more than one possibility, but at some point—sooner in the mind of the satirist, later in that of the more subtle moralist—the various possibilities are stripped of complexity, measured, and judged. Waugh had from the beginning of his career a sense of what was important and what was not: a reputed work of genius is not necessarily important; neither, really, is "a world that has been well travelled by psychologists and satirists—the world of wild aberration without theological significance." [12] This sense of discrimination accounted not only for his more intransigent political and religious stands but also for his tolerance, as a novelist and as a traveler. At twenty-five, in the midst of a belated honeymoon (granted, the bride was in hospital), Waugh delighted in observing the life of jolly brothels in Port Said. At fifty-five, he regarded with great interest the Star Bar in Mombasa, "a notorious dancing-bar, part brothel, part thieves' kitchen; everyone spoke of it with awe. . . . All races and all vices were catered for. I have never been in a tougher or more lively joint anywhere" (*Tourist in Africa*, 47). In his fiction, he could view without apparent shock or disapproval the depredations of Basil Seal or Kätchen; the passions of Captain Grimes, Ambrose Silk, and Anthony Blanche; and the callousness of Mrs. Beaver and Mr. Youkoumian.

---

10. *Decline and Fall* (London: Chapman & Hall, 1962), pp. 113–114. This, from the Uniform Edition, not only has a Preface by Waugh but restores readings expurgated for the first and subsequent editions.

11. *The Ordeal of Gilbert Pinfold* (London: Chapman & Hall, 1957), p. 9.

12. *Monsignor Ronald Knox* (Boston: Little, Brown, 1959), p. 314.

His tolerance had essentially the same root as his lack of empathy. He once wrote, "as happier men watch birds, I watch men. They are less attractive but more various" (*Tourist in Africa*, 12), and his attitude toward them and toward everyone outside his sympathies was essentially that of an observer toward a specimen. He need not condemn them because they are outside the law and not liable to judgment. Of course, since they are not fully human, they get no more sympathy for being sheep than they would for being wolves: Mr. Joyboy is rightfully exploited by Dennis Barlow; the fat and stupid members of the upper middle classes are the natural prey of Basil Seal. In *Remote People* Waugh gave a theoretical basis for his objectivity: "It seems to me that a prig is someone who judges people by his own standards; criticism only becomes useful when it can show people where their own principles are in conflict" (*Remote People*, 61).

Waugh could not maintain this attitude. It was not perversity or religious mania which drove him to abandon his position as detached, ironic observer—quite congenial to one side of his personality—for that of overt moralist and judge. The pressure of events after 1935—for Waugh as for many others the advent of a grim new age—drove him first to a conservatism which could advocate and celebrate Fascist victory in *Waugh in Abyssinia*,[13] then to celebrate the glories of what he thought to be a vanishing aristocracy in *Brideshead Revisited*, and then to express loathing for, indeed resentment of, the postwar world in a manner that was only partly facetious. Beset with vexations and, like Rossetti, with an insomnia that could be alleviated only by drugs, he was assaulted by imaginary voices "in terms of 'gross and unbearable obloquy'" (*Rossetti*, 179).

Unlike Rossetti, whose experience he recalled when he shared it, he did not attempt suicide, but silenced his voices and went on to produce four more books, one of which, *Unconditional Surrender* (titled in the United States *The End of the Battle*), went beyond dis-

13. From the perspective of the 1980's, Waugh's view of Abyssinian officialdom looks very different than it did, say, to Rose Macaulay, who called *Waugh in Abyssinia* "a Fascist tract" and made other animadversions about his political views in "Evelyn Waugh," *Horizon*, 14 (December 1946), 370–376.

tinctions of class, nationality, race, and religion to exhibit sympathy and concern for impoverished Yugoslavian Jews.

Even in this novel, however, Waugh's vision, as differentiated from his opinions, was essentially exclusive, defensive, reclusive. He recognized these impulses and embodied them in Ivo Crouchback, who died alone and insane, just as he recognized the streak of extravagant romanticism in *Brideshead*, which he parodied in Ludovic's absurd and popular novel *The Death Wish*. In positive terms, he advocated local loyalties and ties of custom rather than of rule, and in Guy Crouchback he portrays a definite and limited act of charity.

But it was chiefly in personal and negative terms that the vision found expression. The real theme of much of his work is "Save yourself; others you cannot save." Paul Pennyfeather retreats into theology, William Boot to the shabby comforts and the decaying certainties of Boot Magna, Dennis Barlow to England and the practice of his art, Scott-King to his boys' school and the classics, Guy Crouchback to the "Lesser House" and the placid domestic charms of the safe, conventional, agriculturally inclined Domenica Plessington.

By his own account, Waugh shared this desire to escape, to burrow into the rock, "to create," as an artist, "little private systems of order of his own" (*EAR*, 304); and in *A Little Learning* he linked to "the common English confusion of the antiquated with the sublime" his own tendency to seek "dark and musty seclusions, like an animal preparing to whelp" (44). It would be too simple to say that this reaction to experience made Waugh an escapist, a romantic, or a reactionary. Certainly these were dangerous possibilities that sometimes became actualities, for instinctive condemnation and rejection of unpleasantness, if followed to a logical conclusion, lead either to fantasies of wish fulfillment or to shrill denunciation. However, Waugh did not descend entirely into fantasy, and at his best he could perceive the inadequacy of the refuge as well as that of the world outside it.

The chief danger for such a writer is oversimplification, both morally and, at least for Waugh, technically. His chief means of creating character was caricature; his most common and most successful narrative or expository division was three or four pages, and even in his most consciously complex work he could seldom exceed either of these limits. To attain any degree of real complexity, whether of insight or of narrative, he was forced to multiply, to develop concurrently several points of view and narrative strands. Whenever he did not do so, his work was least successful.

Waugh's need for technical and emotional complexity is seen most clearly in his short stories. Most of them depend for their effect on the manipulation, through surprising turns of plot, of characters less wooden than cardboard. Neither character nor situation is much developed, and Waugh himself often seemed bored by conceptions that must have looked promising but had not worn very well.

The characters in Waugh's novels do not differ markedly in type from those in the short stories, and the actions in which they are involved are if anything less complex than than those in the shorter form. Yet, by superimposing a series of cardboard figures one over the other, Waugh creates something more than a pack of cards. The epigraph from Lewis Carroll, denying that the characters are real, fits *Vile Bodies*: Simon Balcairn, Agatha Runcible, Miles Malpractice, Archie Schwert, and the rest are individually trivial; put together in action and going each to a depressing end, they give an impression of a generation doomed, frustrated, and futile. An even clearer indication of Waugh's technique of reinforcement by repetition is his use of the double, ranging from the Boots in *Scoop* to Guy Crouchback's three counterparts (mentioned on the jacket flap of the English edition) of *Sword of Honour*. Throughout his career, Waugh used these devices, extensive rather than intensive, to construct his novels; such technical innovations as he introduced were designed not only to serve this end but to render less obvious, by interweaving as closely as possible the various characters and motifs, the fact that his basic method was so simple.

Decline and Fall, perfect in its way, is in this respect comparatively crude, introducing and establishing characters chiefly by a series of monologues and then developing and resolving the plot strands in discrete blocks, as indicated by chapter titles such as "Captain Grimes," "The Agony of Captain Grimes," and "The Passing of a

Public School Man." *Vile Bodies*, though a less successful novel, is technically more advanced: Agatha Runcible's delirium, for example, draws together more vividly and effectively than had Professor Silenus' lecture in *Decline and Fall* the central themes and characters of the novel in the metaphor of the endless and meaningless race that is Waugh's objective correlative for the world without theological significance. In *A Handful of Dust*, Waugh brought to full maturity the techniques by which he achieved multiplicity and simultaneity; Tony's delirium, inhabited by the people and formed by the ideas that have betrayed him, is dramatic rather than merely rhetorical, and it represents as great an advance over Agatha's rambling as that in its turn had over Silenus' discursive categorizing. The critics who, Waugh wrote in the Preface to the novel, "date my decline" from *A Handful of Dust*[14] were perhaps correct in a technical sense: there was nothing really new in his subsequent novels except the experiments with first-person narration in *Work Suspended* and *Brideshead Revisited*.

While it is now obvious that Waugh was making a conscious change in his approach to fiction with *A Handful of Dust*—he told Katherine Asquith that "for the first time I am trying to deal with normal people instead of eccentrics" (*Letters*, 84)—he overtly announced a shift in method only with the first-person narrator's comments in *Work Suspended*: "It seems to me I am in danger of becoming mechanical, turning out year after year the kind of book I know I can write well" (167). Furthermore, by the late 1930's Waugh had begun to take a serious interest in religious and political questions. He may have felt that the first-person narrator would enable him to present in his fiction an attitude toward experience more searching, complex, and mature than that exhibited in the earlier novels and especially in *Scoop*, which was a conscious reversion to a simpler method. He may also have seen in this point of view a way of attaining a greater unity of effect. Although the outbreak of World War II drove Waugh to abandon his theme and take

14. *A Handful of Dust* (London: Chapman & Hall, 1964), p. 7. This, from the Uniform Edition, has a Preface by Waugh.

up, in *Put Out More Flags*, the new subject of war in something like his old form, he returned to first-person narrative in *Brideshead* before abandoning it altogether in his fiction.

Whatever his reasons, the experiments cannot be considered entirely successful either in technique or in maturity of point of view. Even Waugh was not satisfied. He revised *Work Suspended* in 1949 to cut extraneous material as well as shape the fragment for independent publication, and he altered the text of *Brideshead* several times before the acknowledged revision of 1960. As his excisions from the latter show, the first-person narrator whose experience, tastes, and attitudes to some extent paralleled his own had tempted him to introduce blocks of analysis, little essays several paragraphs long, that slow the pace and blur the focus. Moreover, the first-person technique could not guard Waugh against exceeding the bounds of his basic vision. Attacking rather than retreating from the world, he seemed querulous and strident because he presented overtly and without qualification opinions regarded as his.

However, the nature of Waugh's vision is less important than the adequacy with which it is embodied: without balance and ironic contrast, Waugh could not personally embody his central subject, the individual in retreat from a chaotic and menacing society, in satisfying forms. Given proper form, the subject could sustain novels that deserve to endure. In these terms, I would argue, *Helena* and *The Ordeal of Gilbert Pinfold* will interest only specialists; *Vile Bodies*, *The Loved One*, and perhaps *Sword of Honour* and *Brideshead* (see Chapters 10 and 13 for qualifications of this view) are of the second rank; *Scoop* and *Put Out More Flags* are greater successes in lesser modes; and *Decline and Fall*, *Black Mischief*, and *A Handful of Dust* will come to be seen as representing Waugh's art and vision at their most effective.

The estimate of the novels put in the second rank may seem surprising. Though they have not been uniformly acclaimed by readers and critics, they have been regarded with general respect, and the sensational quality of *The Loved One* and the popularity of the television version of *Brideshead* make them better known than more accomplished work. But in none of these novels is Waugh's recurring subject rendered adequately, with the result that they are sentimental in the sense that facts are not proportionate to the emotional response demanded. *Vile Bodies* provides the clearest example: the outer world is clearly established as mad and confusing by the events of the novel, but the contrasting place of peace and security sought by Adam and Nina is adumbrated only in the Christmas scene at Doubting Hall. Throughout most of the book Waugh must depend on direct statement in his authorial voice or in that of his characters to indicate to the reader the principles according to which the action is to be judged. Consequently, theme is too blatantly emphasized, while the narrative line, without effective contrast or thickening, is not very convincing.

The case of *The Loved One* is similar but more complex. Waugh is successful in showing the soulless, automatic responses of the people and the disorder of the society of Hollywood and Whispering Glades, inviting and easy targets for the satirist. But the novel lacks a moral center, a clear basis of judgment. Some critics have assumed that Waugh is contrasting Dr. Kenworthy's religion of death as a painless rest home with the Christian view of death, judgment, heaven, and hell. This assumption seems to be supported by Waugh's essay, "Death in Hollywood" (*EAR*, as "Half in Love with Easeful Death," 331–337), on the art and values of Forest Lawn, which explicitly and forcefully makes the contrast between the two eschatologies. In the novel itself, however, no such basis for judgment or moral distinction exists. Aimée's suicide and Dennis' blackmail are the result of promptings of the spirit, remote, austere, amoral, and rather vague. Waugh seems to imply that the possession of any spirit whatever distinguishes these two and Sir Francis Hinsley from the animals, two-and four-legged, that surround them. But even this standard is not consistently applied: Dennis' use of Aimée's death to effect his own withdrawal to England and the demands of his muse may be carried out ironically by both author and character, but the basis of his superiority to Mr. Joyboy and Sir Ambrose Abercrombie has been undermined. If, on the other hand, Dennis is acting under the compulsion of inspiration, of an inner necessity to write work of lasting value, then the dimensions and atmosphere of this refuge need a more convincing presentation.[15]

In its scope and its moral insights, *Sword of Honour* both intends to be and is a more considerable work than any of its predecessors. Like Tennyson's *Idylls of the King*, it is impressive for its goal and method when considered in retrospect. The movement of the main story involves the related processes of stripping away Guy Crouchback's illusions about the institutions of country, regiment, and class; of building in him a sense of his contact with humanity; and of releasing him from his spiritual paralysis. To illustrate and point up these processes, Waugh uses a series of comic scapegoats or doubles to embody and thus to dispel Guy's illusion: Apthorpe as parody of the old soldier, Ivor Claire as detached aristocrat, and Ludovic as thrall, at least in his preposterous novel, to the idea of the type of woman who, like Guy's faithless wife, symbolizes the amoral grace and beauty of the 1920's. Yet, however well it employs these and a number of other devices, *Sword of Honour* is not fully satisfying as a work of art. It may be that the theme and the scope were too large for Waugh to render. Certainly he found it necessary to summarize, explain, and comment more frequently than in earlier novels, and many of these passages make the novel more tedious to read than to recall. The book's length may also have made Waugh conscious of demands on the reader's memory, so that he felt obliged to make quite explicit the comparisons and analogies, the motifs, and the recurrent bits of minor action that might have been more effective if better concealed.[16]

The major weakness of the book is not narrowly technical, though it could be described as formal: it stems from the lack of alternatives and qualifications which also marked *Vile Bodies* and *The Loved One*. Here the weakness is in the kinds of irony directed at Guy Crouchback and other members of the old order who are

15. The theme of Death as an inspiration for Art was introduced at a late stage of composition; perhaps Waugh imposed it on the text rather than integrating it. See my *Evelyn Waugh, Writer* (Norman: Pilgrim Books, 1981), pp. 210–211.

16. In revising the three novels for the one-volume recension, Waugh cut some material, not always happily, but did nothing to conceal joinery. See *Evelyn Waugh, Writer*, pp. 325–332.

finally acceptable, though misguided, and that aimed at almost all left wingers and Americans, who are immediately rejected. The former is understanding if not indulgent: as Waugh wrote to Anthony Powell, Guy "is a prig. But he is a virtuous, brave prig" (*Letters*, 443). The latter is scathing, expressed in names like Scab Dunz and Bum Schlum for the American journalists and Spitz (in the recension Speit) for the American general, and judgment is simply pronounced rather than presented.

But Waugh's political views and anti-American bias are themselves effects of a deeper attitude: a dislike not only of the modern world but of any successful institution. In *Helena*, designating Constantine a symbol of "Power without Grace," he was as censorious of the emperor as he ever was of a modern politician. The difficulty in both *Helena* and *Sword of Honour* is that Waugh seemed unable to conceive of or at any rate to present in fiction the possibility of power *with* grace, or power used with some if not completely moral motive and effect. As a result, he chooses, not quite critically enough, grace without power, institutional forms, as represented by Guy's father, without any secular content, emphasizing the lack of power and making it almost a guarantee of grace. Waugh might not have agreed with Guy that only a fully just cause is worth pursuing, but he does not show clearly, as he does in some novels, the consequences of such an attitude.

Scoop and *Put Out More Flags* are more successful—not necessarily better—books than those I have just discussed because they are less ambitious and because their form balances more perfectly the opposing forces in Waugh's vision. In *Scoop*, Boot Magna is William's refuge from the world of Lord Copper; in *Put Out More Flags*, the desire of Ambrose Silk and Cedric Lyne to remain individuals and aesthetes in a world that is organizing itself for war contrasts to the eagerness with which most of the characters— even, finally, Basil Seal—rush to join one herd or another. The books are less ambitious because the threats to security—popular journalism and the Germans—are not shown as really serious. William escapes Lord Copper's publicity mill by simple stubbornness and by fortuitously provided substitutes, and although the Germans kill Cedric and the British drive Ambrose into exile, *Put Out More Flags* closes with a sense of release and triumph.

Yet these books do have a symmetry of form because both the world and the refuge are developed, so that one continually poses a criticism of the other. William Boot has escaped from the world's confusion, but he has also abandoned the possibility of love and of maturity; and Lord Copper, without gaining either, has forgone tranquility, would not know what to do with it if somehow he stumbled onto it. But it is in his domain that prizes like love are to be won. In the last line of the novel, "Outside the owls hunted maternal rodents and their furry broods," Waugh implies that the world is a more sinister place than either Copper or Boot—or Mrs. Stitch—imagines, and with that single line almost raises the novel above the level of condescending and farcical wish fulfillments on which it has rather complacently run.

Put Out More Flags, a far better book, qualifies continuously. Ambrose is sterile, a homosexual, but he is the only creator in the novel. Ambrose is more sane, Basil and his cohorts more effective. Basil and company are more responsible in social terms, but for reasons that are often insignificant; Ambrose has a high sense of vocation as an artist, but as person and even as artist he is ultimately silenced by events. England at war has no place for Ambrose, but banish him and banish, if not all the world, the part of the world that makes civilization possible. Only the boyish outbursts of patriotic feeling—even, in a fashion not wry enough, from Ambrose—prevent this from being one of Waugh's best novels.

In his three most successful novels, *Decline and Fall*, *Black Mischief*, and *A Handful of Dust*, Waugh presents the madness of the outer world as inevitable and therefore beyond judgment and the refuge as desirable and necessary but not fully secure or satisfying. Like F. Scott Fitzgerald, Waugh notes in the first of these novels that the very rich are different from you and me, but he shows that Paul Pennyfeather can never fully join or participate in the world of Rolls-Royces, country houses, and the Ritz, and that this existence, though glittering and exciting, is fundamentally meaningless, so that when Paul retreats into the shelter provided by Oxford and by the study of theology, he assumes an identity which he could not find in the outer, dynamic world. Paul's retreat is not so much a rejection of that world, however, as a recognition that it is not for the likes of him.

Like *Vile Bodies*, *Black Mischief* shows that there is no refuge or escape, but it maintains a formal and emotional balance lacking in the earlier book. Waugh has written that "The story deals with the conflict of civilization, with all its attendant and deplorable ills, and barbarism" (*Letters*, 77), and, as Frederick Stopp has shown, barbarism comes off rather better than civilization because it has vitality that civilization lacks.[17] In fact, the true barbarians in the novel, especially the Earl of Ngumo and the Nestorian abbot, have an integrity of being and a sense of tradition lacking in most of the other characters, while the superiority of Basil to the rest of the Europeans lies in his dissatisfaction with the trivial and empty forms of civilized life. In London and even in Seth's Ministry of Modernisation, Basil cannot function; confronted with murder, revolution, and chaos, he adopts native dress and customs to become an effective leader. Yet—and this is where the vision expressed in this novel is superior to that in most of Waugh's other works—he shows that one cannot regress. Barbarism has implications which even Basil quite literally finds it hard to stomach, and he is forced back to a London where "Every one's got very poor and it makes them duller."[18] Sonia Trumpington fears that Basil may turn serious too—but there is really no place for him to turn.

Because it confronts directly the ills of modern civilization and embodies them in characters rather than (as in *Black Mischief*) in a series of intellectual fads and because it traces more vividly and uncompromisingly the effects of seeking refuge from the world without adequate resources for the retreat or an ordered, enduring place of withdrawal, *A Handful of Dust* is the most penetrating and formally satisfying of Waugh's novels. The outer world of Polly Cockpurse and Mrs. Beaver is condemned, but, as Waugh implied

17. Frederick J. Stopp, *Evelyn Waugh: Portrait of an Artist* (Boston: Little, Brown, 1958), p. 32.
18. *Black Mischief* (London: Chapman & Hall, 1962), p. 233. From the Uniform Edition, this has a Preface by Waugh.

by saying that "It was humanist and contained all I had to say about humanism" (*EAR*, 304) and as Richard Wasson has shown in detail,[19] Tony's place of refuge is insubstantial and without real foundation, based on empty picturesqueness and private associations rather than a solid tradition. One may go further and say that Waugh is rejecting the aesthetic, the traditional, and the institutional approaches to life. All are forms without content; the world of the novel is hollow. Waugh spares a minimal sympathy for those who embrace some sort of form. Yet both Tony's delusions and the callousness and aimlessness of the Londoners are exposed rather than condemned; both are the result of processes that the individual cannot control or even understand. In a sense, the innocent and the guilty are equally responsible and equally blameless. The novel presents a picture of how things are rather than a moral statement about them.

Ultimately, questions about the value of Waugh's work can be reduced to one crucial question of whether or not he gives in his art a vision not of the truth but of a truth. It seems quite clear that he does. His novels embody a series of variations on one central theme: the individual, to be saved as an individual, must retreat from modern society; institutions are finally not worthy of loyalty, though ideals and people are; power in the world inevitably corrupts, but renunciation of the world and of power entails a real cost; the pressure of events is toward greater confusion, increasing drabness, and vitiation of energy; and private salvation cannot be shared. These views may be partial, but they are neither irresponsible nor foolish, and at his best Waugh presents them in coherent and compelling fashion in novels likely to be of enduring value.

19. Richard Wasson, "*A Handful of Dust*: Critique of Victorianism," *Modern Fiction Studies*, 7 (1961/62), 327–337.

CHAPTER 5

Waugh on Fiction

Even moderately careful readers of Waugh's novels are willing to admit that he knew what he was doing in particular cases, but even after the publication of *Essays, Articles, and Reviews* it seems difficult for many critics to regard him as having any theories about what he and other novelists were doing. It is true that his comments on fiction are neither very numerous nor very extensive. Only 36 of the 237 items in *Essays, Articles, and Reviews* and fewer than 100 of the 1,000 items he published in various genres deal with fiction.

Most of these items are reviews. Moreover, Waugh's situation as a reviewer varied widely during his career. As a young man he struggled to get work of any kind; in the 1930's he established himself as the expert on travel books for the *Spectator*; late in life he commented on books on specialized topics such as furniture and Kipling, on the work of—or memoirs about—his contemporaries, on that of new writers such as Muriel Spark whom he wished to encourage, mostly "in one of the weekly papers which is read by his friends & acquaintances because it is they primarily with whom he wishe[d] to communicate" (*Letters*, 537). Twice—between May and October 1930 in the *Graphic* and in the last six months of 1937 for *Night and Day*—he had his own book page. These venues not only gave him a certain freedom to choose the books he reviewed but also encouraged him to establish a point of view and an individual voice—and at times to reflect in print on formal and technical problems he faced in his own work.

Even when he was most conscious of theory, however, he remained aware of his role as reviewer. He once observed that reviewing "has to be done quickly; there is just time to jot down a

few points before the book fades from memory" and that "the best
we can hope to do is to give our readers some idea of a book's
character so that they will know whether they are likely to want it"
(*EAR*, 208). In simpler terms, the reviewer's job was "telling the
reader why a book is likely to be of use to him" (*EAR*, 277). His
standards were much more flexible than later critics have assumed.
He once defined a prig as "someone who judges people by his own,
rather than by their, standards; criticism only becomes useful when
it can show people where their own principles are in conflict." [1]
Even as a bright young intellectual, he was willing to apply to formula fiction the standards of formula fiction. He praised Alec
Waugh because "he never 'shows off' at all or writes for effect. He
has a mastery of thorough, sober workmanship and he never tries
to be clever." [2] And Waugh is able to use John Buchan's thriller to
condemn Gilbert Frankau's attempt at the same form and notes
with praise for craftsmanship in a minor genre the tight control of
character and language in the machine-tooled, commercial stories
of Sir Philip Gibbs (*Graphic*, 9 August 1930, p. 247).

Of course, Waugh lacked neither standards nor personal agendas.
He was quite willing to condemn, and he was, as Donat Gallagher
has pointed out (*EAR*, 112), always ready to enunciate the principles by which he judged any idea. While there is enough over-
lapping of comments to indicate a fundamental consistency in his
views of fiction, Waugh shifted emphases between his first period
of reviewing, 1929–1931, to his second, 1936–1939, and in the period after World War II was concerned with aspects of fiction which
he had not covered before. Without imposing a rigid classification,
I think it possible to distinguish the theoretical areas of structure,
narrative technique, characterization, and style. When they are in-
terwoven in a single essay or review, I shall not attempt to separate
them.

The comments on fiction published between 1929 and 1931 are
more consciously avant-garde and theoretical than anything he was

1. *Remote People* (London: Duckworth, 1931), p. 51.

2 *Graphic*, 7 July 1930, p. 33. This may seem very faint praise unless it is contrasted with Evelyn Waugh's dismissal of Richard Oke's *Frolic Wind* as "wretchedly
affected and 'stagey.'" *Graphic*, 27 September 1930, p. 509.

to publish thereafter, and like those of many literary men who write criticism, the theories he advocated helped to account for creative work he had just published or was about to publish. Moreover, because he was still in the process of establishing himself not only as a professional writer but as a presence on the literary scene, he displayed in these reviews and essays a more overt interest in the problems and concerns of the writer than he did in his later work.

Waugh's essay on Ronald Firbank (*EAR*, 56–59) was his first conscious attempt to establish an aesthetic. The essay is not entirely accurate; Firbank used far more description and less dialogue than Waugh (who was probably planning *Vile Bodies*) found it convenient to allow. However, Waugh was more interested in Firbank's solution to the peculiarly twentieth-century problem of "making an art form out of [nineteenth-century] raw material of narration," emphasizing the way in which

The talk goes on, delicate, chic, exquisitely humorous, and seemingly without point or plan. Then, quite gradually, the reader is aware that a casual reference on one page links up with some particular inflection of phrase on another until there emerges a plot; usually a plot so outrageous that he distrusts his own inferences.

Waugh cites two instances from Firbank and might well have cited the wounding, wasting, and death of Lord Tangent in *Decline and Fall*. Firbank's means of "bringing coherence to his own elusive humour" with an objective rather than a "subjective attitude to his material";[3] his emphasizing "the fact which his contemporaries were neglecting that the novel should be directed for entertainment"; and his breaking in the process "the chain of cause and effect in fiction"—these, Waugh felt, were Firbank's chief innovations.

Having written his most Firbankian novel, *Vile Bodies*,[4] Waugh next turned to a reexamination of Thomas Hardy's *Tess of the D'Urbervilles*. He was willing to give Hardy full marks, though not in

3. In reviewing Wyndham Lewis' *Satire and Fiction* (*Graphic*, 25 October 1930, p. 174), Waugh praised "the observations about the 'Outside and Inside' method of fiction" and asserted that "No novelist and very few intelligent novel readers can afford to neglect this essay."

4. See Julian Jebb, "The Art of Fiction XXX: Evelyn Waugh," *Paris Review*, 8 (Summer-Fall 1963) and Waugh's Preface to the Uniform Edition of *Vile Bodies* (London: Chapman & Hall, 1965).

this novel, for "the structural magnificence of his plots, his conception of character, and the solidity and continuity of the life he reveals." Modern novelists had little to learn even from Hardy's virtues. Instead, they

direct their efforts mainly towards economy and selection and accuracy;
they attempt a literal transcription of dialogue, choosing each extract only
for its significance in the structure of their story; they convey their narrative, atmosphere and characterisation by means of innuendo rather than
direct description.

He also rejected Hardy's "bogus" pessimism, arguing that "it is so
much more pretentious to write books about sad and cruel people
than about odd and amusing ones." "True tragedy" is achieved by
developing a situation "that seems in conflict with the benevolent
organisation of the universe, and by making an artistic and significant form out of the apparent chaos to reconcile it with the universe."[5] This dictum may not explain tragedy, but it goes a long
way toward explaining the tone of *Vile Bodies* and *A Handful of
Dust*, and it is the opening shot in the minor skirmish which Waugh
conducted against stock unhappy endings (see also *Graphic*, 31 May
1930, p. 476).

Waugh already had an example of the ideal modern novel to set
against Hardy. In June 1929 he had written to Henry Yorke [Green]
that *Living* was an "*important*" book, praising the "absence of that
awful thing they call 'word pictures,'" the way in which no appearances are described," the invention of "an entirely new language,
doing for Birmingham born people what Singe [*sic*] did with
Irish—making an artistic form out of a dialect so that every word
is startling," and the management of plot "which is oddly enough
almost exactly the way Firbank managed his" (*Letters*, 35). His first

---

5. "'Tess'—As a 'Modern' Sees It," *Evening Standard*, 17 January 1930, p. 7. The
dictum about the relevance of dialogue to the work as a whole was applied consistently in Waugh's critical career. In 1921 he warned Dudley Carew not to "bring
characters on simply to draw their characters or make them talk. Fit them into a
design" (*Letters*, 2). And in 1938, reviewing Kate O'Brien's *Pray for the Wanderer*, he
noted the few occasions on which the author was guilty of "recording conversations
for their general instead of their particular interest" (*Spectator*, 160 [29 April 1938],
768). And note the similarities of Ernest Hemingway's views on essays faked into
dialogue and the fact that "Prose is architecture, not interior decoration." *Death in
the Afternoon* (New York: Charles Scribner's Sons, 1932), p. 191.

public review of the book was published as he prepared to finish *Vile Bodies* ("Turning Over New Leaves," *Vogue* [London], 74 [4 September 1929], 43), and when that novel's success brought him a literary page of his own, he devoted much of his third column to praising *Living* as "A Neglected Masterpiece" (*EAR*, 80–82). He warned his readers that there were oddities in language and technique but that "The more I read it the more I appreciate the structural necessity of all the features which at first disconcerted me," and he described more clearly—he never quite defined the term—what he meant by *structural*:

There are no unrelated bits such as one finds in most books. A danger in novel-writing is to make one's immediate effect and then discard the means one employed. Modern novelists taught by Mr. James Joyce are at last realizing the importance of re-echoing and remodifying the same themes. Note, for instance, the repeated metaphor of "pigeons" in *Living*.

He also found "the same technical apparatus at work as in many of Mr. T. S. Eliot's poems—particularly in the narrative passages of *The Waste Land* and the two *Fragments of an Agon*."

Subsequent reviews in the *Graphic* were less militantly avant-garde, and many (like his review of his own *Labels*, 4 October 1930, p. 25) were playful, but there were intermittent attempts to educate his readers to the new type of fiction. Reviewing what was in theme "a simple, commonplace story," he found its real significance in a method which, he asserted,

is going to become more and more the manner for the fiction of the next twenty years. There are practically no descriptive passages, except purely technical ones. The character, narrative and atmosphere are all built up by and implicit in the dialogue, which is written in a vivid slang, with numerous recurring phrases running through as a refrain. (*Graphic*, 12 July 1930, p. 75)

He pointed again to Firbank as the originator of this style and noted that both he and Hemingway had used it.

Waugh's praise of W. R. Burnett's slang and of Henry Green's Birmingham dialect will surprise readers like William Safire who regard him as the patron saint of traditional English, but in fact the young, or youngish, Waugh had a well-developed taste for vivid language. In 1930, he praised a minor mystery story because "It is American in origin and consequently the dialogue gains in pungency and liveliness (*Graphic*, 28 June 1930, p. 715), and he found in John Dos Passos' *The Forty Second Parallel* "phonetically spelt colloquial American which makes one despair of English" (*Graphic*, 11 October 1930, p. 74). Waugh always abhorred clichés, merely local stylistic effects, and any kind of overwriting. For example, in his last review for the *Graphic* he found Graham Greene's style in *The Name of Action* "a little repugnant. It is all metaphor and simile, which often fails in its reason for existing by obscuring rather than illuminating the description" (*Graphic*, 25 October 1930, p. 174). Well into the 1930's he welcomed fresh, surprising, and vivid language. He even praised "The facetious back-chat of flirtation" in a novel about very lower-middle class characters ("A Tale of London Town," *Evening Standard*, 20 August 1931, p. 14).

However, he was by no means uncritical of the form in which it was used. Although he called Dos Passos' novel "from a purely literary point of view . . . by far the most interesting piece of work, always excepting the fragments of Mr. Joyce's *Work in Progress*, which has appeared since Mr. Henry Green's *Living*," he noted what seemed to him defects in construction and observed, very acutely, that the book seemed "incomplete as it stands."

In fact, important though he thought the novel, he gave first place in this particular review to a much more conventional work of fiction, Somerset Maugham's *Cakes and Ale*. Dismissing the controversy over the roman a clèf features, Waugh found far more interesting the "brilliant technical dexterity," by which, in this case, he meant the management of suspense and surprise, of the shifts from past to present and from one narrative mode to another.

Waugh as literary critic was not very different from Waugh as moralist or social commentator. He was able to see the limitations of older ways of doing things, but he did not automatically praise the new, and he was able to recognize that it was very difficult to be both new and significant. Thus, while he rejected old forms, he did not reject form, and while he rejected conventional language, he insisted that all local effects be integrated into a larger whole. In the broad sense, he was a modernist and formalist, but like T. S. Eliot, he was willing to consider the internal form of the individual work rather than impose preestablished rules. In these responses, as in his surprising tolerance for commodity fiction, he was far more tolerant than would seem plausible to those acquainted only with the later Waugh.

However, his tolerance for the whole process of book reviewing was temporarily exhausted, and except for two reviews in the *Evening Standard* in 1931, he made no further printed references to fiction until 1936. In the interim, he was certainly busy with a wide variety of other activities; perhaps, having established himself as a novelist and having reached a point where he could consolidate and develop early methods, he was less interested in theory.

His first comment on fiction after the five-year hiatus was a very negative review of Aldous Huxley's *Eyeless in Gaza*[6] on the grounds that, in order to slow the library borrower and create a demand for more copies and to conceal the fundamental and consistent unpleasantness of the central character, Huxley "has left things to the binder, and has been content, unambitiously, to sew up the chapters in the wrong order. The result is a novel of conventional plan . . . arbitrarily shuffled and redealt."

Waugh was much happier with P. G. Wodehouse's *Laughing Gas*, crediting this "neglected genius" with "inventing the enormously impressive device, cumbrously borrowed from him by Mr. T. S. Eliot, of introducing into demotic speech allusive phrases from technical and poetic English" and of having "a James-Joyce-like fertility in enriching the language with new words." Most important, however, was the creation of a purely literary world. Waugh maintained that "Jeeves stands out as a giant of artistic creation, not as a man of thought but as a man of words" and that Wodehouse was "free from the reigning folly in which novelists believe that they are making their characters live" by "portraying them in all their moods and functions." Instead, Wodehouse limits and controls his

6. "Blinding the Middle-Brow," *Tablet*, 168 (18 July 1936), 84. Waugh was delighted with Cyril Connolly's parody of the novel. See *Night and Day*, 11 November 1937, p. 23.

characters, who "lead patterned lives comparable to the precise regularity of the great Diaghileff ballets."[7]

In part, of course, Waugh is teasing pseudomoderns by placing Wodehouse in the company of their major heroes. Six years earlier, however, Waugh had stated the case against realism in character drawing: characters "cannot be successfully bounded by the limitations of the art-form in which they appear." Unlike the general reader, Waugh regarded this as a defect because "it is the author's business to restrain his own talent to the confines proper to his medium" (*Graphic*, 11 October 1930, p. 74).

Neither the attack on Huxley's sham modernity nor the praise of Wodehouse's virtues represents a new element in Waugh's thinking about fiction. He had made similar if less frontal attacks on other writers in 1930, and his view of the subordination of character to design complements his praise of Firbank. However, in these two essays and in his weekly book pages for *Night and Day*, he was less concerned to support techniques which were no longer quite new and more concerned to uphold traditional standards. He praised the language of Leo Rosten's Hyman Kaplan for its "brilliant quality of undermining the very structure and logic of plain statement" (*Night and Day*, 11 November 1937, p. 23). He enjoyed as much as he had in 1930 the "pungent phrases" and the lack of "unnecessary comment" in an American gangster novel which read "like the most enjoyable kind of 'talkie'" (*Night and Day*, 20 August 1937, p. 26), and he praised the management in shifting from one mood to another (*Night and Day*, 7 October 1930, p. 26).

However, in opposing the slightly younger men who "ganged up and captured the decade" (*EAR*, 394), he turned more and more to commentary on social and political issues. In only twelve of twenty-six *Night and Day* columns did he review fiction at all, and only a third of the sixty-nine books treated were fiction. The most extensive, on 19 August was a send-up of a vulgar and improbable romance which sounds like material for a television miniseries.

7. "An English Humorist," *Tablet*, 168 (17 October 1936), 533. See also Roger Simmonds' experimental play in *Work Suspended* (London: Chapman & Hall, 1942), which the publisher is too dim to recognize as exactly like a ballet.

One reason for this relative indifference to fiction and in particular to theoretical issues was the fact that Waugh was not writing
fiction that required much rethinking of his own practice. *Scoop* is
excellent of its kind, but it is a kind which he had done before.

However, once he turned to a new form in what became *Work
Suspended* in the late 1930's, his comments on writing become more
pointed than they had been in almost a decade. He showed a new
concern for grammar and precision in language (*EAR*, 232, 239,
250–251), presaging the fussier Waugh of the Pinfold era, and he
took a more sober view of "the sudden superb swoop into nonsense" as, "for the man of words, one of the bitterest denials possible; the denial that anything is more worth saying than anything
else" (*EAR*, 234). To be sure, he was writing for the Catholic newspaper, the *Tablet*, but he was more serious in other venues as well.

He was also growing more precise. In reviewing Cyril Connolly's *Enemies of Promise* (*EAR*, 238–241) he explained that the distinction between the critical and the creative writer "is an added
energy and breadth of vision which enables him to conceive and
complete a structure." Because Connolly did not have this sense,
he thought, he faked some transitions between disparate elements.
Waugh preferred the term *architectural* to *creative*, and it is worth
noting that while he had delighted in the extravagances of Gaudi in
1929[8] by 1938 he was advocating a return to the Vitruvian Orders
followed by English architects of the eighteenth century (*EAR*,
215–218), in part because they are more universal: "By studying
'the Orders' you can produce Chippendale Chinese; by studying
Chippendale Chinese you will produce nothing but magazine covers." And he showed a new solemnity about style which consists,
not as Connolly's discussion implied, in "isolated passages" like a
mouthful of wine, but in "the whole" because

writing is an art which exists in a time sequence; each sentence and each
page is dependent on its predecessors and successors; a sentence which he
admires may owe its significance to another fifty pages distant. I beg Mr.
Connolly to believe that even quite popular writers take great trouble
sometimes in this matter. (*EAR*, 235)

8. *A Bachelor Abroad* (New York: J. Cape/H. Smith, 1930).

Waugh had taken trouble, of course, and in fact this passage accords with and develops what he had said about Firbankian and Joycean use of motifs as structural principles. But he was no longer invoking Firbank and Joyce.

Waugh was a great deal happier with Somerset Maugham's *Christmas Holiday* in a review titled "The Technician" (*EAR*, 247-248). As in the review of *Cakes and Ale* for the *Graphic*, Waugh praises Maugham's mastery of technique, but here (perhaps transferring the new concern for architecture and furnishings aroused by his own furnishing of Piers Court, his first real home as an adult) he adds the comparison of "watching a first-class cabinet-maker cutting dovetails; in the days of bakelite that is a rare and bewitching experience." Maugham becomes for Waugh "the only living studio-master under whom one can study with profit. He has no marked idiosyncrasies which threaten the pupil with bad habits. His virtues of accuracy, economy and control are those most lacking today among his juniors." Waugh concentrates on the long narration in the middle of the book, praising especially "the transitions from direct speech to stylized narrative, the change of narrator as Simon takes up part of the story, the suspense that is created even though the reader already knows what the climax will be" as "models of technique."

Waugh had apparently not begun writing *Work Suspended*[9] when he wrote this review, but his praise of Maugham's craftsmanship is very close to the terms he uses for the elderly painter in that novel. When he reviewed *The Week-End Wodehouse* in June 1939, he had thought enough about the novel to be able to tell A. D. Peters that he was not working on it (*Catalogue*, E370). Less overtly but no less clearly than in the case of *Scoop*, thinking about Wodehouse ran parallel to thinking about his own work. He expanded his earlier discussion of Wodehouse's irrealism to argue that

It is the half-real characters of the ordinary popular novelist who disappear. Literary characters may survive either through being so real and round that they are true of any age and race, or through being so stylized that they

9. Christopher Sykes, *Evelyn Waugh: A Biography* (Boston: Little, Brown, 1975), pp. 181, 189, thinks that Waugh began this novel in 1937 (or 1938; he is a little vague on the score) but apparently inserts *new* before *novel* in the diary entry of 22 Novem-

carry their own world with them. Of the first group is the Pooter family, whose physical circumstances now correspond to those of no existing class; of the second are Mr. Wodehouse's characters. They live in their own universe like the characters of a fairy story. (*EAR*, 254–255)

In *Work Suspended*, Waugh, or at least his first-person narrator, modified the distinctions. Plant asserts that "There is no place in literature for a live man, solid and active." The writer can display Dickensian oddities who come into the spectators' view

dazzled, deafened, and doped, tumble through their tricks and scamper out again, to the cages behind which the real business of life, eating and mating, is carried on out of sight of the audience. . . . The alternative, classical expedient is to take the whole man and reduce him to a manageable abstraction. Set up your picture plain, fix your point of vision, make your figure twenty foot high or the size of a thumb-nail, he will be life-size on your canvas; hang your picture in the darkest corner, your heaven will still be its one source of light. Beyond these limits lie only the real trouser buttons and the *crepe* hair with which the futurists used to adorn their paintings. It is, anyway, in the classical way that I have striven to write. . . .[10]

Once again, this does not contradict anything Waugh said about Firbank's method, but it is stated in the personal voice rather than from precedent and, paradoxically, appeals to classical rather than modernist canons which turn out to be not all that different in theory, although Waugh's fictional practice was becoming more conventional.

The outbreak of war terminated rather than suspended his experiment with retrospective first-person narration in *Work Suspended* and interrupted his comments on contemporary fiction for more than eight years. For much of that time he was on active service or writing *Brideshead Revisited* or engaging in more remunerative work. What leisure he had for minor literary matters was devoted to a variety of general topics.

However, Waugh's review of Robert Graves and Alan Hodge's *The Reader Over Your Shoulder* (*EAR*, 275–277) is the first indication

---

ber 1937 (*Diaries*, 247) and thus misses the obvious inference that Waugh is referring to *Scoop*, which he was then revising.

10. *Work Suspended* (London: Chapman & Hall, 1942), pp. 82–83. The passage appears only in this edition.

of an attitude toward style which persisted until the end of Waugh's life. He had praised vivid slang and demotic speech in fiction as late as 1937; now he attacked "the present decay of literary decency that is abundantly apparent in many quarters. This is the century of the common man; let him write as he speaks and let him speak as he pleases." According to Waugh, this creates a problem for the artist (from this point on, he puts writers in this class, very often implicitly), who has the choice between "anarchic bohemianism and ascetic seclusion" as refuges from the state. "The Bohemians," he continued, "will have a valuable function in teasing, it may be hoped to madness, the new bourgeoisie, but I believe it will be left to the ascetics to produce the works of art in which, if at all, English culture will survive."

Like Basil Seal's in *Put Out More Flags*, Waugh's own days of teasing the burgesses had depended on "a peace-loving, orderly and honourable world in which to operate." [11] Even in his most political book, *Robbery Under Law*, [12] he had talked of Western civilization in general rather than English culture in particular. And he had praised Arthur Calder-Marshall's fiction as that

of an anarchist, not a Marxist—and anarchy is the nearer to right order, for something that has not developed may reach the right end, while something which has fully developed wrongly cannot. . . . The disillusioned Marxist becomes a Fascist; the disillusioned anarchist, a Christian. A robust discontent . . . is good for a writer. . . . (*EAR*, 206)

But by 1943 the robustness was gone, and in his diaries from this period through the late 1940's Waugh's desire to retreat from the world is especially strong. His immediate solution to the problems of the writer, however, was not heroic virtue but "Aristocracy," which supported the artist with money, attention, capricious encouragement of experiment, skeptical exposure of popular nonsense, and, most important, "a continuous tradition of gentle speech, with all its implications—the avoidance of boredom and vulgarity, the exchange of complicated ideas, the observance of subtle nuances of word and phrase—[which alone] can preserve the

11. *Put Out More Flags* (Boston: Little, Brown, 1942), p. 56.
12. *Robbery Under Law* (London: Chapman & Hall, 1939); published as *Mexico: An Object Lesson* (Boston: Little, Brown, 1939).

written tongue from death . . ." (*EAR*, 276). Here he sounds rather like Anthony Blanche contrasting civilized discourse with Sebastian's bubblings, but neither he nor Blanche is being frivolous.

A dozen years later, Waugh developed these ideas more fully in "Literary Style in England and America" (*EAR*, 477–481), more fully, in fact, than he was ever again to develop any ideas about fiction. Here he went beyond his statements in the review of *Enemies of Promise* to maintain that style "is of the essence of a work of art" and even further to define literature as "the right use of language irrespective of the subject or reason of the utterance." Turning on James Joyce, in whose *Work in Progress* he had once expressed great interest, he argued that though Joyce was "possessed by style," he failed as a writer because, though he certainly had "individuality," he lacked the essential "lucidity" and "elegance." The criterion of "elegance," "the quality in a work of art which imparts direct pleasure," he defended against puritanical modern critics.

By this point his personal pantheon of contemporary writers included not Dos Passos and W. R. Burnett but Max Beerbohm, Ronald Knox, E. M. Forster (especially the first half of *Pharos and Pharillon*), Raymond Mortimer, Graham Greene, Henry Green, Ivy Compton-Burnett, and (to me, most unaccountably) Anthony Powell. The American language and American writers had ceased to enchant him. Like English women, the Americans had not learned Latin and therefore "wrote as though they were babbling down the telephone." The result he found "repetitive and slangy." Even when he admired an American writer, as he did J. F. Powers, he found the "light, free, colloquial language . . . not only unfamiliar but unintelligible, not only in dialogue but in direct narrative when he speaks in *propria persona*" ("Scenes of Clerical Life," *Commonweal*, 63 [30 March 1956], 667]. Perhaps the two dialects were in fact becoming separate languages, he conjectured. Whatever the language, he insisted, as he had in the review of Graves and Hodge and in "Fan-Fare" (*EAR*, 302), that the artist should concern himself more and more with style in order to avoid being bored with his own work or, by turning prophet, boring others.

In fact, Waugh resisted any temptation to regard the artist or writer as in any way special outside the exercise of his art. Early in his career he compared the writer to the carpenter: the second is inclined to shape timber into a finished object; the first "is not really content to leave any experience in the amorphous, haphazard condition in which life presents it; and putting an experience into shape means, for a writer, putting it into communicable form."[13] After World War II, he was more inclined to argue, as he did to Lord David Cecil, that

God's order is manifest everywhere. You and I, as men specially concerned with writing, are entitled to see it specially in writing, so long as we recognize writing as differing not at all from gardening or needlework or any other activity, and so long as we regard all humanism as recreation—a harmless way for fellow [?] men to occupy their leisure and earn their livings. The danger is to say "a Poet is a lovesome thing, God wot.'" (*Letters*, 305)

Waugh is responding to a point in Lord David's inaugural lecture at Oxford, and other dismissals of art at an end in itself can be found in Waugh's writing and interviews.

However, he could turn against his own view that "most men and women of genius have entertained preposterous opinions"[14] and that therefore content matters little to confute John Mortimer's view that writers are "not to be judged by the quality of their thoughts." On the contrary, Waugh argues, "writing is the expression of thought. There is no abstract writing. All literature implies moral standards and criticisms—the less explicit the better" (*Letters*, 574).

While ideas—better still, a vision; better still, a conception of a God-centered fictional universe—might be important to Waugh's post-*Brideshead* concept of the novelist, certain moral qualities such as humility were a handicap. He argued that Chesterton was too nice a man to be a major writer:

It is often pride, emulation, avarice, malice—all the odious qualities—which drive a man to complete, elaborate, refine, destroy, renew, his work

13. *Ninety-Two Days* (New York: Farrar and Rinehart, 1934), pp. 4–5. Waugh may have been driven to discuss first principles by desperation at the lack of material. See *Catalogue*, E231.
14. "The Man Hollywood Hates," *Evening Standard*, 4 November 1947; *EAR*, 338. See also the remarks on Voltaire and Gibbon in the review of Graves and Hodge. "The Man" is Charlie Chaplin.

until he has made something that gratifies his pride and envy and greed. And in doing so he enriches the world more than the generous and good, though he may lose his own soul in the process. That is the paradox of artistic achievement. (*EAR*, 560)

There was also the possibility, admitted in *The Loved One*, confronted directly in *The Ordeal of Gilbert Pinfold*, and analyzed obliquely in a review of Muriel Spark's *The Comforters* (*EAR*, 518–519), that the writer's imagination was near allied to madness. When his own career as an imaginative writer had ended and he was trying to force himself to work on a number of uncongenial tasks, he wrote of Kipling's consciousness of a daimon

who entered him from outside and directed his work. Most story-tellers are aware of this influence. They do not know where they are tending; worse, they fear the ending of this guidance from some undiscovered place in their minds. (*EAR*, 624)

Two months later he implied that the daimon needed editing as much as any other being when he saw the danger for Muriel Spark of becoming its "mere amanuensis" (*Spectator*, 207 [7 July 1961], 28).

Most of the time, however, he was able to avoid disquieting considerations about the sources of inspiration. When he reviewed fiction, he remained for the most part in familiar territory. He was aware that the experiments in the novel written almost entirely in dialogue, like those of Ivy Compton-Burnett and Henry Green, belonged essentially to the 1930's. He was also aware of generic and period differences when he contrasted the early novels of Anthony Powell, "brilliant studies in the grotesque," with *A Dance to the Music of Time* series, in which "the characters behave as anarchically but . . . are seen as cohesive. They have not merely the adventitious connection of crossing the path of a single observer; they all hang together apart from him. There is homogeneity and rule in apparent chaos . . ." (*EAR*, 550).

It was not so much that Waugh did not have challenging material for new theoretical discussion but that he did not seek it out. As he told the editor of an experimental literary magazine, "A writer should have found his *métier* before he is 50. After that he reads

only for pleasure; not for curiosity about what others are doing"
(*Letters*, 536). He did not define pleasure, but the context indicates,
and his letters and diaries confirm, that he read and reread his contemporaries and predecessors rather than seeking new aesthetic experience. And some of his early enthusiasms had waned. In 1928
he thought that in *South Wind* Norman Douglas had written "the
only great satirical novel of his generation" ("Turning Over New
Leaves," *Vogue* [London], [17 October 1928], p. 59); in 1952 he tried
to reread the novel "and to my horror found it very heavy going"
(*Letters*, 370). In 1962 he told an interviewer that he could no longer
read Firbank and that "there would be something wrong with an
elderly man who could enjoy Firbank" ("The Art of Fiction XXX,"
81). Privately, in letters and diaries, he was less satisfied with the
work of Powell and Green than previous or concurrent responses
in print would indicate. For example, he blamed Green, perhaps
with not pure facetiousness, for creating the vogue of proletarian
literature (*Letters*, 398), and with less humor criticized the jumbled
and jangled diction of *Nothing* and suspected that "Henry never
could write dialogue at all & has been bluffing all the time" (*Letters*,
328).

Perhaps the best illustration of Waugh's postwar views on fictional method is his recurrent involvement with the work of Graham Greene. In 1930, he had praised the "sturdy sense of drama
. . . and the ability to 'put across' sex appeal" in *The Name of Action*, though he did wish that Greene "would write more freely and
directly" (*EAR*, 101). In 1936 he added some suggestions to
Greene's idea for a race of professional travelers, proposing that at
least five compete, "not in time but economy" (*Letters*, 108–109),
and the following year he worked for Greene, then assistant editor
of *Night and Day*. In 1942, he reviewed Greene's *British Dramatists*
(*EAR*, 272–273), calling him "a writer of outstanding imaginative
power" and a "splendid novelist" but withholding full praise for
this volume because Greene emphasized popular rather than aristocratic audiences and ecclesiastical and didactic rather than secular
and pleasurable sources for English drama.

After the war, however, Waugh reviewed three of Greene's novels
and the notebook for another. His review of *The Heart of the Matter*

(*EAR*, 360–365), the longest he ever wrote on a single novel, spends a good deal of space on the theological implications of the action and gives a very shrewd analysis of Scobie's character, in the process noting that "Scobie is a man of independent soul" and thus abandoning his earlier theory that character should be subordinated to a design.[15] Moreover, he uses Greene as an example of the writer's relationship to the zeitgeist (perhaps the only German philosophical term Waugh ever used straightforwardly): "he is in spite of himself in the advance guard. Men of affairs stumble far behind." Of course, Waugh seeks to claim Greene as an ally in shifting emphasis "from sociology to eschatology" as he had done in *Brideshead Revisited* and about to do again in *Helena* and the war novels, already in the planning stage.

In this respect, Waugh's review essay is typical of his postwar concerns, but in analyzing technique he emphasizes many of the same elements he had praised almost twenty years earlier. For example, he admires the "severe modern surface" of the earlier novels and describes approvingly a style which

is not specifically a literary style at all. The words are functional, devoid of sensuous attraction, of ancestry and of independent life. Literary stylists regard language as intrinsically precious and its proper use as a worthy and pleasant task. . . . [But Greene's] words are simply mathematical signs for his thought.

Of course, Greene had taken advice which Waugh had no doubt forgotten, but more important, Waugh was emphasizing the art of the novelist over the art of the writer as he had done before the war.

The most significant aspect of Greene's technique for Waugh was that "no relation is established between writer and reader" through either a commenting narrator or an observer. Instead,

It is as though out of an infinite length of film, sequences had been cut which, assembled, comprise an experience which is the reader's alone,

---

15. This accords with Waugh's argument in 1946 that modern realistic novelists fail not because a complete man cannot be shown but because "They try to represent the whole human mind and soul and yet omit its determining character—that of being God's creature with a defined purpose." He promised in future novels to "attempt to represent man more fully, which, to me, means only one thing, man in his relation to God" (*EAR*, 302) and later worried because *The Loved One* broke that promise (*Catalogue*, E548).

without any correspondence to the experience of the protagonist. The writer has become director and producer. Indeed, the affinity to film is everywhere apparent. . . . It is the modern way of telling a story.

Yet, Waugh continued, all kinds of technique were less important than "the natural qualities of the narrator's mind, whether or no he sees events in a necessary sequence. Mr. Greene is a story-teller of genius." Especially notable are Greene's "statement of the scene," not only in physical but in moral, spiritual, even psychological terms.

Three years later, Waugh was even more delighted with *The End of the Affair*, not only because of Greene's "defiant assertion of the supernatural" but because of the substitution for "an omniscient and impersonal recorder" of a "chief character giving his distorted version; a narrator who is himself in course of evolution, whose real story is only beginning at the conclusion of the book, who is himself unaware of the fate we can dimly foresee for him" (*EAR*, 404–406). In both theme and technique, as Chapter 13 demonstrates, Greene's practice was very close to Waugh's in *Brideshead Revisited*. Also praised are Greene's "variety and precision of . . . craftsmanship" in managing the "crazy mutations of pity, hate, comradeship, jealousy and contempt" in the relationship between the narrator and the husband.

Waugh was by no means uncritical of Greene either in detail or in general. He sent Greene two corrections for the printed version of the novel (*Letters*, 350) and questioned the theological accuracy of Greene's presentation of baptism and the plausibility of the heroine's not noticing the theft of her diary. In fact, in reviewing *The Quiet American* (*Sunday Times*, 1 December 1955), he argued that the theme of its predecessor was "so sublime as to strain the author's splendid skill. His resort to the diary in that book was an admission that his normal method of story-telling was inadequate to the story he had to tell."

The review of *The End of the Affair* was the highest point of Waugh's professional regard for Greene. *The Quiet American* he found less intense and more mundane; privately he called it "a masterly but base work" (*Diaries*, 747), probably because of the unreliable, morally odious, professionally incompetent, and generally ignorant narrator. He reread all of Greene's and of Anthony Powell's works in 1960 (*Letters*, 541).

Seven months later, however, he found *A Burnt-Out Case* so distressing in theme that he refused to review it at all, adding, "What is more—no, less—Graham's skill is fading" and giving several examples. Both the subordination of method to morals and the need to remind himself to make it are characteristic of Waugh, who was less militantly the Catholic novelist than he had been. As for his response as a Catholic and friend, Waugh's own disappointment with the changes in the Church introduced after the second Vatican Council probably increased his distress; and many letters written after the war show how deeply and genuinely distressed he was at the apostasy of any Catholic, especially an old friend. Therefore, he was particularly unsettled at Greene's coming out "as specifically faithless" (*Diaries*, 775). Two days later he wrote to Greene apologizing for his own part in labeling him a Catholic novelist and acting like the smarmily pious Rycker in the novel. Greene replied that he had wanted Waugh to review the book in the *Month* in order to dispel or at least to focus any Catholic hostility to the novel, that Waugh had not acted like Rycker, and that in Querry's loss of faith he was trying "'to give expression to various states or moods of unbelief.'" At this point Waugh was not satisfied, replying that Greene had "made a plain repudiation." [16]

Greene responded that he was rather weary of "the confusion between the functions of a novelist and the functions of a moral teacher or theologian," and perhaps as important as Greene's facetious postcard in ending the stiffness between the two friends was Waugh's memory of his own position thirteen years earlier, in which he argued that the Catholic writer had only to ask himself if, first, "when I write *in propria persona*, am I correct in Faith and Morals? Secondly, do I always do my best to produce a workman-like product that is fair value for my hire?" (*Duckett's Register* [March 1948], 3). Greene obviously felt that he could answer yes to both questions.

Waugh never again raised doubts about the artfulness of the

---

16. See *Letters*, 557, 559–560; *Diaries*, 775. For Greene's point of view, see *Ways of Escape* (New York: Simon and Schuster, 1980), pp. 262–267.

book, and in his review of *In Search of a Character*, the notebooks Greene kept while visiting Africa in search of background, he sidestepped both theme and technique. But by the time he wrote "Sloth," almost a year after he first read the novel, he had resolved the issue by distinguishing, as he had in the case of Scobie, between the moods of character and author: "Artists often express vicarious experiences (most erotic writing is the work of the impotent). It would be impossible for a man who was really guilty of Sloth to write about it, for he would be incapable of the intense work required to produce a novel like *A Burnt-Out Case*" (*EAR*, 574).

Waugh himself was not reduced to literary impotence or guilty of Sloth in the last few years of his life, though he frequently complained of failing powers. But he no longer seemed much interested in formal and technical questions. The prefaces he wrote for the Uniform Edition of his novels between 1959 and 1966[17] are, with one exception, disappointingly brief and confined to the circumstances of composition and in the cases of *Vile Bodies* and *Brideshead Revisited* to what he regards as weakness of style or technique.

His last recorded comments on his fiction, in the *Paris Review*, must be the shortest and contain the highest percentage of simple sentences of any in that long and garrulous series. In fact, his comments on his own novels were a reprise or anticipation of the prefaces, and his more general remarks on technique echo his comments of the 1930's. Asked, for example, about the Forsterian distinction between flat and round characters, he replied that

All fictional characters are flat. A writer can give an illusion of depth by giving an apparently stereoscopic view of a character—seeing him from two vantage points; all a writer can do is give more or less information about a character, not information of a different order.

To the obvious question about the difference between characters such as Prendergast and Sebastian, he responded that "There are the protagonists and there are characters who are furniture. One gives only one aspect of the furniture." When Julian Jebb pursued

17. These prefaces are to *Brideshead Revisited*, 1960; *Decline and Fall* and *Black Mischief*, 1962; *A Handful of Dust* and *Scoop* 1964; *Vile Bodies*, *The Loved One*, and *Sword of Honour*, 1965; and *Put Out More Flags*, 1967. As in the last case, the prefaces were written a year before they were published.

the point, Waugh replied that he had given most information not about Charles Ryder but about Guy Crouchback and then, with some impatience, rejected the whole line of inquiry because

your questions are dealing too much with the creation of character and not enough with the technique of writing. I regard writing not as investigation of character, but as an exercise in the use of language, and with this I am obsessed. I have no technical psychological interest. It is drama, speech and events that interest me. (*Paris Review*, 79)

Although the comment on style recalls his views of the 1943–1955 period, the final emphasis returns to the essay on Firbank and the comments on objective, even cinematic fiction presented most strongly in his review of *The Heart of the Matter*.

In fact, though Waugh's emphasis changed—from structure in 1930 to style in 1955, from character as mere counter in 1942 to character as existing in the divine order in 1950, from the writer as craftsman in 1938 to the writer as child of the zeitgeist in 1948—there is an underlying consistency in his views about form and method in fiction. Style should be congruent to form and, finally, subordinated to it; technique should serve to modulate from one mood, mode, narrative technique, style, place, or time to another; the structure of the whole is most important of all. As a novelist he was aware of the need "to hold the whole of a book in my head" (*Paris Review*, 78) in order to complete a structure. As a critic, he was impatient with portentous discussions of work that operated on more than one level,[18] but he knew that "any book worth discussing at any length exists in three dimensions, a solid thing which can be viewed from any angle and cut in any section. Most good novels vary in mood and method—satire, comedy, drama, allegory, analysis, description, comment and criticism, all have their part" (*EAR*, 421).

At the time of Waugh's death, his emphasis on craft caused the Jamesians to regard him as technically negligible. His emphasis on the novel as entertainment caused disciples of Leavis and Trilling to

18. Waugh praises Anthony Powell as "a happy example of a writer who works on one level," arguing that books of writers who do not are "inferior exercises in the art of communication." *Spectator*, 24 June 1960; *EAR*, 547–548.

feel a little abashed if they were so frivolous as to enjoy his novels.[19] Since then, the debate about depth and scope of representation of fiction has shifted considerably because of the practice of novelists (largely American) of the 1960's who were more inclined to share Waugh's views about objectivity and detachment in fiction and because of new or newly discovered theorists such as M. M. Bakhtin who emphasize, if not the "elegance" which Waugh so loved, the "variety of contrivance" which he admired and advocated.[20]

19. See, for example, Steven Marcus, "Evelyn Waugh and the Art of Entertainment," *Partisan Review*, 23 (Summer 1956), 348-357; D. S. Savage, "The Innocence of Evelyn Waugh," *Western Review*, 14 (Spring 1950), 197–206; and A. E. Dyson, *The Crazy Fabric* (New York: St. Martin's Press, 1965), pp. 187–196.

20. *The Ordeal of Gilbert Pinfold* (Boston: Little, Brown, 1957), p. 3.

CHAPTER 6

Waugh as Editor

Every piece of writing that Evelyn Waugh read, from letters by his children to books by established writers, met his unremitting scrutiny for grammar, style, and structure. In the strict sense, Waugh reviewed everything that he or anyone else wrote. His standards were clear and, his victims may have felt, remorseless. Because of those standards and that habit of mind, he was a brilliant editor as well as a self-editor. Not everyone was tough enough to submit to his criticism—Frank Pakenham refused to bother with Waugh's suggestions[1]—but those confident or humble enough to stand the strain found him eager to help.

Waugh's editorial skills were developed and called on very early. In his *Letters*, the first (1–2) not sent to a member of his immediate family contains his criticism of a short story which Dudley Carew had submitted to him—by no means the last or most severe criticism he wrote to Carew.[2] Waugh liked the theme—"contentment is the only failure"—and in fact, judging from his *Diaries*, had probably given Carew the idea. He was less happy about the embodiment of that theme, which he foresaw "degenerating into long conversations and descriptions of the weather." His advice was practical: make one character adopt another's natural attitude; imi-

1. Frank Pakenham, *Five Lives* (London: Hutchinson, 1964), pp. 15–16. Pakenham, who was stung by Waugh's increasingly blunt criticisms of the manuscript of *Born to Believe* and somewhat mollified by Waugh's offer to spend a month going over the manuscript, later regretted refusing the offer. He reports that Waugh distinguished between politicians like Pakenham who "think in sentences," and a real writer, who "thinks in words."

2. Dudley Carew, *A Fragment of Friendship: A Memory of Evelyn Waugh When Young* (London: Everest Books, 1974).

tate the cinema; and "bring home thoughts by actions and incidents" rather than by dialogue alone; "MAKE THINGS HAP-
PEN"; "don't bring characters on simply to draw their characters
and make them talk. Fit them into a design." Above all, "GO TO
THE CINEMA. . . ."

Thirty-five years later, having read Fr. Aelred Watkin's attempt
to tell the story of his grandmother's life, Waugh gave very much
the same advice: make the account more pictorial, dramatize contrasts, perhaps

conceive of Maria Pasqua's life as a film...in the *mechanics* of the *imagination*. Instead of seeing it as an historical document, imagine yourself watching a film—each incident as precise and authentic as in the present version,
but with the *continuity* (in the technical cinematographic sense) and selec-
tive dramatic emphases and scenery of a film. And then write as though
describing the experience. (*Letters*, 464–465)

Even when he was less encouraging, Waugh could be frank without being brutal. In 1938, given the manuscript of a novel by Alex
Comfort, he rejected it as encouragingly as possible. Although he
found the incidents not credible and badly structured, the rural dialect badly done, and one character "a great bore," the real problem
was that

the book owes its origin to an impulse to write *a* book, not this particular
book. Your imagination was not so obsessed by your subject that it had to
find literary expression. And that is the only way—at least while you are
learning the trade—that a good book can result.

He added, however, that Comfort could take heart because the
manuscript showed definite talent and the effort in writing it was
part of the apprenticeship demanded of every writer (*Letters*, 117–
118).

None of these manuscripts was published, though Carew and
Comfort both became professional writers, and Fr. Watkin's sister
completed and published *Maria Pasqua* in 1979 (*Letters*, 461 n1).
Nancy Mitford was more successful and certainly more resilient:
Waugh examined very carefully the manuscripts of several of her
novels. However, the advice preserved in the *Letters* is less detailed
than structural. Waugh argued that themes in *The Pursuit of Love*

(1945) could be emphasized by major revision in structure and development. Even though the book had been published, he enjoined her to "Start rewriting it *now* for the Penguin" because "a real writer . . . cares to go on improving after the reviews are out & her friends have read it & there is nothing whatever to be gained by the extra work" (*Letters*, 213).

Three years later, he wrote that the manuscript of *Love in a Cold Climate* has "a work of art there, lurking in a hole, occasionally visible by the tip of its whiskers," but "it isn't a book at all yet. No more 40 hour week. Blood, sweat & tears. That is to say if you want to produce a work of art." He gave very specific advice about establishing contrasting styles in dialogue and development and disposition of characters and then argued that the first two chapters were superfluous (*Letters*, 285–286). When he read the published version, however, he conceded that he had been wrong about those chapters, praised "all the descriptive & narrative passages," and stoutly maintained that "*all* the fashionable talk is awful" and that the incident on page 28 is "hell" (*Letters*, 301).

In 1951, Waugh praised Mitford's *The Blessing*, told her not to give away the allusion to Little Lord Fauntleroy, asked her to reconsider two characterizations because they rang false, and responded to her confession of weariness with "No complaints about headaches. Revision is just as important as any other part of writing and must be done con amore." He did support her rejection of the publisher's criticism, and a week later conceded that "it is just officiousness & bossiness that prompts half the suggestions. Writers are the worst advisers because they can't help thinking how they would write it themselves" (346, 338). In the rest of the published letters, he confined his comments to quibbling—her view—about the usage of particular words and to intelligent but not very specific praise of her books.

The evidence of these letters shows Waugh in the role of adviser, but his work on the English editions of two books by Thomas Merton shows that he was even more effective when given a free editorial hand. When he edited *The Seven Storey Mountain*[3] for

---

3. Thomas Merton, *The Seven Storey Mountain* (New York: Harcourt, Brace and Company, 1948). Cited here is the Garden City Books Reprint Edition of 1951,

Burns and Oates, he found the book "intensely moving" and thought it "likely that American monasticism may help save the world" (*Letters*, 283). Sympathetic though he was, however, he knew that piety is no substitute for technique. While it is not accurate to say that Waugh had no piety and Merton no technique, Waugh as editor approached the book not as a believer but as a craftsman, and his editing was intelligent and ruthless.

In his preface to the English edition, Waugh considerably understated his role, writing that "The present text has been renamed and very slightly abridged in order to adapt it to European taste. Nothing has been cut out except certain passages which seemed to be of purely local interest."[4] In his diary, Waugh was more frank: "Tom Burns gave me the enthralling task of cutting the redundancies and solecisms out of Tom Merton's *The Seven Storey Mountain*. This took a week and resulted in what should be a fine thin volume" (*Diaries*, 700).

In fact, Waugh cut over 20 percent of the original text, occasionally in blocks of paragraphs but more frequently a sentence here, a phrase there, in order to make the narrative move more rapidly, to give it point and emphasis, and to focus it, as the English title, *Elected Silence*, implies, on the central issue of the book: Merton's movement away from the secular world to the life of contemplation.

To this end, Waugh eliminated the casual, autobiographical aspects of *The Seven Storey Mountain*. Merton's father, for example, plays far less part in *Elected Silence* than in the original: analysis of his painting style, the progress of his critical reputation, anecdotes about his native spirituality, even Merton's eulogy are omitted. Similarly, a long tribute to Mark Van Doren is omitted, though later Van Doren's active though incidental role in helping Merton to understand his vocation to the priesthood is left unchanged.

Waugh treated places as he did people: if they support the central line of narrative, they remain more or less intact; if they are merely

---

which has identical pagination. In paired references to this text and to *Elected Silence*, this is cited first.

4. Thomas Merton, *Elected Silence* (London: Hollis and Carter, 1949). Cited second in paired references.

places where Merton lived or passed through in his wandering about Europe or England, they are omitted. Thus Merton's description of the landscape around St. Bonaventure College and that observed on his trips to New York or to Gethsemane, the Trappist monastery, are all retained because Merton makes the landscape reflect his various spiritual states or creates suspense about the destination's effect on his progress toward the contemplative life. For example, Merton describes the harmony between the words of his Breviary and "the sun blazing on the trees and moist rocks, and flashing on the surface of the shallow river and playing in the forest foliage along the line" as he journeys toward Olean; later he uses the increasingly desolate landscape on the journey to Gethsemane to set off his first view of the peaceful, moonlit monastery.

But passages of mere travelogue are cut: an impressionistic first view of Paris; two paragraphs of a tourist's view from the train of the Aveyron valley (though Waugh leaves untouched the final stage of the journey to prepare for the climax of arrival); two paragraphs listing the sights of the area surrounding his home; a list of the Roman churches he is sorry to leave. On the other hand, Waugh preserved descriptions of the interior of these churches, for they have a direct bearing on Merton's apprehension of spiritual reality. Even so, the editorial pencil eliminated the redundancy, indirection, and impressionistic art criticism in order to focus on the effect. (Here and throughout, brackets are used to indicate material cut from Merton's original.)

These mosaics told me more than I had ever known of the doctrine of a God of infinite power, wisdom and love [W]who had yet become Man, and revealed in His Manhood the infinity of power, wisdom and love that was His Godhead. [Of course I could not grasp and believe these things explicitly, But since they were implicit in every line of the pictures I contemplated with such admiration and love, surely I grasped them implicitly—I had to, in so far as] [t] The mind of the artist reached my own mind and spoke to it his conception and thought. [And so I could not help but catch something of the ancient craftsman's love of Christ, the Redeemer and Judge of the World.] (110/96)

[So for once I put my favorite aside.] And I read more and more of the Gospels, and my love for the old churches and their mosaics grew from day to day. Soon I was no longer visiting them merely for the art. There was something else that attracted me: a kind of interior peace. I loved to be in these holy places. I had a [kind of deep and strong] conviction that I belonged there [: that my rational nature was filled with profound desires and needs that could only find satisfaction in churches of God]. I remember that one of my favorite shrines was that of St. Peter in Chains, and I did not love it for any work of art there [, since the big attraction, the big "number," the big "feature" in that place is Michelangelo's Moses. But I had always been extremely bored by that horned and pop-eyed frown and by the crack in the knee. I'm glad that the thing couldn't speak, for it would probably have given out some very heavy statements.] (110–111/96)

Merton's reaction to visual art may have been casual and uninstructed, though he consistently describes the effects on his sensibility of ecclesiastical art and architecture, but he took great pains to learn about literature and to write it, taking a Columbia University M.A. with a thesis on "Nature and Art in William Blake," at least beginning research for a doctoral dissertation on Hopkins, and writing a number of novels and poems as well as literary journalism before he entered the monastery. In fact, the conflict between Merton's desire to be a man of art and his vocation as a man of God is a major undercurrent of *The Seven Storey Mountain*, a current which surfaces in the epilogue when Merton the Trappist confronts "this shadow, this double, this writer who had followed me into the cloister. . . . Nobody seems to understand that one of us has got to die." Waugh left this passage untouched, though he did eliminate the scene just before it in which Merton, having received a copy of his first volume of poems, "went out under the grey sky, under the cedars at the edge of the cemetery, and stood in the wind that threatened snow and held the printed poems in my hand." And some of the redundancies and melodramatic phrases are cut from Merton's analysis of his doubts, notably "Maybe in the end he will kill me, he will drink my blood" (410/364). Waugh preserved the essential climactic material, which helps to define Merton's spiritual position, but he was not really interested in Merton the struggling literary man or the student of literature. Much of the material about Blake's poetry and his place in intellectual history, as distinct from his religious vision, has been eliminated. Indeed, most of Merton's discussions of literature, which are impressionistic and sometimes vague and exclamatory, have been cut.

Merton's literary efforts met a similar fate: all of the poems printed in *The Seven Storey Mountain* were left out of *Elected Silence*, as are accounts of his youthful attempts to write "rough, raw Skeltonic verses" and of a "partly autobiographical" novel based on his early life. One might suspect that Waugh did not take Merton very seriously as a literary man. He points out in the Foreword that "Columbia not Cambridge formed his literary style," and in letters to Merton he tries to indicate Merton's defects of style and construction and to foster in him a professional attitude toward his writing. However, the contrast between Columbia and Cambridge would be more instructive if Waugh had ever had anything good to say about the English university, and a formal rather than a critical impulse may have dictated his deletions. *The Seven Storey Mountain* is in part a *Künstlerroman*; *Elected Silence* is a spiritual autobiography.

The operative term is *spiritual*, which is not synonymous with *theological* or *apologetic*, a distinction of which Waugh, as his deletions show, was far more acutely aware than Merton. Merton noted in himself a tendency toward "wholesale and glib detraction" (79/71) in a passage which Waugh omitted, and the original text of the book has occasional passages indicating that Trappist vows had not entirely eradicated Merton's tendentiousness. He condescends to a Protestant minister who explains parables to schoolboys: "I don't remember that there was any particularly deep spirituality about it, but there was nothing to him to prevent him from showing us the obvious moral lessons" (53/47). The Church of England he scorns because it is characterized by "sterility and inefficacy . . . in the moral order" caused not only by "lack of vital contact with the Mystical Body of the True Church" but also by "the social injustice and the class oppression on which it is based: for, since it is mostly a class religion, it contracts the guilt of the class from which it is inseparable." The condemnation is followed by the lame "But this is a guess which I am not prepared to argue out" (66/58). Later Merton asserts, feebly tempering his assertion, that "sometimes Protestant theology does, in certain circumstances, amount to little more than a combination of sociology and religious history . . ." (84/75).

Merton's prejudices were not exclusively theological. He was similarly condescending to the Scots, concluding a list of characteristic activities with the sarcastic "and all those other noble institutions" (71/63) and toward the "virtues of the watchmaking Swiss . . . which I have now forgotten" (116/99). And in a passage two pages long he pictures Cambridge and then most of upper-class England as "pretending . . . to act as if it were alive," affected by "Some kind of a moral fungus" (126/106).

Even a common religion and vocation did not convey immunity from Merton's criticism. Announcing to a Franciscan that he is to make a retreat with the Trappists and receiving the answer "Don't let them change you," he glosses the remark as meaning "Don't go reminding the rest of us that all that penance might be right, by getting a vocation to the Trappists" (318/268). In the epilogue, writing about the necessity for the contemplative life, he expends considerable space quibbling with St. Thomas Aquinas' distinction among active life, contemplative life, and a mixture, defending the second against what he regards as St. Thomas' illogical, Dominican preference for the third.

All of these remarks are missing from *Elected Silence*. Many of them would have offended Waugh, who in youth professed a romantic attachment to Scotland and who never lost his loyalty to England's class structure, however much he might criticize its members. The argument with St. Thomas, he might have thought, spoiled the climax of the book; and aside from the artistic reason, he once cautioned Merton about the "slight hint of bustle and salesmanship about the way you want to scoop us all into a higher grade than we are fit for. . . ."[5]

Waugh's awareness of different emphases in English and American Catholicism may also account for his omission of several theological passages which are not, to American Catholics over forty-five, tendentious. Merton interrupts his account of his French lycée

---

5. Waugh to Merton, 29 August 1949, in Sister M. Thérèse, "Waugh's Letters to Thomas Merton," *Evelyn Waugh Newsletter*, 3 (Spring 1969), 2.

to beseech parents to send their children to Catholic schools and to inveigh against those who "have the consummate audacity to weep and complain because God does not hear their prayers for peace, when they have neglected not only His will, but the ordinary dictates of natural reason and prudence, and let their children grow up according to the standards of a civilization of hyenas." Waugh preserved the contrast between lycée and the neighboring college of the Marist Fathers, but he eliminated the sermon. Elsewhere, Merton asserts of the Virgin Mary that "Sanctity comes to us through her intercession. God has willed that there be no other way" (230/184). As a Catholic, Waugh could assent to the first statement. The second may have seemed excessive; at any rate, he cut it.

Still another passage recounts the artfulness of a friend in telling "the *mendacium jocosum* or 'humorous lie,'" gives a not very humorous anecdote in illustration, and concludes, stuffily, that "Moral theologians say that the *mendacium jocosum* in itself does not exceed a venial sin" (182–183/146). The anecdote and another paragraph of analysis Waugh cut, undoubtedly prompted by his comic instinct. The final sentence was also cut, perhaps on the grounds that it was hyperscrupulous applied to oneself and impertinent applied to anyone else. And Merton's qualification of "There is nothing wrong in being a writer or a poet—at least I hope there is not" (231/185), was removed. Waugh admitted in his article on the American Catholic Church (*EAR*, 377–388) that the artist was not essential to the Church, but he was not, like Merton, willing to say that what is inessential might therefore be illicit.

Other theological discussions were removed on clearly artistic grounds. Merton sometimes introduces doctrine that is overspecific or irrelevant. Writing of the death of his father, for example, he expresses the hope "that, in the living Christ, I shall one day see my father again," a hope comprehensible to anyone likely to read eighty-five pages of his narrative. However, Merton continues: "that is, I believe that Christ, Who is the Son of God, and Who is God, has power to raise up all those who have died in His grace, to the glory of His own Resurrection, and to share, body and soul, in the glory of His Divine inheritance, at the last day" (85/76). The passage might be defended on the grounds that non-Catholic American readers might take the first sentence to mean some vague, pleasant beyond, a sweet by-and-by, and that the further definition both specifies and instructs. Waugh had a higher opinion of the potential readers of *Elected Silence*, where the definition is omitted.

Occasionally, Merton's desire to instruct not only impedes but contradicts the narrative. Recording his brother's movement toward conversion, Merton at two points lists the doctrines which he explained to John Paul. However, Merton recognized that his brother "had not come here to find out a lot of abstract truths" but was impelled by an "insatiable thirst for peace, for salvation, for true happiness" (395–396/350). Seizing, perhaps, on this statement, Waugh cut the irrelevant passages.

Even when Merton is simply recording his actions, Waugh sometimes eliminates and compresses in order to give the narrative a faster pace. One instance of backtracking to explain why Merton, having begun to read his copy of St. Ignatius' *Spiritual Exercises*, had not done so before, was cut to emphasize his first attempts at mental prayer. Merton's first of many ordeals at the dentist took two visits in the original; Waugh eliminated the first, unsuccessful treatment and retained the second, in which the tooth is pulled. Much later, after Merton receives notice to take his physical examination for the draft, he goes to New York; visits friends; writes "a fancy poem about javelins and leopards and lights through trees like arrows"; and, "an Englishman wearing a shamrock which I had bought from a Jew, went walking around the city" on St. Patrick's day (314–315/265). Then he returns to take his physical examination. The pleasant but inconclusive interlude carries the action no further forward, and it does not survive in *Elected Silence*.

On the whole, however, Waugh seemed to approve of the narrative passages, for they alone are almost free from all the kinds of excisions, from paragraph to single word, that he made. Toward the nonevent he was ruthless. The imputation of motive to the Trappist-fearing Franciscan; the supposition that because Merton "decided to make my meditations sitting cross-legged on the floor. . . . the Jesuits would have had a nasty shock if they had walked in and seen me doing *Spiritual Exercises* sitting there like Mahatma Gandhi" (269/220); the speculation about the place of his father in eternity and about the reasons in the supernatural order for his being given the name *Frater Louis* and about the Third Order and about what God was *not* asking him to do are all missing from the English edition. So also is a paragraph recording his state of mind after he was rejected by the Franciscans:

> God had kept me out of the cloister: that was His affair. He had also given me a vocation to live the kind of life that people led in cloisters. If I could not be a religious, a priest—that was God's affair. But nevertheless He still wanted me to lead something of the life of a priest or of a religious. (300/253)

To Waugh, the paragraph had no redeeming value. The first sentence is not clearly true of the event; it is certainly not true of Merton's later career. There are several kinds of repetition; the "But" and "nevertheless" are redundant. And the whole paragraph is rendered superfluous by the surrounding paragraphs, which record Merton's decision to abandon the worldly life and by his statement to a priest, "I am going to try to live like a religious."

Merton had the unfortunate habit of saying the same thing twice, and sometimes he had difficulty in deciding what he really wanted to say. This is shown most clearly in Waugh's treatment of the beginnings and ending of paragraphs and of larger divisions of Merton's narrative. If, for example, Merton buried the topic sentence under a needlessly long transition, Waugh pared the superfluous material in order to begin the paragraph with a clear and emphatic statement of purpose. Thus Merton spends most of a page describing his reaction to the art he found in Roman churches. The next paragraph begins, "I was fascinated by these Byzantine mosaics. I began to haunt the churches where they were to be found, and, as an indirect consequence, all the other churches that were more or less of the same period." This passage is cut, leaving as transition and thesis the third sentence, "And thus without knowing anything about it I became a pilgrim" (108/95). When Merton discovers that his mother is dying, he writes: "Prayer? No, prayer did not even occur to me. How fantastic that will seem to a Catholic—that a six-year-old child should find out that his mother is dying, and not know enough to pray for her! It was not until I became a Catholic, twenty years later, that it finally occurred to me to pray for my mother" (14/14). Waugh retained only the last sentence, which becomes all the more effective because of its brevity and understatement.

Whole paragraphs were cut at the beginning of sections, notably in the Epilogue, where Merton begins:

> Day unto day uttereth speech. The clouds change. The seasons pass over our wood and fields in their slow and regular procession, and time is gone before you are aware of it.
> Christ pours down the Holy Ghost upon you from heaven in the fire of June. . . . (407/361)

Waugh began the epilogue of *Elected Silence* with the second paragraph, subordinating the cycle of the seasons to the cycle of the liturgical year, what neither would have felt necessary to explain was post-Pentecostal.

Waugh paid even more attention to extraneous or anticlimactic material at the end of a paragraph or section, for Merton characteristically tried to reinforce his point by repeating it or by adding detail or paraphrase. Discussing the sustaining mercy of God, Merton asks,

> How could all this be possible without the merciful love of God, pouring out His grace upon us? Can there be any doubt where wars come from and where peace comes from, when the children of this world, excluding God from their peace conference, only manage to bring about greater and greater wars the more they talk about peace? (128/107)

Because the paragraph is about God's mercy rather than man's evil, Waugh cut the last sentence, leaving its predecessor in climactic end position. Or in a paragraph on perfectibilitarian social theories Merton not only repeats the idea of the first sentence but slides away from the emphatic point in the final subordinate clause, which Waugh cut, in "And yet it is still just as naive to suppose that members of the same human species, without having changed anything but their minds, should suddenly turn around and produce a perfect society, when they have never been able, in the past, to produce anything but imperfection and, at best, the barest shadow of justice" (135/113).

Merton was just as likely to blur the climax of a section as that of a paragraph. Ending a section on the charm of life in France with his father, he describes a book filled with pictures over which he pored. Waugh not only cut a list of cathedrals in order to begin the last paragraph with the boy's looking at a photograph of the Grand Chartreuse—an obvious foreshadowing of Merton's vocation—but deleted the final sentence dealing with the boy's "obscure but half-realized woe, that I could not be in all . . . at once" to end paragraph and section with "I knew my heart was filled with a kind of longing to breathe the air of that lonely valley and to listen to its silence" (43–44/38). Later Waugh cut two paragraphs about the influence of Merton's godfather to leave at the end a paragraph about his standards of value and the anticipation, "This was a distinction [the contrast between theory and practice] which I did not grasp until it was too late" (80–81/73). These examples come early, but Waugh did not relax his vigilance: three-fourths of the way through the book, Merton decides to continue teaching and writing because he feels that, if he cannot enter a monastery, these activities constitute his secular vocation:

And the emptiness and futility and nothingness of the world once more invaded me from every side. But now it could not disturb me or make my unhappy.

It was sufficient to know that even if I might be in it, that did not compel me to have any part of it, or to belong to it, or even to be seriously begrimed with its sorry, unavoidable contact. (352/303)

Once again, Waugh removed the redundant generalization of the second paragraph to let the emphatic simple sentence end the section.

One can imagine Waugh's making all of these deletions fairly calmly, but it seems likely that more trivial infelicities annoyed him. Although he may not have reacted precisely like his character Gilbert Pinfold—"Shocked by . . . a fault in syntax, his mind like a cinema camera trucked furiously forward to confront the offending object close up with glaring lense; with the eyes of a drill sergeant inspecting an awkward squad, bulging with wrath that was half facetious, and with half simulated incredulity"[6]—he was moved to send Merton a copy of Fowler's *Modern English Usage*, as Frederick Stopp says, "to assist him in cleaning up his prose style."[7] Sentences beginning "In other words," "To say it better," "There is no need," "I had no way of saying," "I can hardly identify," "For some reason," and all similar phrases were expunged; transitional and exclamatory uses of "Yet," "No," "Now," "But," and "So" met the same fate. Expletive constructions were reduced to normal syntactic order, as in the removal of "It is a matter of common belief among Catholics that" from a sentence which then read, "When God promises to answer our prayers, He does not promise to give us exactly what we ask for." Exclamatory sentences were pruned, as were repetitions, dead metaphors and colloquial redundancies of all kinds. Waugh may have been more amused than annoyed at "I was free. *I had recovered my liberty*" and "In its January, I was to *have my twenty-sixth birthday, and* enter upon my twenty-seventh, most momentous year." Whatever his attitude, he did excise the italicized words. "Old thirteenth century houses" became "thirteenth century houses"; "fragile web," "web"; "First of all," "First"; "starts out," "starts"; "opened up," "opened"; "flame and fire," "flame"; and "a bad case of pneumonia" simply "pneumonia." Trite phrases like "the tender mercies," "crowded together like sardines," and various analogies and metaphors including a paragraph beginning "Souls are like athletes" failed to survive Waugh's scrutiny.

These changes would be made by any copy editor; the longer deletions could be made by anyone with adequate rhetorical training and the faculty of unremitting attention. Waugh rose above adequacy, which, rare, is not to be disparaged, and demonstrated most clearly his genius as careful reader and highly trained writer in his delicate surgery on individual paragraphs, eliminating superfluities to leave them terse and effective. Speaking of a Hindu monastery, Merton writes and Waugh emended:

[Of all that they do, they attach most importance to prayer, to praising God. They have a well-developed sense of the power and efficacy of

6. *The Ordeal of Gilbert Pinfold* (London: Chapman & Hall, 1957), p. 8.
7. Frederick J. Stopp, *Evelyn Waugh: Portrait of an Artist* (Boston: Little, Brown, 1958), p. 52.

prayer, based on a keen realization of the goodness of God.] Their whole spirituality is childlike, [simple, primitive if you like,] close to nature, [ingenuous, optimistic,] happy. [But the point is, although it may be no more than the full flowering of the natural virtue of religion, with the other natural virtues, including a powerful natural charity, still] [t] The life of these pagan monks is one of such purity and holiness and peace, in the natural order, that it may put to shame the actual conduct of many Christian religious, in spite of their advantages of constant access to all the means of grace. (192/152)

Elsewhere, writing of his suddenly expressed decision to be a priest:

I cannot say what caused it: it was not a reaction of especially strong disgust at being so tired and so uninterested in this life I was still leading [, in spite of its futility. It was not the music, not the fall air, for] [t] This conviction [that had suddenly been planted in my full grown] was not [the sick and haunting sort of a thing that an] emotional [urge always is. It was not a thing of passion or of fancy. It was a strong and sweet and deep and insistent attraction that suddenly made itself felt, but not as a movement of appetite towards any sensible good]. It was something in the order of conscience, a new and profound and clear sense that this was what I really ought to do. (253/205)

Or, commenting on his new draft card:

Yet it was enough to remind me that I was not going to enjoy this pleasant [and safe] and stable life forever. [Indeed,] [p]Perhaps now [that I had just begun to taste] my security[, it] would be taken away again, and I would be cast back into the midst of violence [and uncertainty and blasphemy and the play of anger and hatred and all passion, worse than ever before]. It would be the wages of my own twenty-five years: this war was what I had earned for myself and the world. [I could hardly complain that I was being drawn into it.] (308–309/260)

Anyone who takes real pleasure in words must appreciate the skill with which needless detail is eliminated, awkward or otiose constructions reduced to simplicity and clarity, and in general lean and graceful statement freed from the tissue that imprisoned it.

Finally, a supreme example of Waugh's triumphant revision. Merton begins the final chapter of Part One with a transitional voyage from England, the subject of the previous chapter, to America, where he is to live and continue his spiritual struggles. To make this important transition, Merton characteristically calls on inflated language:

> I had a long way to go. I had more to cross than the Atlantic. Perhaps the Styx, being only a river, does not seem so terribly wide. It is not its width that makes it difficult to cross, especially when you are trying to get out of hell, and not in. And so, this time, even though I got out of Europe, I still remained in hell. But it was not for want of trying. (131)

Waugh, operating on the principles of clarity, economy, and understatement, reduced this to:

> I had more to cross than the Atlantic. Though I got out of Europe, I still remained in hell. (110)

Yet one is left with a quibble. Why retain the word *still*? Perhaps it implies a temporary state, though the distinction, if there is one, is supersubtle. Perhaps it is a fault, and for a second Waugh's attention lapsed—proving him preternaturally but not supernaturally attentive.

Both Merton and Waugh were pleased with *Elected Silence*, and in May 1949, Waugh gratefully accepted Merton's dedication of *The Waters of Siloe* (*Letters*, 308). When he read the book, he was less happy. Already committed to editing the English edition, he became so frustrated with the task that, without the encouragement of Katherine Asquith, he would have abandoned it.

As Waugh's *Letters* show time and again, he was very conscious of his audience, and while he rarely lied outright, he modified his views out of consideration for his correspondent. His letter of thanks to Merton was a model of tact, and only when one examines the (incomplete) text carefully and with a knowledge of other documents can one see how extraordinary it is. He called the subject matter "enthralling" and suggested ("If your superiors intend you to go on writing") that Merton write a comprehensive "middlebrow history" of Catholicism in the United States—an extraordinary suggestion to make to a man who had a reputation as a poet, mystic, and analyst of the higher spiritual realms. Turning to the book itself, Waugh argued that "The arrangements seem to me a little loose." The "Prologue" and "Note on Contemplative Orders" seemed unnecessary: the first "strikes the wrong *artistic* note, smacking of popular journalism in the way you try to catch the attention with an anecdote"; the second anticipates information later given "better and more fully." The narrative passages Waugh praised, but he noted the inconsistency of styles which ranged from "literary English" to slang (*Letters*, 308). Other passages resembled *The Seven Storey Mountain* in their redundancy and diffuseness, and Waugh argued that these faults not only waste material but corrupt readers, who "will not trouble to study a sentence for its proper meaning if they have learned to expect much the same thing to be said again later on" (*Letters*, 308).

To Sister M. Thérèse, whom he had met in Milwaukee early in 1949, he was still guarded but more pointed: "One would like to think of [Merton] wrapped in silence, not typing out articles every day. I must admit that I think the *writing* of *Waters of Siloe* rather inferior to his earlier work. I don't think it possible to combine a Trappist's life with that of a professional writer. Cheese and liquers [*sic*] are the proper products of the contemplative life." [8]

The problem, Waugh implied in a much more frank letter to Katherine Asquith, was that Merton's religious superiors did not seem to distinguish between books and cheese, "& as a result when the other monks go out into the fields Merton is set down at a typewriter & told to produce books. . . . it is for his directors & superiors to decide if that is good for his soul. From a literary point of view the prospect seems depressing." Waugh viewed *The Waters of Siloe* as a predictable result: the structure was chaotic; "the historical chapters most interesting but the prologue painful"; the sense of audience confused or non-existent, "sometimes . . . people who had never heard of a monk & sometimes . . . people far advanced in spiritual growth."

Mrs. Asquith's praise of the book gave Waugh some hope that he could produce something creditable, but, as his outline of alternatives indicates, not a great deal:

I had thought of cutting it ruthlessly into a history of American Cistercians with a single preliminary section culled from all over the book giving a description of contemplative prayers. Would it do just to cut out obvious

8. Quoted in Sister Thérèse Lentfoehr, "My Meeting with Evelyn Waugh," *Evelyn Waugh Newsletter*, 11 (Spring 1977), 3–4.

gaucheries & leave the structure as he planned, or failed to plan, it & write a foreword explaining why a Trappist is publishing books at all (which has disconcerted even sympathetic critics)? Or not even that? Publish and be damned? (*Letters*, 309)

Despite his reputation for ruthless frankness, Waugh was not prepared to follow the last course, but his Foreword to *The Waters of Silence*, the English edition, follows—somewhat disingenuously, given his earlier remarks—the course outlined in the antepenultimate question. Waugh repudiates the view that "the Cistercian Rule requires such absolute seclusion from the world that any contact with it constitutes an irregularity" as "a romantic and untheological view of the character of the contemplative life."[9] All monks support themselves; Merton's superiors have directed him to do so by the more difficult labor of writing; he may be expected to produce "a number of books in the future." After this laconic—and secretly glum—prediction, Waugh repeated some of his remarks to Sister Thérèse:

We have long been accustomed to drink liqueurs and to eat cheese manufactured by contemplatives. Now we have the opportunity of reading works designed to popularize the idea of the contemplative life. It is not for us, living in the world, to cavil at this generous decision.

Nor, for that matter, to rejoice or, except to note that *Elected Silence* "has been widely read and . . . very respectfully criticized," to praise even by implication.

A comparison of *The Waters of Siloe* and *The Waters of Silence* indicates that Waugh did his best to remedy the book's most obvious defects but that, as in the case of the Preface, he did not commit as much energy to what he saw as a hopeless task. The most obvious difference, the title, may have been the publisher's decision,[10] though Waugh disliked allusion for its own sake and may have preferred the directness of the English version. However, his

9. Thomas Merton, *The Waters of Siloe* (New York: Harcourt, Brace and Company, 1949). Thomas Merton, *Waters of Silence*, with a Foreword by Evelyn Waugh (London: Theodore Brun Ltd. [Limited Edition]; London: Hollis and Carter, 1950).
10. Thomas F. Burns, the publisher, thinks that he was "responsible for the change of title and also for inviting Waugh to do an editing job" but cannot remember whether Waugh "just got tired or approved of what he did not cut." Letter to RMD, 26 November 1982.

letters make it clear that the order of *Silence* is his. He cut entirely
Merton's Prologue and Note on the Function of a Contemplative
Order from the beginning of *Siloe*, and he removed Chapter XIII,
"The Cistercian Character and Sanctity" and "Glossary of Some
Monastic Terms" at or near the end. He moved "The Daily Life of
a Cistern Monk in Our Time" from its place between Contents and
Prologue in *Siloe* to a position just before the Bibliography, perhaps
to avoid beginning a historical account with an anachronistic sched-
ule. His other major structural alteration, also dictated by the desire
to preserve historical continuity, made Merton's Chapter XII, "Cistercian Life in the Twelfth Century," Chapter 2 of *Silence*. Despite
the fact that Chapter I (and 1) moves from straight chronological
to a less determinable structure, it takes the Order to "the height of
its spiritual vigor" (*Siloe*, 29; Waugh cut this phrase), and Chapter
II begins "By the middle of the seventeenth century" and deals with
reform in the Order. Merton had placed Chapter XII at the beginning of Part Two. Since Waugh had removed all but one of the three
chapters in that section, he abolished the division into parts.

In his role as copy editor, Waugh was less enthusiastic and attentive than he had been in shaping *Elected Silence* out of *The Seven
Storey Mountain*. At the beginning—perhaps before he wrote to
Mrs. Asquith and before he discovered that "I have bitten off more
than my failing teeth can chew" (*Letters*, 309)—he was alert, cutting four of the first five sentences of Chapter I and some words on
a majority of pages through the end of Chapter III/4. In Chapter
IV/5 he cut "Greece," used by Merton to distinguish "the Athens
of Kentucky" from its original (65), and, three pages later, the
vague "and so on." Only "evil-smelling," to describe a monastery
destroyed by fire, failed to survive in Chapter V/6, and though
Waugh made three alterations in the first three pages of VI/7,
Chapters VII/8 and X/11 have only one substantive change each,
and Chapters VIII/9 and IX/10 have none. Waugh did manage to
rouse his critical faculties to make eleven changes in the first third
of Chapter XI/12, but in the final chapter he changed only "that
way" to "poor" where Merton had tried to avoid repeating the ad-
jective.

Even this kind of minor change, made in various ways over and over again, allows us to see a master craftsman at work, weighing matters of rhythm, tone, and precision that might be more difficult to see in his own work. Although Waugh did not edit *Siloe* with the rigor and enthusiasm he brought to *The Seven Storey Mountain*, he did reveal in various ways not only his training as a writer and critic of English prose but—the spirit of his embattled history tutor at Oxford must have smiled grimly—as a historian.

Most obvious are the cuts of verbal deadwood: "off" and "with" from "go off to" and "joined with"; "kind of" from "some kind of purpose" (8), "anything like" (7), "to do so," "were not slow to" (29), "and so on" (68), "into the bargain" (103), "in any case" (229), "More elemental" (236). Dead or distracting metaphor also caught Waugh's attention. He changed Merton's "the central warmth of peace and beauty among men in a world that seemed wrestling with the ice of death" to "among men in that icy world" (6) and cut the image of a labyrinth applied to journeys by the founders of monasteries (7). "At one blow" (10) and "a sea of moving vestments" (16) were rejected, as were the description of judges pouncing "with the satisfaction of hungry lions on their prey" and a discussion of monks as "something more than transplanted athletes playing the spiritual equivalent of football in a strange, eleventh-century uniform" (239).

Waugh disliked excessive emotion as much as he did surplus language. He literally cut an exclamation (12), and he did the same with words, phrases, and even sentence-paragraphs like "tremendous" (16), "exceedingly" (240), "marvelous" (3)), "the most sincere monk it would be possible to find" (61), and "It was to be a fierce purgation of society which La Trappe would survive, but not without a wonder!" (49)

More complex were the deletions of generalizations which were implied in the description of specific events. For example, Merton wrote, "So great was the number of monks that *all life was depersonalized*. There was no intimate contact with superiors" (5). Waugh cut the words I have italicized and made one sentence of two. Thirty pages later, Merton asks, "What was the mental atti-

tude of the average monk of the Common Observance? How did
he live? What did he live for?" and gives a generalized and specu-
lative paragraph about a stereotyped monk's desire for salvation
with not too much discomfort. Waugh cut this to move directly to
the evidence, letters written by a novice in the eighteenth century.

Like any well-trained historian, Waugh detested fruitless, obvious, or irrelevant speculation: about why families chose monasteries "for their less talented sons" (36); about the possible expectations of Trappists and Revolutionists in 1789 (51; the passage
about lions quoted previously is part of this narrative); about what
Trappists do not feel or think (238). Moreover, Waugh rejected
anachronistic language which raised irrelevant associations: characterization of "Cistercian insistence on manual labor" as based on
"what the Communists call 'social consciousness'" (17), and the
desire by the French revolutionary government that the monks not
exist at all as "the final solution" (53).

Readers made sensitive to language by Waugh's editing can discover many other passages which might have received his attention,
such as "These two things, obedience and the presence of God, the
two foundation stones of Benedictine spirituality, were absolutely
all he had left. Everything else had been taken away" and so on for
the rest of the paragraph (198) or "a sigh that had, perhaps, much
secret satisfaction in it" (84). However, as the statistics indicate,
Waugh attended less and less to stylistic lapses of these and other
kinds in *The Waters of Siloe*. Perhaps, a reluctant and not very dedicated teacher in his youth, he despaired of a pupil who could not
learn from one extended lesson, for he ended his letter to Merton
about *Siloe*, "I wish I saw the faults of *The Seven Storey Mountain*
disappearing and I don't."

Merton responded to Waugh's editing of *Siloe* gratefully and gen-
erously. He agreed with the structural criticism; told Waugh that he
had tried to delete the Prologue and had been overruled; confessed
that "The Note is my fault"; and conceded, somewhat hyperboli-
cally, that "I have no difficulty in accepting you as the delegate of
the Holy Ghost in this matter" (*Letters*, 309, n. 2). Waugh acknowledged Merton's generosity, adding, truthfully enough as far as he
went, "It was a difficult book to prepare for the European

reader. . . ."[11] His payment, he noted, was "in Church candles for the dining-room table," but he did not say whether they were worth the game.

The chief point about Waugh as adviser and editor is not to establish his superiority to other writers but to show that his approach was thoroughly professional. He was obsessed with language, consulting the dictionary almost daily for thirty years or more to learn, as he put it, the "subtle difference of nuance" between nearly synonymous words.[12] His own work he revised at every opportunity, and his comments on that work are expressed with characteristic bluntness and candor. Furthermore, he had a respect for the craft of writing which outweighed his concern for individual feelings. Anyone who sought to publish a book he assumed to be a professional writer, and Waugh held him or her to professional standards.

11. "Waugh's Letters to Merton," p. 3.
12. *Tourist in Africa* (Boston: Little, Brown, 1960), p. 119.

Applying Theory

CHAPTER 7

Waugh's Juvenilia

A man of principle and taste, Evelyn Waugh always deprecated his juvenile work. However, the rest of us can be amused and enlightened by the foreshadowings of mature achievement even in his earliest work. Of course, even casual perusal of Waugh's diaries reveals that a great deal of material—drawings, school essays, diaries, jeux d'esprit in various forms—was not preserved. But a great deal has been, and it shows that Waugh's style did not emerge fully formed but was based on a long and active apprenticeship for someone who strongly resisted the career of writing.

The juvenile items at The University of Texas and elsewhere[1] include work in most of the genres and media practiced by the mature Waugh—diary, autobiography, cartoon, reporting, fiction—as well as those, such as watercolor, drama, libretto, and verse, which he abandoned or practiced sparingly in later years. Waugh matured at different ages in different media. Thus as illustrator and versifier, he attained by the time he was eighteen a degree of skill which he never greatly surpassed, though the wit and finish of his pastiches increased until their culmination in the collages he gleefully assembled for the illustrations to *Love Among the Ruins* (one labeled "Canov fec. Moses delin. Waugh perfec.") and Major Ludovic's sonnet on the Sword of Stalingrad in *Unconditional Surrender*.

Waugh always worked in various media concurrently, but in general it can be said that he could draw before he could write, write

1. The juvenilia in verbal form are collected in *Evelyn Waugh, Apprentice: The Early Writings, 1910–1927*, ed. Robert Murray Davis (Norman: Pilgrim Books, 1985). It is not sold outside the United States.

before he could spell, and narrate before he was willing to undergo the rigors of presenting character and setting in verbal form. From the vantage point of his ultimate choice of career, the impulse toward narrative is the most interesting aspect of the juvenilia.

The HRC *Catalogue* lists forty-eight items under "Drawings," two of those sketchbooks used at Heatherley's Art School. The earliest dated materials, "aged 4 and 9 month" (July 1908) and "4 years 11 months" (September), are drawings of various objects, exhibiting more mimetic ability than most children's but not differing markedly in interest: ships, Indian villages, flowers—all outlined in pencil and filled in with crayon. (An unconscious irony, in view of Waugh's mature laments about Inland Revenue, can be observed in the first: it is done on the blank verso of printed instructions for obtaining income tax refunds.) By the time he was eight, Waugh had progressed to ink as a medium and to an interest in situation, producing a drawing of a besieged castle. Still more advanced and more exotic are watercolors—the most accomplished of Waugh's juvenile artwork—of daggers, "Changes in Indian Writing," and "Types of Eastern Dress," the whole titled "The Beauty of the East." Most of the drawings can be divided into two classes, ecclesiastical and bellicose, foreshadowing, perhaps, *Sword of Honour*.

Even more interesting are two narratives, "The Slaves of Hurre Len. A Revised Rajah Shoo" and "In Quest of Thomas Lee," which tell their stories in pictures accompanied by brief captions. The first combines a taste for the exotic with an interest in melodrama and involves the capture of an airplane pilot by a villainous Hindu and a rescue, with danger and surprise improbable enough to satisfy even Princess Jenny Abdul Akbar of *A Handful of Dust*, whose account of her very beautiful and very wicked Moslem husband is probably drawn from the same kind of source. The second deals with Lee's capture by South American natives and his fortuitous meeting with his brother Christopher and his friend Lenard [*sic*], an outcome parallel to but more fortunate than that of *A Handful of Dust*.[2]

2. For additional discussion of Waugh's art and some reproductions, see Alain Blayac, "Evelyn Waugh's Drawings," *Library Chronicle of the University of Texas*, n.s. 7 (1974), 42–57.

The written material has, of course, considerably more interest for the student of Waugh's career because it gives evidence of the impulses that pushed him toward what he came to call the family trade of literature. These were at least fourfold. First, as he explained in the self-dedication of his untitled schoolboy novel, he was born into an intensely literary family in which the writing, reading, and making of books were regarded as natural if not inevitable activities. His father, Arthur Waugh, was director of Chapman & Hall, a solid if not leading publishing firm, and a firmly established if not a leading reviewer and man of letters. Moreover, as both Evelyn and Alec Waugh later testified, much of the family's social life involved literary men and occasional literary women.[3]

A second kind of impetus to authorship came from what would now be called Evelyn's peer group. With neighbors, some of them older, he organized "a patriotic league named The Pistol Troop," conducted battles with what he called "gutter children" and later "street cads," and produced a magazine to which adults as well as children contributed. In less bellicose moods, and without military sanction, Waugh, the Fleming children (called the Roland family in *A Little Learning*), and others "produced a number of plays, written by ourselves and acted in home-made costumes before home-made scenery" (60). Alec Waugh testifies that The Pistol Troop was succeeded by "the W.U.D.S. (Wyldesmead Underhill Dramatic Society)" and mentions programs, "very professional . . . illustrated with photographs of the chief performers" (*My Brother*, 168).[4]

Two plays and the libretto of a comic operetta survive. "A Woman's Curse" is melodrama, with an Oriental villain, Tse Feng (alias the Red Hand); sudden disappearances; delightful dialogue including "You cur," "Thou art doing things about which thou knowest nothing," and "Nay, cool thy temper and drink tea." The villain, rejected and rebuked by the heroine, drinks the poisoned tea pre-

---

3. See Alec Waugh, "Authors at Underhill" in *My Brother Evelyn and Other Portraits*, Chapter 2, and *A Little Learning* (Boston: Little, Brown, 1964), p. 62.
4. Two such programmes survive at the Humanities Research Center (HRC) (*Catalogue*, G1–2). Except for the photographs in one, they resemble that given in the notes to "A Woman's Curse" (See *Evelyn Waugh, Apprentice*) in casting and in variety of turns.

pared for her father. A second play, "Come to the Coach House Door, Boys," is set in wartime England. David Malaher, son of a family noted for traditional cowardice, sounds a zeppelin alarm in order to escape his music lesson and with his parents breaks down the coachhouse door seeking shelter. Faced with punishment, he advises his parents to claim that the damage was caused by enemy action, a ruse that succeeds and illustrates the first use of the familiar Waugh theme of impudence triumphant.

Less realistic but more delightful is the gem of Waugh's early work, "The Sheriff's Daughter," a libretto which demonstrates that young Waugh had at least intuitive knowledge of the structure of New Comedy. Written more or less in tetrameter couplets not unworthy of Bottom and his friends, the play deals with the love of Jack, a poor but honest cowboy, for Celia, the eponymous heroine. She will marry, she says, the man who captures the notorious outlaw El Maduff. Ciril [sic], an itinerant detective, and the chorus of cowboys all determine to win her hand, and while Jack is capturing the real Maduff, Ciril mistakenly apprehends a Professor Lazmouse. Ciril is consoled, however, when the professor produces a daughter for him to wed, whereupon Maduff points out "That an outlaw cannot be / led / to the gallows, or even shot / dead / when more than one couple is wed." Struck by his knowledge of the laws of comedy, his captors free him—and the sheriff brings out another daughter for him.

Malefactors fare less happily in two short stories written before he went to Lancing. "The Curse of the Horse Race" was the only youthful work to escape Waugh's blanket condemnation of his early writing and the only prose juvenilia published in his lifetime.[5] It contains murders, attempted murders, and swordplay and concludes with the villain satisfactorily hanged and a moral: "I hope this story will be a leson to you never to bet." "Fidon's Confetion," composed a bit later, judging from the use of ink rather than pencil,

5. In *The World of Evelyn Waugh*, ed. Charles J. Rolo (Boston: Little, Brown, 1958), pp. 3–5. Chapters 1 and 9 are published in *A Little Learning*, p. 62; the first page of the manuscript is reproduced opposite p. 15. The story was first published in *Little Innocents: Childhood Reminiscences*, ed. Alan Pryce-Jones (London: Cobden-Sanderson, 1932).

also begins with gambling—"Midnight boomed from the old clock tower and stil the two men played on"—but shifts from Ralfe Cantonville's debts and further losses to the villain Baycraw to Baycraw's murder of Ralfe's father and Fidon in an unrelated act of revenge. The murder weapon implicates Ralfe—" 'Why,' cried Barbarous his sister, 'that's Ralfe's knife' "—and his athletic but not very clever brother Tom floors Baycraw for sneering and resolves to clear Ralfe. He is aided by the confession of Fidon because "whatever faults Fidon might have had he was not a cad and upon hearing of Ralfe's arrest he quickly resolved to turn evidence." As he hands his written "confetion" to Tom, a shot through the window fells him and the confession disappears. After various chases, Baycraw is accidentally hanged on a tree branch and Tom bursts triumphantly into the courtroom with the document. The third surviving story from this period, "Multa Pecunia," was included in the *Pistol Troop Magazine*; it involves hidden treasure stolen from Queen Elizabeth, a villainous butler named Smith, and doubts of the youthful hero's sanity. Waugh accurately called this work "imitative of the worst of my reading" (*A Little Learning*, 62).

In fact, this kind of imitation of both fictional and dramatic forms was probably less rare among children (and, judging from stories about Arthur Waugh's love of theatrics both formal and informal, adults) than those of us raised with movies, radio, and television can now imagine. Evelyn seems to have differed from his contemporaries not only in being more talented but, as his diaries and letters show, in having a much stronger competitive nature.

As early as 1916, when he edited *The Cynic: Cynical Without Being Cheaply So: Piquant in Moderation: Racy in Excess*, and had it mimeographed at his father's office, he asserted himself. In his opening "Editorial" and manifesto he proclaimed his victory over the official school magazine. His campaign was premeditated if not planned. In a diary entry for early 1916 not given in *Diaries*, Waugh anticipated the beginning of the winter term at Heath Mount School:

> By George when the term begins things will hum. I think it's my last so I'm going to raise Hell. Our first shell to smash the ramparts of convention is "The Cynic" the most gorgeous paper out.

In fact, he continued at Heath Mount until the end of 1916. Issues appeared 21 January, 8 February, 7 March, 5 May, and September. The gap in publication, Waugh explained in the last number, occurred because he was waiting for a rival paper to appear "so as to deliver some helpful criticisms to the youthful journalist."

However, as his editorial indicates, the chief object of criticism was the *Heath Mount Magazine*. Waugh made helpful criticisms of the masters' efforts and predicted that "when they have had a little more experience [they] will be able to produce quite a presentable little paper." Later he apologized for criticizing false rhymes in comic verse: "Believe me we had no idea it was humourous or we should have been more lenient."

If the authorities did not not actually repress this schoolboy cheek, they did not encourage it. Waugh noted in his diary that Mr. Hinchcliffe, his form master, "has of course forbidden the 'Cynic' to be sold but nevertheless we have already sold out [at 3 pence each] . . . we have after paying for the printing got about halfe a crown over for the war fund which we are collecting." Later, describing another project, he carefully distinguished between the war fund and the Waugh fund.

In *A Little Learning*, Waugh gives the impression that his bellicose impulses gave way, about 1915, to the religious period in which he composed *The World to Come*, described as "a deplorable poem in the metre of Hiawatha . . . describing the experiences of the soul immediately after death" (93). In fact, the poem must have been composed during the run of *The Cynic*, and Waugh's ability to separate satiric from religious impulses persisted, even more notably in his personal than in his professional life, as long as he lived. Although Waugh was ashamed of the poem, it is by no means discreditable for a boy not yet thirteen. The first canto represents the narrator's sensations on dying—"All was blackness, all was nothing, / Everything was utter blackness . . ."—his passage to the stairway leading to heaven's gate, and Michael's announcement that

Thou must make the wondrous journey
Through the Kingdom of the Heavens,
Thou must see how man was modelled,

See how prayers ascent to Heaven,
See the torture of the wicked.

Only then may he face the Trinity. In Canto II, the guardian spirit Cyprian conducts him to a mountaintop for two visions, one of Christians slaughtering each other and exulting in victory, the second of a charitable Moslem's prayers' finding favor. In the final canto, the narrator overlooks hell and Satan, who is "swept away in laughter, / laughing to his own damnation," before turning from Cyprian toward the entrance to Heaven.

Two elements of the poem are noteworthy: Waugh the religious versifier is considerably less bellicose and more realistic about war than Waugh the cartoonist or chronicler of the Pistol Troop's gutter wars or the editor of the *Cynic*; and the figure of Satan, scorning the timid righteous and extolling the virtues of those who "had the courage / To rebel against the Tyrant," is a lurid version of the role Waugh tentatively assumed and finally, from indifference and ambition, rejected in his later years at Lancing College.

The classical, historical, and literary training he received at Lancing was another important influence on and impetus to his juvenile writing. Summing up the content and effect of his education in *A Little Learning*, Waugh concludes that "My education . . . was the preparation for one trade only; that of an English prose writer" (140). As Waugh's diaries and relatively few surviving manuscripts demonstrate, public school boys of that period were asked to do a good deal of writing. Waugh asserted that "our written work was seldom read and then only to criticise style or meaning; spelling was regarded as too elementary for attention" (139–140), but "Essay" and "The House: an anti-climax," preserved by his friend and literary disciple Dudley Carew,[6] demonstrate more careful attention by the master than he recalled. Both stories are very much in the vein of Waugh's potboiling short fiction of the 1930's, full of rueful irony about convention's triumphing over genuine emotion (or its absence) and originality. "Essay" is in fact a framed monologue by Lunnstein, a Jew educated to be a society painter who

6. See Dudley Carew, *A Fragment of Friendship* (London: Everest Books, 1974).

defects to the Futurists and the Cafe Royal, is disappointed in love and burns his original drawings, and at the end of a year returns to his backers and his Mayfair haunts. Now a member of the Royal Academy, he leads what most would call a good life and brusquely dismisses his longing to do significant work by turning to the portrait of the narrator. In structure, of course, if not in tone, the story resembles *Decline and Fall*, and the monologue, more individuated and more lively, continued to be a favorite device by which Waugh's characters revealed themselves at least through *Brideshead Revisited*. Later, as here, it was a device by which Waugh allowed characters as unlike him as possible to justify themselves and, however outrageously, to gain the sympathy of the audience.

In contrast to this desire for objectivity is Waugh's autobiographical impulse, notable from "The Balance" thorough *Basil Seal Rides Again*, where a hatcheck man describes Basil, as one had Waugh, as "florid" (*Diaries*, 773) and where Waugh converts to disreputable paternal triumph his own feelings for his daughter Margaret. "The House: an anti-climax" illustrates this tendency. A prudently disguised version of Waugh's attempt during March 1921 to embarrass the authorities by having his OTC platoon win the drill competition, the story is set in 1917, when the school is in disarray, and the reader is enjoined to understand the special circumstances "when reading a story which at any other time period would have been utterly impossible." Ross, a sixth former, finds himself head of the House, attempts to restore order among his demoralized and disorganized underlings, and runs afoul of Steward, who rejects "corps mania" and refuses to run for his House in the five-mile race. Ross tries to substitute, collapses, and after a week in the infirmary emerges to discover the House Platoon's drilling marvelously, their new loyalty elicited by his failure. The omniscient narrator comments that "It would make a splendid ending if the House could be allowed to win the Shield, but this is a story of School life and everyone who knows the House will know that it is out of the question"—in real life as in fiction. However, Ross and Steward are reconciled, and Ross earns the narrator's commendation for making it seem, solely by his manner, as though he has forgiven his underlings rather than they him.

There is no way of knowing whether these were typical responses to assignments, but it is clear from the diaries that Waugh sometimes regarded assignments as challenges to his ingenuity and to his skill, that he took some pains with them, and that on occasion he sent them to his father and noted, without pain or rancor, even the unfavorable responses.

At least as much energy went into extracurricular writing, some of it officially approved, much of it not. Waugh was acutely, perhaps needlessly, sensitive to the danger of keeping a diary, once destroying part of it and on other occasions exercising prudent self-censorship. He did not express and perhaps did not have a clear motive for keeping it; perhaps he did so because of what he later called the writer's desire to give written shape to his experiences.[7]

However, his desire to write was also a result of his recurrent desire to emulate and surpass his brother Alec. Throughout the period at Lancing College covered by his diaries (September 1919–December 1921), visits by Alec, already established as a novelist and man of letters, spurred him to a rivalry that seems not to have been conscious. Perhaps some of the earliest stories and almost certainly the schoolboy novel (see Chaper 11) were written with the intention of going his predecessor one better.

There is no question that in the play "Conversion" he dealt head-on with a number of stereotypes, including Alec's in *The Loom of Youth*. Act I portrays "School as Maiden Aunts Think It Is" at "Dr. Grimthorpe's Academy for the education of the sons of Gentlemen." The good boys talk an incredible and delightful mixture of cant and of clichés about "the old gray stones." Apprised of his friend's activities during vacation, a hero replies that such pursuits are permissible, "Always provided, of course, that instruction is not used as a mere cloak for indulgence." The villain, exposed and thwarted, is told to think of his aunt whenever he is tempted to do a mean thing and shows nauseating signs of repentance.

Act II, "School, as Modern Authors Say It Is," contains passages directly traceable to the novel, as the following passages indicate

---

7. *Ninety Two Days* (New York: Farrar and Rinehart, 1934), p. 5.

(originally published 1917; I quote the Richards Press edition of 1947):

"You know I think Meredith goes a bit too far at times," came a voice from the middle of the room.
Bradford rose at once. "What the hell do you mean? Meredith go too far? Why, he is a splendid wicket-keeper, and far and away the finest half-back in the school. You must allow a good deal to a blood like him."
"Oh, I know he is a magnificent athlete and all that, but don't you think he does rather a lot of harm in the House?"
"Harm? Who to?"
"Well, I mean there's Davenham now and—"
"Davenham!" came the scornful retort. "What does it matter what happens to Davenham? He's absolutely useless to the House, rotten at games and spends his whole time reading about fossils. . . . Meredith is simply a glorious fellow. Do you remember the way he brought down Freeman in the Two Cock? Why, the House simply couldn't get on without him." (p. 23)

[Jeffries has just been expelled, and speaks]
"it is unfair. Who made me what I am but Fernhurst? Two years ago I came here as innocent as Caruthers there; never knew anything. Fernhurst taught me everything; Fernhurst made me worship games, and think that they alone mattered, and everything else could go to the deuce. . . . And now Fernhurst, that has made me what I am, turns round and says, 'You are not fit to be a member of this great school!' and I have to go. Oh, it's fair, isn't it?" (p. 60)

In a passage too long to quote, Tester, a member of the Sixth form, converts the protagonist to an aesthetic view of life by reading aloud "the great spring Chorus in *Atalanta*, into which Swinburne crowded all that he ever knew of joy and happiness" (147–149).

Evelyn's Fernhurst, "one of the largest and wickedest of our Public Schools," has athletes who defend Collier, a good fellow, because "he may be half-witted and a cad, and he may not wash much, but he's got a wonderful hand-off." He also steals—and gets the push for doing, he laments, what Fernhurst taught him to do, after which he bursts uncontrollably into a verse of Dowson's "Ceonera" [*sic*]. Overheard by a sympathetic master, Collier confesses that he is at heart a pagan; he is enjoined to rise above small sins and, when tempted to do a mean thing, "think of a chorus from Atalanta." The last act, "School as we all know it is," draws on the author's situation as a rebel who wants the perquisites of the establishment. Through the dialogue of minor characters, very skillfully managed, Waugh implies that Townsend has been "ragging chapel" and prepares for a confrontation between Townsend and Maine, one of the prefects. Unmoved by Maine's appeals to reason, Townsend is more impressed by arguments from power: those who have it can keep honors and prizes from those who will not give at least surface acquiescence: "We can't have you in a position of authority . . . if you persist in making an ass of yourself." Rebellious in no particular cause, Townsend agrees, in the most cynical of the three "conversions," to behave.

In other types of writing, like speeches prepared for debates or, like "The Twilight of Language," for clubs, Waugh was equally self-assertive but less obviously bellicose. And of course various literary prizes could bring him money—to be spent about equally on books and on food—as well as the regard of masters and contemporaries. He debated often and won several prizes for poems and essays, but only one debate speech is preserved in his diary, and only his prize poem, "The Return of Launcelot," in Spenserian stanzas, survived among the other materials transmitted to the University of Texas. When Waugh began to pursue the larger prize of an Oxford scholarship in the summer and winter terms of 1921, he abandoned everything but a few debate speeches and editorials for the Lancing College Magazine.

Once he reached Oxford, however, he abandoned serious attempts at study and devoted himself to an extensive social life and to various literary projects for undergraduate magazines, including the Isis, whose "sole attraction" for Waugh "was that it paid its contributors"; the Cherwell, which after an episode with a Philbrickian publisher was financed and edited by Waugh's friends, and the Oxford Broom, founded by Harold Acton.

Waugh later regarded his literary contributions as "not . . . much better or much worse than most undergraduate journalism" (A

Little Learning, 187). However, he goes on to say that one (probably "Edward of Unique Achievement") "was a quite funny short story in which an earnest student might find hints of my first novel" and that another ("Antony, Who Sought Things That Were Lost") "betrays the unmistakable influence of that preposterously spurious artifact, which quite captivated me at the age of nineteen, James Branch Cabell's *Jurgen*" (*A Little Learning*, 189). Earnest students who read the stories in light of Waugh's still earlier juvenilia can trace the continuation of the split between the anarchic impulses of *The Cynic* and, heavily disguised by melancholy or necromancy, the spiritual impulses of *The World to Come* and between social satire and self-critical justification observable in "The Balance" and in more subtle fashion in *Vile Bodies*.

The undergraduate stories, "The Manager of 'The Kremlin'" and "The Sympathetic Passenger," and for that matter Waugh's later short stories were mostly written to formulas that changed less because of Waugh's development than because of the audience for whom he wrote. "The Balance," however, shows Waugh's attempt to extend his range both technically and thematically. He began it while he was teaching in Wales and after he had destroyed "The Temple at Thatch," which "concerned an undergraduate who inherited a property of which nothing was left except an eighteenth-century classical folly where he set up house and, I think, practised black magic" (*A Little Learning*, 223). To readers of Waugh's undergraduate stories, the themes sound familiar, and there is no evidence that the technique was markedly different. In "The Balance," however, Waugh used cinematic devices by which to present as objectively as possible material drawn from his own painful experiences as failed painter and unsuccessful suicide. By using methods which he had studied as a reviewer of films and in the films which he made with Terence Greenidge and other contemporaries at Oxford, he was able to turn away from the subjectivity which he described in "The Twilight of Language" and was later to condemn in "Ronald Firbank" (*EAR*, 56–59). Moreover, though he used Oxford as a setting, he placed it in the framework of the London social scene which he was to exploit for part of *Decline and Fall*, most of *Vile Bodies*, and in fact most of his mature fiction.

Although "The Tutor's Tale: A House of Gentlefolks," about a young nobleman kept secluded from the fashionable world he is brilliantly able to inhabit by aged guardians on the grounds that he is feebleminded, was less experimental than "The Balance," it does show the youthful Waugh's using the same London setting and one of the same characters, Ernest Vaughan, and thus beginning to create the setting and cast of characters for what came to be called the world of Evelyn Waugh.[8]

Although "The Tutor's Tale" was solicited while Waugh thought of himself as a schoolmaster with literary interests, it was written after he had been fired and had concluded, reluctantly, that "the time has arrived to set about being a man of letters" (*Diaries*, 281, 21 February 1927). Technically, one could argue, the period of his juvenilia ends here, or hereabouts. When it concluded, or shaded into professional authorship, Waugh had worked through mere imitation of commercial and conventionally aesthetic models and was on the verge of understanding his real style and subject.

8. See *Evelyn Waugh, Writer* (Norman: Pilgrim Books, 1981), pp. 32–37, for a more thorough discussion of "The Balance" and "The Tutor's Tale."

CHAPTER 8

Context and Structure in *Vile Bodies*★

Just over a year after Evelyn Waugh published *Decline and Fall* and eloped with Evelyn Gardner, he returned to England to try to establish more firmly his status as an author and as a married man and householder. He and She-Evelyn "found bills of over £200 waiting for us and each overdrawn at our banks so I must write a lot quickly" (*Letters*, p. 36). By retiring from the London scene to a quiet inn near Oxford and by abjuring even the party of Bryan and Diana Guinness, he was able to realize his hope. By the end of June, he wrote to A. D. Peters, his agent, that he was sending ten thousand words of the novel.[1]

A month later, he wrote to Henry Yorke (Green) that he had "written 25,000 words of a novel in ten days. It is rather like P. G. Wodehouse all about bright young people. I hope it will be finished by the end of the month & then I shall just have time to write another book before your party" (*Letters*, 36). To Harold Acton, however, he confessed that he felt "chained to this novel" and called it "a welter of sex and snobbery written simply in the hope of selling some copies. Then if it is [at] all a success I want to try and write something more serious. I have done half of it and hope to get it finished in another three weeks" (*Letters*, 37).

In early July, however, Evelyn Gardner Waugh confessed her love

★ The material drawn from popular journalism and social history is based on research by Charles E. Linck, Jr., incorporated in our article, "The Bright Young People in *Vile Bodies*," *Papers on Language and Literature*, 5 (1969), 80–90.

1. *Catalogue*, E186. This is probably the material in the carbon typescript preserved at the University of Texas. See *Catalogue*, item A10, and my "*Vile Bodies* in Typescript," *Evelyn Waugh Newsletter*, 11 (Winter 1977), 7–8.

for John Heygate,[2] and the attempted reconciliations, negotiations for divorce, and emotional turmoil made it impossible for Waugh to continue writing the novel or anything else. But Waugh had decided to be a professional writer, and a professional was once defined as someone who does what he does even when he doesn't feel like it. By mid-August he had decided to attend a motor race in Belfast "in the hope of finding an honourable grave" (*Letters*, 39) but found only an incident for his novel. Once there he recovered enough to telegraph Peters about placing a satiric piece on the race and drivers (*Catalogue*, E109) and shortly thereafter accepted a commission to write the article which became "Let the Marriage Ceremony Mean Something" (*Letters*, 39, but c. 25 August 1929, rather than the September date which Amory assigns).

By September, he retired to another inn to try to finish the novel but confessed that "It has been infinitely difficult and is certainly the last time I shall try to make a book about sophisticated people. It all seems to shrivel up & rot internally and I am relying on a sort of cumulative futility it may have" (*Letters*, 39). By 1 October he was back in London and on his way to Paris, probably finished with at least a draft of the novel and willing to seek consolation for the end of his marriage.

Judging from this account, Waugh's memory was quite accurate when he recalled thirty-five years later that *Vile Bodies* was "a totally unplanned novel," written at a time when he could "set a few characters on the move, write 3000 words a day, and note with surprise what happened." The shift in tone midway through the novel "from gaiety to bitterness" he explained by the uncharacteristic circumlocution "a sharp disturbance in my private life."[3] He also noted the journalistic appeal of the subject and the novel's great popularity. Implied in his comments are two principles of structure, social and moral, and while they overlap, they are complex enough to be discussed separately.

---

2. Martin Stannard, *Evelyn Waugh: The Early Years 1903–1939* (London: Dent, 1986), pp. 180–185, establishes the chronology of the failure of the Waugh marriage.

3. *Vile Bodies* (London: Chapman & Hall, 1965), p. 7. This is the Uniform Edition, the last prepared by Waugh. Cited in the text is the first American edition

It is clear from Waugh's letters that he was quite conscious of capitalizing on a popular subject. The world from which he drew the material has faded into the pages of nostalgic memoirs and social histories, and the reader who contrasts their tone with that of *Vile Bodies* may suspect that Waugh was not only exaggerating for the purposes of satire but escaping into fantasy. However, contemporary gossip columns not only give a lively account of the period and reveal the originals of some characters and incidents in the novel but also chronicle and embody a set of attitudes and a process of social change which Waugh satirized and made into a structural principle of his novels: the process by which a coterie becomes mere newspaper copy. The stages of the process are described in the newspapers as well as the novel: private fun publicized by members of the group; increasing numbers of spectators, emulators, and gate-crashers attracted by the publicity; recognition by the coterie's members that they are being stereotyped; and final dissolution of the group.[4]

The bright young people commemorated and satirized in *Vile Bodies* were the second group to bear that label. In 1924, as Waugh was taking his examinations at Oxford, *The Daily Mail* headlined "The Prince in a Treasure Hunt, Midnight Chase in London, 50 Motorcars, The Bright Young People."[5] Though this group had room for celebrities such as Tallulah Bankhead and Gladys Cooper, entrée seems to have depended largely on wealth or social standing or both: Lady Eleanor Smith and the Jungmann and Guinness girls were among the founders and moving spirits of the group. To some extent, this set overlapped that of Oxford.[6] Many of Waugh's friends served as links between the two: John Sutro, Robert Byron,

---

(New York: J. Cape/H. Smith, 1930), readings of which are preserved in the current Little, Brown editions.

4. See James Hall, *The Tragic Comedians* (Bloomington: Indiana University Press, 1963), pp. 45–65, for an excellent discussion of "Stylized Rebellion" in the early novels of Waugh. See also Steven A. Jervis, "Evelyn Waugh, *Vile Bodies*, and the Younger Generation," *South Atlantic Quarterly*, 66 (Summer 1967), 440–448.

5. July 26, 1924. As far as Charles Linck and I can determine, this is the first use of the phrase in print. See also the account by Robert Graves and Alan Hodge, *The Long Weekend: A Social History of Great Britain, 1918–1939* (London: Faber and Faber, 1940), p. 125.

6. Cecil Beaton, *The Wandering Years: Diaries: 1922–1939* (London: Weidenfeld and Nicolson, 1961), pp. 18–21.

Brian Howard, Harold Acton, Bryan Guinness,[7] Lord Ava, and Frank Pakenham. Some were wealthy, some well born, some both, but the second group was noted more for wit than wealth and for imagination and audacity than social position. By 1927, most of the male members of the younger set had come down from Oxford, and the gossip columns were ready to record their activities.

Lady Eleanor Smith, perhaps the most important link between the two generations of bright young people, began her column, "From a Window in Vanity Fair," for *The Weekly Dispatch* in January 1927. Her contacts gave her access to information and sympathy for her subjects, and her prediliction for the audacious and unusual was reflected in her column. Its content and spirit were soon imitated by Lord Donegall, whose "Almost in Confidence" began in the 5 June 1927 issue of *The Sunday News*, and, a year later, by the Hon. Patrick Balfour (later Lord Kinross and the "Pauper" of Waugh's letters), who became "Mr. Gossip" in "Echoes of the Town" for *The Daily Sketch*.

Lady Eleanor's column dealt with Mayfair café society almost to the exclusion of off-Season of the county or the hunt. In the same column (26 March) as more traditional society-page material such as the announcement of Kitty Kinlock's engagement to Lord Brownlow were items calculated to announce and enforce a trend, such as the report that the Berkeley Restaurant was always filled by the bright young people. Two weeks later she remarked that the chic Mrs. W. S. Maugham always had them about, and on 15 May she included among their numbers two brilliant and unabashed conversationalists, Edward Marjoribanks and Harold Acton. A fortnight later she reported that Brian Howard's mother had numerous "sleek young men" at her party. The most sensational event of the social season was the Kylsant-Henderson wedding, for someone had literally set the Thames afire with gasoline and two hundred "bogus" wedding invitations had been circulated. As a

---

7. *Vile Bodies* and *Labels/A Bachelor Abroad* were dedicated to him and to his wife, Diana Mitford. See the *Letters* for their importance to Waugh in the months after his marriage dissolved. He gave them the manuscript of *Vile Bodies*. See Martin Stannard, "The Mystery of the Missing Manuscript," *Times Higher Education Supplement*, 1 June 1984, p. 13.

known prankster herself, she was compelled to deny a part in either practical joke. But then boredom set in. By 17 July, she was complaining about too many parties and the horrors of the debutante season, though Martin White's "Sailor Suit" party and Nina Hamnett's "Bloomsbury" party were novel enough to seem interesting.

Though Lady Eleanor was bored, the bright young people had only begun to be famous. Captain Neil McEachern's party both launched a new era for their second wave and established a pattern followed by many subsequent parties (including, rather wearily and at a distance, the one given by Archie Schwert in Chapter 4 of Waugh's novel), for it enthralled the more conventional socialites and led to wider publicity for the group. Captain McEachern's party was fully chronicled by modish writers in *The Tatler* and *Eve*, the latter with photographs by Cecil Beaton. The *Tatler's* style was new for that journal:

> This last week or two has brought out an entirely new craze in the shape of fancy-dress dances of one kind or another. They are fancy dress, but new style. No longer do we go hoping to look pretty, handsome, decorative or picturesque. To be amusing and arresting is the chief idea. Undoubtedly, Captain Neil McEachern's, which happened last week in Brook Street, and was followed by several more, and several tentative ones no doubt inspired by the success of his, was the best of all. We had a good band, and a good supper, and Hutchinson, the coloured singer from Chez Victor, but the best part of the entertainment was provided by the guests who all impersonated living people. Daring, yes. But really terribly amusing.

The reporter was particularly interested in new names and original costumes:

> One of the main ideas seemed for the men to come as women and the women to come as men. I was not present at the wedding of Lord and Lady, or rather Mr. and Mrs. Asquith as they were then, but young Mr. Cecil Beaton, who had already made himself famous by his dress designs and his photographs, achieved a huge success by his conception of the bride. A golden wig wreathed in orange blossoms and a thick net veil reaching to his feet, while the long white satin train stretched half across the room. . . . Mr. Bryan Howard, who is Mrs. Francis Howard's son, and gave another of these parties himself on Friday with Mr. David Plunkett-Greene, was Everybody's Mother with a big hat, well trimmed with ostrich feathers perched high up on the hair frame, a sequin bodice

and velvet skirt, black cotton stockings and low-heeled shoes. Not too good really for those who can remember the beauties of the "nineties."[8]

The list of impersonations included Elizabeth Ponsonby as Iris Tree, also a guest; Tallulah Bankhead as tennis star Jean Borotra; Oliver Messel as Tallulah; and a dozen King Fuads.[9]

By the summer of 1929, as Waugh worked on *Vile Bodies*, the gaiety had become more brilliant but more hectic. Audacious originality was replaced by shock value, and the presence of spectators had turned the Bright Young People from an elite acting for its own amusement into a sideshow performing for a more and more obtrusive audience. The *Bystander* resumé contrasts with the 1927 accounts:

The Kindersley-Guinness wedding started the carnival . . . and even the spacious Guinness mansion in Grosvenor Place seemed to bulge. . . . The night following saw a clash of some half-dozen dances. . . . Then, of course, there was a much-trumpeted party on board the old sailing ship that is moored at Charing Cross Pier. Though the invitation was to embark for "Cythera," the good ship never once budged from her moorings. . . . It was a fancy dress party, inspiration to be taken from Watteau, but now-a-days such routs seem to be seized upon not so much for fancy dressing but for fancy undressing.

There was a cosmopolitan and bohemian mixture of guests, that included . . . the Hon. Nancy Mitford and the Hon. Mrs. Evelyn Waugh, whose husband has isolated himself in the country in an attempt to excel his first novel success, *Decline and Fall*.[10]

If Heygate attended, the reporter did not record his presence.

The bright young people had become one of the sights of London: parties aboard the *Friendship* drew large crowds of onlookers, who were rewarded when someone in a bathing suit (responding, it was rumored, to Dean Inge's plea for dress reform) was arrested to the delight of the press and of crowds of men, women, and "darling little things who did not know quite *what* they were" nearly five thousand strong.[11] Mr. and Mrs. Evelyn Waugh were among

8. *Tatler*, 27 July 1927, p. 142.
9. *Eve*, 3 August 1927, pp. 217, 254, and passim; *Sunday News*, 24 July 1927, p. 7.
10. *Bystander*, 3 July 1929, pp. 4–5.
11. *Bystander*, 10 July 1929, p. 77.

the five thousand who witnessed "The Gate-Crasher as Zulu" at the next party aboard the ship and were photographed in their Egyptian whites, "attired," the caption read, "for the 'Tropical' party—which was hot in more ways than one. . . . The author of *Decline and Fall* looks somewhat scared, although there were no fierce Zulus on board." [12]

Some of the gaiety was more imaginative and less accessible to sightseers and gate-crashers—and to reporters vulgar enough to write for the *Bystander*. During the same period, Waugh participated in the "Bruno Hatte" hoax played on the art world by Bryan Guinness and his friends. Lady Eleanor Smith had been given advance information about similar hoaxes during the season, and she helped to set the stage for this one:

> What will be almost a cocktail party is the private view of the exhibition of paintings by Bruno Hatte, to be held next week—on Friday, I think it is.
>
> Bruno Hatte is a painter of German extraction, and his work is mainly of the abstract type, seemingly derivative from Picasso and Chirico. But the queer thing is that his work is not derived from any painter—he was discovered by Mr. Brian [*sic*] Guinness near Clymping. [13]

The brochure describing the exhibition, written by Waugh and Brian Howard, gave details of the artist's background—some of them, such as his German origin, his shyness, and his physical debility, calculated to prevent his being exposed as a fraud. Postexhibition gossip items gave elated descriptions of awed art lovers who had not penetrated Brian Howard's disguise.

The parties were less ingenious and probably wearing enough to warrant Adam's comment in *Vile Bodies*: "Oh, Nina, *what a lot of parties*" (170). Moreover, as Martin Stannard has shown (see note 2), Evelyn Gardner Waugh had already confessed her love for Heygate, and a futile attempt at reconciliation was in process. If this is so, then Adam's attempt to find solace in Nina is autobiographi-

12. *Bystander*, 17 July 1929, pp. 178–179.
13. "Bruno Hatte," *Sunday Dispatch*, 14 July 1929, p. 4. The hoax has often been described. See Jessica Mitford, *Daughters and Rebels* (Boston: Houghton Mifflin, 1960), and Patrick Balfour, *Society Racket* (London: John Long, 1932). For contemporary accounts, see *Daily Sketch*, 25 July 1929, p. 5, and "He Is So," *Sunday Dispatch*, 28 July 1929, p. 4.

cally even more pathetic than the fictional text. In any case, the parties went on. Among them were Mrs. Maugham's "White" party for stage people[14] and Mrs. Bryan Guinness' "1860" party— perhaps the one which Waugh missed.[15] More exclusively for the younger set were "The Theatrical Garden Party," featuring the antics of Elizabeth Ponsonby, Denis Pelly, and Brian Howard;[16] Norman Hartnell's "Circus" party, at which "Archie" Campbell and Mrs. Evan Morgan shied coconuts at windows and to which Lady Eleanor Smith took a pony;[17] and the "Second Childhood" party at Rutland Gate at which guests arrived in prams and baby clothing and which they ended by racing cars around the square "in the wee sma' hours of the morning, to the accompaniment of shouts, yells, cat-calls and the hooting of motor-horns."[18] There was Elizabeth Ponsonby's wedding to Denis Pelly, at first more conventional than expected: wedding at St. Margaret's, Westminster; cabaret reception; cocktails. But "Finally Mrs. Denis Pelly . . . sprang into the arms of Mr. Brian Howard, whose white velvet tie needs no further advertisement, and opened the ball."[19]

In addition to the standard social events, new diversions such as moonlight bathing and river parties on the Thames were prompted by a late July heat wave. But some of the spontaneity had passed, and one account stresses the weariness of the actors. One evening Nina Hamnett caught the boat at Westminster Pier and witnessed dancing to accordions and people in bathing dress sitting on mattresses. The hot trip to Tilbury and back soon produced claustrophobia in the guests, and "Evelyn Waugh was particularly cheering, reminding us from time to time how many more hours it was before reaching Tilbury." Miss Hamnett's group sat disconsolately, watching various rowdies, strange inebriates, and Elizabeth Pelly playing a slot machine while "on the top deck the mattresses were filled with sleeping people under tarpaulins, as they had all passed out." By the end of the trip, however, they had recovered enough

14. *Sunday Dispatch*, 30 June 1929, p. 4.
15. *Tatler*, 19 June 1929, p. 4.
16. *Tatler*, 19 June 1929.
17. *Tatler*, 3 July 1929, p. 49, and 17 July, p. 134.
18. *Bystander*, 10 July 1929, pp. 20–21.
19. *Tatler*, 17 July 1929, p. 98.

to perform as advertised: "they climbed up the lamp-posts on the pier and were 'shot' by the Press photographer."[20]

The world of the bright young people faded after the heat wave and the end of the summer Season (and the Waughs' marriage), and the gossip columnists themselves were becoming disenchanted. Lady Eleanor abandoned her column in September, and many members of the older generation of the "Society of the Bright Young People" began to protest being included in the category, for by this time a third generation, less admissible as equals, had begun to crowd into the spotlight. Viola Tree, who succeeded Lady Eleanor, summed up the state of affairs. Marriages, financial crises, and other disorders were breaking up the group, but

once when bright young people *were* bright young people it meant these four: Miss Elizabeth Ponsonby, Mrs. Babe Plunkett-Greene, Mr. Brian Howard, Mr. Eddie Gathorne-Hardy. Elizabeth married charming Mr. Pelly and became Mrs. Pelly. Babe Green married Tony Bosardi, and became Countess Bosardi. And now Brian Howard has gone to the South of France. So that there is only Eddie Gathorne-Hardy left. And to what he has come!

"I feel that there will be no more parties," he said. "And I feel that if there are I shall not be there."[21]

By this time Waugh himself had finished his novel and fled England.

While he had not been prominent in the bright young set, he was accepted and labeled as a member of it, and in writing *Vile Bodies* he used the vantage point of the insider to establish the omniscient narrator as a knowledgeable, even knowing, observer who reported and interpreted to the uninitiated reader the activities and attitudes of his set. The list of parties that begins to oppress Adam, among them "Masked parties, Savage parties, Victorian parties, Green parties, Russian parties, Circus parties, parties where one had to dress as somebody else" (170), was clearly recognizable by readers of the gossip columns. The airship party is clearly based on the parties aboard the *Friendship*, and the Bruno Hatte hoax fur-

20. Nina Hamnett, *Is She a Lady? A Problem in Autobiography* (London: Allan Wingate, 1955), pp. 57–59. See also *Sunday Dispatch*, 21 July 1929, p. 4.
21. *Sunday Dispatch*, 13 October 1929, p. 4.

nished the inspiration for Adam's invention of the sculptor Provna.

Agatha Runcible was soon identified as "a composite character" of Elizabeth Ponsonby Pelly and Babe Bosardi, and Miles Malpractice and perhaps Johnny Hoop have characteristics similar to those of Brian Howard and Eddie Gathorne-Hardy.[22] The omniscient narrator not only alluded to real people and events but served as guide and interpreter for his readers in parenthetical comments about hangovers; in footnotes on types of invitation cards; in remarks on the younger generation such as "The truth is that like so many people of their age and class, Adam and Nina were suffering from being sophisticated about sex before they were at all widely experienced";[23] and in short essays on gossip columns and racing cars.

Yet, as Waugh later declared, he "was a member rather on the fringe than in the centre" of the bright young people (Preface, 7), and this assertion can be taken in a psychological as well as a social sense. It was not simply a matter of class—he had, after all, been intimate with the wealthy and titled at Oxford—but of circumstances and temperament. After he went down from Oxford in 1924, he was obviously unhappy. Poor, undecided about a career, unhappy in love, he attempted to cling to Oxford. When he drifted into teaching, he felt himself exiled from a glittering world where

22. For Agatha Runcible's identity, see "Now Which Is It?" *Sunday Dispatch*, 16 March 1930, p. 4. The name *Runcible* was probably drawn from the parody of scholarly writing by Richard Pares, Waugh's "first homosexual love" (*Letters*, 435), in which *runcible* was arbitrarily glossed as "about to crash" or "liable to crash": A. Snell (Pares' pseudonym), "A Disquisition on the word 'Runcible' in Edward Lear," *Cherwell*, 2 February 1924, pp. 44, 46. The other identifications are less certain. However, in the third impression of *Decline and Fall*, the names "Miles Malpractice" and "Lord Parakeet" replaced "Martin Gaythorne-Brodie" and "Kevin Saunderson" because these were too close to Eddie Gathorne-Hardy and Gavin Henderson. See "Tasting Power" and "Titular Legerdemain," *Sunday Dispatch*, 18 November 1928, p. 4; "Froth and First Novels," *Bystander*, 21 November 1928, p. v. Waugh somewhat disingenuously commented that he had invented the hotel and Lottie Crump as fantastically as he could and was surprised to receive threatening letters from women who imagined themselves portrayed. Agatha he described as "a young lady of crazy and rather dissolute habits" in whom no one "would see herself . . . without shame." However, a great many people claimed to be the original from which she was drawn (*EAR*, 73).
   For other identifications, see Paul A. Doyle's forthcoming *A Reader's Companion to the Novels and Short Stories of Evelyn Waugh*.
   23. This sentence does not appear in the Chapman & Hall Uniform Edition of 1947 or the New Uniform Edition of 1965, but is printed in every American edition that I have seen.

all his friends prospered, and he came close enough to despair to attempt suicide.[24] Yet even in his partial and intermittent exile he began to be aware that the delights of society were illusory. The bright young people of the early story, "The Balance,"[25] are even more trivial and foolish than those of *Vile Bodies*. Waugh's own reveling was far more spirited than Adam Doure's in the story, but when he turned his experience into fiction, he made the gaiety seem empty and the friendships shallow. This may have been due in part to moral hangover and in part to the not uncommon discovery by young men that a life of pleasure is not entirely satisfactory. Whatever the cause, the result was a certain critical detachment from the antics of his contemporaries when, after the publication of two books and marriage, he became more closely identified with the bright young people.

Even then he had reservations. Two months before he began *Vile Bodies*, he argued, in "The War and the Younger Generation," that "Freedom produces sterility. There was nothing left [after the dislocations of the war] for the younger generation to rebel against, except the widest conceptions of mere decency. . . . The result in many cases is the perverse and aimless dissipation chronicled daily by the gossip-writer of the press." Though he saw, perhaps desiring to reassure readers of the *Spectator*, faint signs of hope, he closed by condemning his own "crazy and sterile generation" (*EAR*, 62–63).

Waugh's detachment from his subject gives an edge to the tone of *Vile Bodies* missing from the gossip columns. Even Archie Schwert's party, the first in the novel, has far less glamour and liveliness than Captain McEachern's. Only Miss Mouse is excited, and she is an outsider: "It was too thrilling to see all that dull money her father had amassed, metamorphosed in this way into so much glitter and noise and so many bored young faces" (64).

24. See the last chapter of *A Little Learning* (Boston: Little, Brown, 1964) and the relevant entries in *The Diaries of Evelyn Waugh*, ed. Michael Davie (Boston: Little, Brown, 1976).

25. "The Balance: A Yarn of the Good Old Days of Broad Trousers and High Necked Jumpers," in *Georgian Stories, 1926*; in *Evelyn Waugh Apprentice*, ed. Robert Murray Davis (Norman: Pilgrim Books, 1985).

Yet, even though he begins the process at a later stage, Waugh reflects in the structure of his novel the increasing boredom and desperation and finally the dissolution of the group. As the novel progresses, the parties become duller and the movement more frantic. The revellers at Archie's party are bored, or affect boredom, but they are not physically constricted and nauseated like those at the airship party in Chapter 8; and the vigorous self-assurance of Lady Circumference's rejection of Mrs. Melrose Ape as judge of the group's morals (Chapter 6) gives way to the prime minister's moral uncertainty and Father Rothschild's melancholy prophecies at the Anchorage House party (Chapter 8). Ginger Littlejohn, introduced midway through the book, is another indication of social decline. Neither witty, daring, nor obliging, he is merely rich. But unlike Miss Mouse in the first section, he asserts his own standards in place of those of the Bright Young People, and finally he uses his money and position to displace Adam as Nina's husband and to oust Archie Schwert, the climber and "The *most* bogus man" of the first chapters, as an undesirable alien.

This social pattern is clear enough, but Waugh apparently planned to use the title *Vile Bodies* as far back as we can trace the composition of the novel,[26] and judging from the source—Philippians 3:21—something more than social commentary is involved. The context of the phrase is the following:

Brethren, be followers together of me, and mark them which walk so as ye have us for an ensample.

(For many walk, of whom I have told you often, and now tell you even weeping, that they are the enemies of the cross of Christ:

Whose end is destruction, whose God is their belly, and whose glory is in their shame, who mind earthly things.)

For our conversation is in heaven; from whence also we look for the Saviour, the Lord Jesus Christ:

Who shall change our vile body, that it may be fashioned like unto his glorious body, according to the working whereby he is able even to subdue all things unto himself.

---

26. See Martin Stannard, "The Mystery of the Missing Manuscript," for a general description of the manuscript.

The key phrases are used in the Church of England's prayer at graveside which accompanies the casting of earth on the body.[27] Initially, perhaps, Waugh may have meant the title as a joke. Certainly the disclaimer in the carbon typescript—"all characters are wholly imaginary (and you get far too much publicity whoever you are)"—accords with Waugh's characterization of the novel as Wodehousian. But two things about the finished novel are clear: matters become more serious as the novel progresses, and the shift from funny to serious is used as a major structural principle.

This is not to say that the novel is overtly religious. Although Father Rothschild, S.J., and Mrs. Melrose Ape, the evangelist, are the first characters mentioned by name, neither is an ideal spiritual guide. Rothschild is the wily Jesuit of English literary convention[28]—Waugh notes in the 1965 preface that he had never met a Jesuit when he wrote the novel—a multifarious and omniscient plotter, immersed in politics. Only seasickness can remind him of religion. Mrs. Ape is immune even to seasickness. Later she enjoins the Bright People, young and old, to "Just . . . look at yourselves," and while, objectively speaking, this is good spiritual counsel which should give the sinner a conviction of his sin, it is uttered solely for dramatic effect and is rightly rejected, Waugh implies, on purely social grounds with "the organ voice of England, the hunting-cry of the *ancien régime*": "What a damned impudent woman" (137–138). Secure in their superiority, the characters can reject message as well as speaker, spare themselves the disquieting process of conversion, and return to their trivial concerns. At a later party avoiding disquiet is more difficult. Speaking to the next prime minister and to the power behind the English cabinet, Father Rothschild characterizes eloquently the plight of the young, summed up as "an almost fatal hunger for permanence" (183) in which they recognize the "bogus" but are unable to find the truly valuable. Rothschild does not give what, considering his orders, should be the obvious answer; instead he blames history both for

27. For other liturgical uses of the passage, see my "Title, Theme, and Structure in *Vile Bodies*," *Southern Humanities Review*, 11 (Winter 1977), 26.
28. See also Neil D. Isaacs, "Evelyn Waugh's Restoration Jesuit," *Satire Newsletter*, 2 (1965), 91–94.

what has already happened, including the loss of faith, and for the war which he knows is to come.

Mrs. Ape and Rothschild retain vestiges of their religious heritage; other characters see religion either as obstacle—Agatha Runcible thinks the market cross against which she wrecks the race car "an enormous stone spanner" (257)—or as incomprehensible anecdote, like those who film the life of Wesley, complete with duels, elopements, and all the paraphernalia of historical costume drama. Even at Doubting Hall (one character drops the *H*), Colonel Blount's home and in some ways a bastion of tradition, the vicar is little more than a lower-level servant, reduced to waiting on the movie projector, and Christmas is almost purely a social ritual of songs, food, and gifts. Only hymn titles and the inescapable Matins recall the true meaning of the feast.

Whether or not he began the novel with a serious religious theme in mind, by the time of publication Waugh had decided to add an "Author's Note" (it disappeared from English editions in 1937), ostensibly to clarify the chronology of events. Chapters 1 through 6 take place on November 10 through 12; Chapters 8 through 13 take place during December, concentrated on December 2 through 5 (the auto races), December 15 through the 17 (Nina's defection from Adam to Ginger and Agatha's death), and the vigil and feast of Christmas—"observed," Waugh adds sardonically, "by the Western Church on December 25th." He does date the epilogue, titled "Happy Ending," but Nina has not delivered the child which presumably was conceived on Christmas Eve.

In liturgical terms, the novel is divided into three periods: pre-Advent, Advent, and Christmas. These periods celebrate, respectively, the normal life of the church, the special penitential life, and the Nativity and promise of mankind's redemption. The novel, however, chronicles not salvation but destruction, not unity but dispersal. The events of the first section present movement without direction, those of the second, suffering without penitence, those on Christmas not "a child is born" or "peace on earth" but "*War has been declared*"; those of the "Happy Ending" a modern Armageddon on "the biggest battlefield in the history of the world." In the terms of the King James Version's chapter headings, the novel traces the fall of Babylon without the creation of a heavenly Jerusalem.

In structural terms, Waugh's prefatory note implies that the novel has an opening section of six chapters, an interim Chapter 7 which covers in summary fashion the events of twenty-eight days, and another section of six chapters, followed by "Happy Ending."

The first section assembles the cast of characters, alludes glancingly to Armistice Day, and compresses into three days the private scandals of Lottie Crump's hotel and the public scandals at Number 10 Downing Street which accompany (but do not cause) the fall of the government, Archie Schwert's party, Adam's trip to Doubting Hall and seduction of Nina, and, closing the section with a flourish, the party for Mrs. Ape which leads to Simon Balcairn's imaginative and libelous account of mass conversions and detailed public confessions in high society, followed by Simon's suicide. Although Waugh does not ignore the pathos of Simon's diminishing popularity and increasing desperation or the intermittent despondency of Adam and Nina, the press does exhibit a flattering interest in the parties, everyone enjoys seeing and being seen, and the social cataclysm produced by Simon's story leads to "an orgy of litigation," with publicity and money for all. In the interim Chapter 7, the consequences of the scandal and Adam's manipulation of the readers of his gossip column leave the novel in the realm of social comedy, for nothing is really at stake and the characters, even Simon, have suffered indignity rather than pain. In the terms of the epigraph from *Alice Through the Looking Glass*, they are not crying "real tears."

The second section moves from social comedy to the operation of nemesis as cause and effect. Chapter 8, which opens this section, seems to begin like the first with an embarkation—this time at a party in a captive dirigible. Here, however, the passengers do not have even the illusion of progress, since the dirigible is firmly tethered, their physical movements are even more constricted than on board ship, and glimpses of nauseated revelers open and close the evening. (On the channel ferry, the characters are only sick in the middle of the trip.) Furthermore, the Bright Young People are beginning to experience moral qualms. The title passage, which concludes a list of party themes and ends "all that succession and repetition of massed humanity. . . . Those vile bodies. . .)," (170–171)[29] comes in this chapter. Their elders fare no better at Anchorage House, center of the highest values of the older generation. This chapter sets the tone for those ensuing: malaise, confusion, misgiving, dispersal, death—a series of catastrophes, beginning with Lady Ursula's loveless engagement to Edward Throbbing as a continuation of the "ancien régime" (Waugh used these words as title for the first section in the typescript), through Agatha's racing accident and subsequent death, Nina's marriage to a wealthy bore, to the outbreak of war. Unlike Chapter 7, the coda to the first section, "Happy Ending" presents a battlefield on which "the sounds of battle began to return" (321) as the novel ends.

In order to unify these sections, Waugh introduces a series of paired and contrasted situations. Ferry and airship in Chapters 1 and 8 have already been mentioned, and religious motifs figure strongly in Chapters 1, 6, 8, and 13—the first and last of the two major sections. Similarly opposed are Adam's trips to Doubting Hall in Chapters 5, 9, and 13. On his first the Hall is a refuge of Victorian somnolence in which he is well fed, treated to bound volumes of *Punch*, and dismissed in blissful ignorance with a check for a thousand pounds on the strength of which he hires a limousine and spends the night with his girl before discovering that it is signed "Charlie Chaplin." On his second trip he encounters not hospitality and hope but the frenetic activity of the film company, and he returns to London to find that he has lost his job. His third trip, in Chapter 13, begins better than the first, since he is welcomed as Nina's husband, but ends worse than the second as war breaks out.

Also contrasted are the motor trip to Arundel in Chapter 5, when Adam sleeps with Nina, and the motor trip to the races in Chapter 10, when no one sleeps at all in the anaphrodisiac atmosphere of petrol and sordid inns; the arbitrary censorship by the customs officer in Chapter 2 which destroys Adam's manuscript and leaves him penniless and Lord Monomark's whimsical firing of

29. Stannard notes, pp. 202–203, that this passage is not in the manuscript.

Adam from the gossip column in Chapter 9; and the deaths of Simon Balcairn in Chapter 6 and Agatha in Chapter 12. In the last two pairs, the first instance is at least partly funny: Adam can fulfill his contract with his publishers by writing twelve books in a year, and Simon has to line the gas oven with paper to avoid the grease on the oven floor. In the second half, matters are more serious: Adam is left with no options, and Agatha dies in a delirium, driving (or being driven by the role she has assumed and the crowds' expectations) toward "nothing at all" without even Simon's chance to strike a comic blow at society. The most comprehensive paired situations oppose the easy departure from the delights of Europe in Chapter 1 to the European battlefield in "Happy Ending" from which no escape is possible. Judgment, or perhaps nemesis, can be ignored, Waugh implies, but it cannot be escaped.

As Agatha notes from her hospital bed,

How people are *disappearing* . . . I had the most awful dreams. I thought we were all driving round and round in a motor-race and none of us could stop, and there was an enormous audience composed entirely of gossip writers and gate crashers and Archie Schwert and people like that, all shouting at us at once to go faster. (266)

At this point, Waugh is moving from commentary to prophecy, from social comedy to moral satire. The bright young people mentioned in Viola Tree's elegiac column felt that they could end the cycle of activity. Agatha knows, with the peculiar clarity of the dreamers, the delirious, and the mad in the novels of Waugh, that she and her cohorts cannot stop, that they are doomed to play their roles—not as actors to be hopelessly emulated and envied but as puppets to be manipulated. When she dies, there is "*nothing at all . . . nothing*" (285).

The novel ends with the bright young people dispersed or dullards like Ginger and the publisher Benfleet prospering, and the sounds of battle beginning to return.[30] In bringing the novel to completion, Waugh had not only begun the process of compensa-

---

30. The outcome of the novel was more spectacular but not more ironic than some of the events that followed the publication of *Vile Bodies*. Fate pursued many of the smart set more leisurely but no less inexorably: Brian Howard, "an incorrigible homosexual, subject to a succession of delusions . . . died by suicide at the

tion for the loss of Evelyn Gardner which extended through *A Handful of Dust* and perhaps *Scoop* and was perhaps completed with the death of and eulogy to Virginia Troy in his last novel, *Unconditional Surrender*, but had solved the formal problems of joining social commentary and moral satire. And in writing a second novel, though some months later he was still able to characterize himself as someone who "had only written two very dim books and still regarded myself less as a writer than an out-of-work private schoolmaster,"[31] he had become a professional writer.

---

time when he at last became rich" (*A Little Learning*, 205); Elizabeth Ponsonby, soon divorced from Denis Pelly, died an alcoholic in 1940; David Plunkett-Greene, her cousin and the first husband of Babe, committed suicide a few years later (Baron Ponsonby to Charles E. Linck, Jr., 1 March 1962).

31. *A Bachelor Abroad* (New York: J. Cape/H. Smith, 1930), p. 27. Although the book describes the events of early 1929, Waugh wrote it after he completed *Vile Bodies*, and his comments on Paris may result not from his trip with Evelyn Gardner but from a visit in late 1929. See *Letters*, p. 41.

CHAPTER 9

Toward a Mature Style:
The Making of *Remote People*

When Evelyn Waugh left England to attend the coronation of Haile Selassie in early October 1930, he had published a biography of Dante Gabriel Rossetti, which was a critical success; *Decline and Fall*, which amused critics as well as readers; *Vile Bodies*, which brought him widespread fame and lucrative contracts in journalism; and *Labels*, in which he was faced with the interesting rhetorical problem of writing about his honeymoon after the divorce had been granted. He had just completed a lucrative series of articles as spokesman for fashionable youth for the *Daily Mail* and a weekly book review column for the *Graphic*; he had contracted to write a biography of Jonathan Swift; and he had just become a Roman Catholic amid considerable publicity.

His decision to abandon Europe and his particular brand of celebrity for a trip to Ethiopia is not really explained in his discussion of his movements—he is silent about any motive deeper than curiosity—but perhaps he consciously planned what in retrospect is the clear shift from the position of leading specialist on the younger generation to that of a serious analyst of adult concerns. External evidence from his various accounts of the journey supports this view: his pieces in the *Graphic*,[1] drawn in some cases almost verbatim from his diaries, falling between reportage and self-exploitation, are intended to be picturesque and amusing. His reports to

---

1. Waugh's three articles in the *Graphic* are "A Journey to Abyssinia," 22 November 1930, p. 350; "A Journey to Abyssinia—Alarums and Excursions," 13 December 1930, p. 504; and "A Journey to Abyssinia—Champagne for Breakfast," 20 December 1930, p. 544.

the *Times* and the *Daily Express*,[2] more sober and factual by their very nature, present or imply a wider context than his own personal amusement. In *Remote People*, sometimes on the manuscript page itself, he worked to fuse two voices—that of the observer of amusing details and that of the urbane, detached, and objective reporter—and create a single persona who could turn from recording human folly to analyzing serious contemporary issues. If my account of the process emphasizes style more than substance, it does so for two reasons: Waugh was more concerned to write a book than he was to resolve issues and he was increasingly obsessed by style.

Waugh's first written responses to his journey were either notations or slightly augmented transcriptions of notations. The first *Graphic* article and the diary are very similar not only in incident but in language.[3] Waugh felt it necessary to begin the article for his sophisticated audience by discussing the prosaic beginning of all trips, even of "what should prove one of the few really amusing journeys left in the world." In the parallel accounts, which focus on the ship's passengers and their activities, the diary is naturally more spare, but in a few instances it contains touches of description which did not make their way into the article. Obviously Waugh was keeping the account for more serious literary purposes than casual journalism, even if he had no time to polish it.

His use of standard travelogue material is best shown in the ways in which he described the arrival at Djibouti at dawn after two days

2. For a discussion of journalistic coverage of the coronation in general and of Waugh's participation in particular, see Donat S. Gallagher, "Black Majesty and Press Mischief," *London Magazine*, 22 (October 1982), 25–38. Dr. Gallagher is preparing an extended discussion of the contexts of Waugh's nonfiction. For a more general analysis of Waugh and of the context in which he wrote, see Paul Fussell, *Abroad: British Literary Traveling between the Wars* (New York: Oxford University Press, 1980).

3. It is impossible to determine whether the articles for the *Graphic* or the diary entries were written first. Because Waugh mailed the articles to the magazine—the first, describing the train and ship journeys and the arrival at Djibouti, appeared on 22, November 1930—and because he left London on 10 October, he would have had to send it almost immediately after arriving. The first diary entry is dated "London-Addis Ababa Friday 10 October-Sunday 26 October 1930," which may indicate either that it was composed in retrospect or that, most uncharacteristically, Waugh did not bother to distinguish between separate entries.

of celebration. The diary is almost as telegraphic as the despatches in *Scoop*: "Djibouti arrived dawn. One couple still dancing, grey faces" (330). The *Graphic* is slightly more detailed: "Rising at six . . . I found two grey-faced couples in extravagant paper hats still dancing on a deck which was being swabbed about their feet by a Chinese steward" (*Graphic*, 22 November). The first is a mere reminder; the second may be intended to illustrate the commonplace and wearisome aspects of the journey to an exotic place.

By the time that Waugh began to write his travel book, he had come to view the scene not as a mere incident but as a frame in which to present the prosaic details of the journey and as a keynote in his temporary farewell to the lees of European culture, and he had reduced the two couples to one, perhaps in order to underscore the pair in weary isolation, prolonging the dance as long as they can:

> They were still dancing when, just before dawn on October 19th, 1930, the *Azay le Rideau* came into harbour at Djibouti. The band—a pitiably hot quartet in alpaca dinner jackets—had long ago packed up their instruments and retired to their remote and stifling cabin. An Anamite boy was swabbing the deck and pushing into the scuppers sodden masses of paper streamers. Two or three stewards were at work pulling down the flags and festoons of coloured lights with which the ship had been decorated. One couple remained.[4]

The next paragraph describes the couple: a mixed-blood girl in Tyrolean costume and a French Foreign Legion officer, shorter than his partner, sloppily dressed and potbellied. The details added for the book version not only emphasize the discomfort and exhaustion of the couple but create an atmosphere in which they move.

In other instances, Waugh took the opportunity to work on comic timing. Describing the honor guard of picked troops drawn up to meet trainloads of visitors, he gives a series of details:

> This body of troops, picked from [the Emperor's] own southern provinces, had been specially trained in ceremonial drill for the coronation by Belgian officers. They wore khaki uniforms, puttees and bare feet. They

4. *Remote People* (London: Duckworth, 1931), p. 11. The U.S. edition is titled *They Were Still Dancing*.

stood a little unsteadily presenting arms with fixed bayonets. A brass band, similarly dressed, struck up the Ethiopian anthem. (*Graphic*, 13 December)

In the final version, the details are sharper, but more significant is the order.

These were squat, coal-black boys from the Soudanese border. They wore brand-new, well-cut, khaki uniforms; the lion of Judah shone in polished brass on cap badges and buttons; with bayonets fixed and rifles of recent pattern. Beside them a band of bugle and drums, with a little black drummer poising crossed sticks above the big drum. But for the bare feet below their puttees, they might have been the prize platoon of some Public School O.T.C. In front of them with drawn sword stood a European officer. This was a squad of Tafari's own guard. (27)

The passage goes on to explain that the unit was formed after all the serious fighting for the throne had ended, but the point has already been made: the process of Europeanization has not proceeded from the ground up, and the result is the more comic because the detail about bare feet has been delayed and therefore the pretensions of the emperor are more effectively undercut.

But as Waugh explains at the end of this paragraph, the purpose—to form "the nucleus of an organised national army" (28)—is not. The *Graphic* articles barely acknowledge purpose of any kind. In contrast, even when his *Times* articles record confusion, they do so in a serious context; in fact, the phrase just quoted is adapted from his *Times* report (8 November 1930, 11). In writing these accounts, Waugh restrained but did not eradicate his sense of the ridiculous. For example, the unveiling of the statue to Menelek revealed certain ironies of situation and did not go at all smoothly, but Waugh's account in the *Times*, understated even for him, merely notes that the square newly cleared for the statue was recently the site of public executions, that "Half an hour before the arrival of the delegations men were still at work planting shrubs and flowers . . ." (3 November 1930, 12), and that the statue was set in "a circular plot sown with grass, the first shoots of which are appearing." As for the confusion, Waugh notes merely that "the police were largely successful in their efforts to keep a space clear for the ceremony" and that the band from HMS *Effingham* was denied entrance to the square. However, the structure of the news story emphasized not details but the succession of events: the procession, including "a body of servants running on foot and carrying gilt chairs"; the emperor's speech emphasizing Menelek's greatness and its connection with current foreign policy; and the unveiling of the statue "in gilded bronze, made from the design of the European architect of the Imperial Court."

The policy of the *Times* allowed for, if it did not demand, a certain reservation about Ethiopia's claims to have entered the twentieth century,[5] and the details about the rawness of the converted place of execution and the large degree of success in controlling the crowd show an observant if not a critical spirit. In *Remote People* Waugh allowed himself much freer rein. The incident is structured not by the official events but by the comic frustrations of the marine band, first denied entrance because the Belgian colonel knows no English and the bandmaster no French; then relegated to the outskirts after negotiation; finally, triumphantly, marched into the center of the square to perform their duties and receive the approval of the emperor. The rather bald general account in the *Times* is here reduced to the personal and then ornamented. For example, the Belgian colonel's dignity is somewhat compromised by the actions of his horse, so that in the conference with the bandmaster "the two officers covered a large area of ground, conversing inconclusively the while with extravagant gestures"; later the colonel "was borne momentarily backwards through the ranks, capered heroically among the crowd, and reappeared at another corner of the square" (46, 47). The statue itself, not simply "covered by the Abyssinian colours" as in the *Times*, is "shrouded in brilliant silk," and the unveiling of the statue, "a vast equestrian figure in gilt bronze," is a shambles. Part of the covering cannot be dislodged; workmen poke at it with long poles; "One piece, out of reach of their efforts, obstinately fluttered over the horse's ears and eyes. The Greek contractor mounted a ladder and dislodged the rag."

---

5. Donat Gallagher has discovered an unsigned article, "British Policy in Aden; A Conference of Tribal Chiefs," *Times*, 17 March 1931, p. 13, and cites evidence that Waugh wrote it to support the policy of the British Foreign Office. See Robert Murray Davis, Paul A. Doyle, Donat Gallagher, Charles E. Linck, and Winnifred M. Bogaards, *A Bibliography of Evelyn Waugh* (Troy: Whitston, 1986), item A321.

Furthermore, the procession is made anticlimactic. When all is ready for the emperor's arrival and everyone is at attention, there is a long pause and "Suddenly up that imposing avenue there appeared a slave, trotting unconcernedly with a gilt chair on his head. He put it among the others, looked round with interest at the glittering uniforms, and then retired." By reducing the train of bearers to an individual and by allowing him to react, Waugh is able to undercut the pomp of the ceremony and allow not a "servant," the official designation, but a slave to upstage the emperor.

However, the Abyssinians are not, for Waugh writing in his personal voice, any more ridiculous than the Europeans, especially the cameramen, who seem more unruly than the native crowd. And more bizarre than lion skins (not even mentioned in the book) is the dress of a photographer in "a violet suit of plus-fours, a green shirt open at the neck, tartan stockings, and parti-coloured shoes."

In another instance, however, the *Times* and *Remote People* are much closer to each other in style and spirit. A comparison of "Ethiopia Today" (22 December 1930; *EAR*, 119–122) and the corresponding passage in *Remote People* (29–34) reveals that Waugh did straighten out the chronology for the book version but that otherwise he tended to find synonyms (perhaps to make the second seem new) rather than to reconstruct. More important than any textual differences are the formal tone and the objective overview of Abyssinian politics which prepared for his writing of the pseudohistory of Azania in the opening pages of *Black Mischief*.

Although he could sustain this new persona for several pages at a time, his self-conscious transition from the material drawn from the *Times* to that derived from direct observation shows that he was still not quite confident about using it. The manuscript of *Remote People* (the first of a travel book to survive intact and the only one, save *Tourist in Africa*, publicly accessible) reveals not only that, as in all of his manuscripts, he took second and third thought to achieve effective rhythms and add telling details and that he continued and extended his deadpan interest in bizarre personalities but that he labored consistently and effectively to strengthen the serious, discursive passages which are the major evidence of his growth as thinker and writer.

The manuscript of *Remote People*[6] is atypical of those I have described in the *Catalogue* only in being comparatively straightforward. Obviously unfamiliar with other Waugh manuscripts, the dealer who sold it to the Berg Collection of the New York Public Library judged that "The corrections are very heavy and there is a great deal of rearrangement." In fact, there is less reshuffling than in the novels, for there the difficulty in deciding on the order of incidents and the number and identity of the characters who would enact them led Waugh to clip, paste, cancel, rearrange, and augment at later stages. In *Remote People*, however, Waugh relied with one exception on the sequence of events recorded in his diary—the trip to Jemjem to chase monkeys in fact occurred before rather than after the trip to the monastery of Debra Lebanos—and drew on his experience as a light essayist to fill gaps occasioned by the lack of external diversion. Judging from his diary and from his letters to his agent, A. D. Peters (*Catalogue*, E153–159), the writing of the book went smoothly, though Waugh did not push himself hard.

While the trip was still in progress—in the Congo 5 to 11 February 1931—he fought boredom "by the desperate expedient of writing" the first two chapters, on down to the eve of the coronation. Thereafter his journey and his first weeks in England—he arrived early in March—must have been more diverting than he allows in *Remote People*. Not until June did he write to Peters, and then he gave instructions to fend off the American publisher who was clamoring for the book. About June 11 he sent Peters the third chapter and corrected versions of the first two and promised the rest in a month. In fact, he sent the last pages on 14 August and on 22 August corrected typescript of the final three chapters. A little over three weeks later he had completed the first chapter of what was to become *Black Mischief*.

Although the coronation of Haile Selassie and the revelations

6. The manuscript, bound and cased, has a specially printed title page: REMOTE PEOPLE / *Travels in British Somaliland and Abyssinia* / by/ EVELYN WAUGH / *THE AUTHOR'S ORIGINAL MANUSCRIPT* / *1931*. Waugh gives an approximate word count at the beginning of the first eight chapters of the manuscript. The manuscript was acquired by the New York Public Library from George F. Sims. Manuscript material is quoted by permission of the Henry W. and Albert A. Berg Collection, The New York Public Library, Astor, Lenox, and Tilden Foundations.

about an exotic civilization almost unknown to Europeans (who, judging from Waugh's account of the press reports, would have been no better informed after reading them) provided the impetus for Waugh's journey and the main interest of *Remote People*, Waugh's stay in Ethiopia provided enough material for exactly half of the book. To make weight, Waugh was forced not only to recount his experiences in Aden, Zanzibar, Kenya, and Uganda but to insert three "Nightmares": being stranded in Dirre-Dowa, making his way through the Congo burdened by various petty annoyances, and dining out in London on the night of his return. Furthermore, throughout the book he was at least as interested in speculating about the meaning of what he saw and felt as in the direct experiences themselves.

Nevertheless, Waugh was quite aware that his potential readers would be attracted largely by the promise of strange sights and people, and though he was too observant, intelligent, and principled to invent details as had colleagues in the press corps and too much the ironist to present a "disgusting spectacle of barbarism" to an audience he held in no higher regard, the manuscript shows that he took considerable pains to add color to his account. Thus, when he first becomes interested in Abyssinia, he gleans fascinating and scarcely credible details from the guests and library at a country house, ending his account in first draft with a history of the country beginning with the Deluge and concluding, "Everything I heard added to the glamor of this astonishing country." At some point after writing this account he discovered or recalled (or invented) "an obsolete encyclopedia" which called the Abyssinians "deplorably lax in their morals, polygamy and drunkenness being common even among the highest classes and in the monasteries" (14). The sentence about glamour, placed after this insertion, gives an entirely different impression of the author and the account to follow, promising the sensational as well as the fanciful.

However, Waugh did not ignore gruesome details about the tropics. He inserted another traveler's account of the horrible processes by which tropical parasites infest and debilitate their hosts, though he seems more interested in the relish of the teller than in the prospects for his own health.

When he reached Abyssinia, Waugh was not inclined to take a romantic view of what he saw even if his persona had allowed him to. A long insertion (all of page 36) does begin with the emphatic "Every man in Ethiopia carries arms . . ." and concludes with a description of the street traffic, exotic enough for the most jaded, but Waugh notes that most of the rifles are antiquated and the cartridges useless; the women, far from being attractive, are veiled "so that only the two eyes appear, like those of a hooded rider of the Ku Klux Klan."

Elsewhere Waugh added material to create a context rather than to exploit striking detail. Describing his journey to Harar, he first gives the perspective from which Burton described it in *First Steps in Africa* to contrast with his own approach from the highlands, from which it appears as "an irregular brown patch at the foot of the hills." Some time later he inserted on the back of the previous page of manuscript a long sentence, which provides both visual and political perspective, on the mountain behind the town where the Abyssinians, uneasy Christian conquerors of Arab territory, had prepared a refuge in case of insurrection (98). Later, as if to emphasize the charming pointlessness of his stay in Zanzibar, he added two paragraphs about his visit to the Arab lord of the manor at Bububu, a trip which gives Waugh a chance to refer to the Oxford Railway Club founded by his friend John Sutro, to disparage Oriental preference for fake Oriental products from the West, and to emphasize subtly the obsequious dependency on British goodwill of the Arab aristocracy and give point to the ensuing generalization, found in the original draft, that "it is the absence of any kind of political issue which makes Zanzibar so depressing" (164–165).

Even more frequent than these insertions in the manuscript were the hundreds of emendations which underlined or revealed a situation or setting with the proper emphasis. The simplest example is Waugh's treatment of the end of "First Nightmare." Originally, the final paragraph read: "Next morning we arrived at Aden. That was the end of four exceedingly painful days and the beginning of a delightful interlude in my African journey." On reflection, Waugh obviously saw that he had spoiled the climax. He struck through the second half of the compound, leaving the blunt "that was the end of four exceedingly painful days" to conclude the chapter (123). Elsewhere he augmented and refined rather than simply adding or cutting. The approach to the monastery of Debra Lebanos is in the manuscript so full of deletions that, despite the fact that a difference in time of composition cannot be assumed, it is easier to represent the passage as two separate drafts.[7] Waugh and his companions approach a great canyon.

I do not know how deep it was but I should think at least three thousand feet, partly divided by strata of timber. At the bottom a river [illegible] between green banks; it was practically dry at this season, but delicate threads of water (shone) split and reunited in delicate threads of light. A narrow path led down the face of the cliff and it was towards this that we were clearly making.

I do not know how deep it was, but I should think at least two thousand feet, descending (steeply) abruptly in tiers of sheer cliff broken by strips & patches of timber. At the bottom a river ran between green banks to swell the Blue Nile far in the South; it was practically dry at this season except for a few (delicate) shiny channels of water which split and reunited in the sandy bed in delicate threads of light. (Far below) Poised among trees, two thirds of the way down on a semi-circular shelf of land, we could discern the roofs of Debra Lebanos. A cleft path led down the face of the cliff and it was to this that we were clearly making. (74)

Insertions such as those about the Blue Nile and the roofs of Debra Lebanos provide physical context for the material in the foreground. More frequently Waugh revised to present more accurate detail, as in the change from three to two thousand feet; still oftener he sharpened the image, as in the change from "strata" to "strips and patches," from "narrow path" to "cleft path," and, most emphatically, in the elaboration and reconstruction of the long unit which twice postpones "delicate threads" until the climactic end of the view from two thousand feet above.

Artfully described as it was, however, the scenery was not the major attraction of a book by Evelyn Waugh even in 1931. As biog-

7. In transcribing manuscript material, I enclose deleted material in parentheses, inserted material in diagonals. Exceptions to this practice are noted.

rapher, novelist, and traveler he was known chiefly for his gallery of odd and sometimes oddly endearing characters. *Remote People* was no exception: it contained not only the originals of Mr. Youkoumian and others in *Black Mischief* and Mr. Baldwin in *Scoop* but a number preserved only in these pages. And Waugh worked as hard to recreate them as he did the landscape. Even minor characters were reworked. On the first page of the manuscript Waugh cut a description of French officials to expand the treatment of the people at his table on board ship (12). And in describing the Cook's agent, he changed the commonplace "a mine of inaccurate information for the journalists" to "an unfailing source of inaccurate information, on all local topics," piling excess on excess to create a minor comic monster who never appears again (44). The Seventh Day Adventist accountant occupied Waugh's attention for a slightly longer period, but never more happily than when Waugh went back to revise the lines containing his first dialogue: "I offered him a drink and he said 'Oh, no, thank you,' in a (voice) /tone/ which (expressed)/in four (words) monosyllables contrived to express first/surprise, then pain, then reproof, and finally forgiveness" (221). "Contrived" is a brilliant afterthought, for it makes the young man pompous as well as priggish. The shift from "words" to "monosyllables" illustrates the difference between competent writing and a style.

On a slightly larger scale Waugh was able to create Mr. Hall, the press attaché who handled all of a long list of errors and omissions with consistent equanimity. In first draft, the end of the paragraph, which generalized from the large number of particulars in the body, was rather flat. The revisions made Mr. Hall an almost androgynous prodigy whose absolute inaction seems Olympian. Waugh notes that everyone in bad temper would go to Hall,

who would understand /and sympathize; with almost feminine delicacy he would/ calm him /&/ compliment him; /with masculine decision he would/ make a /bold/ note of the affair on his pad; /he would rise, bow &/ smile (the) his pacified visitor out with every /graceful/ assurance of good will—and do /absolutely/ nothing (at all) about it. (43)

Waugh took similar pains to elevate Professor W. (Whittemore in the *Diaries*) to a figure of fantasy worthy of the Alice in Wonderland

atmosphere of Addis Ababa during the coronation ceremonies. At
first Waugh introduced him as having "made a study of coptic ritual" but saw the opportunity to begin on a high note and substi-
tuted "an expert of high transatlantic reputation on Coptic ritual"
(57), all the funnier since the professor is wrong about every possible detail of the ceremony. Furthermore, Waugh moved the introduction and Professor W's dialogue from after to before the inves-
titure to extend the distance between his confusion about details of
the Mass and the climactic single-sentence paragraph, "Then the
Mass began." A few pages later, moving into the luncheon party
with the emperor, Waugh began very generally with "There were
about eighty guests. . . ." At some later time he inserted the professor's anticipation of talking privately with the emperor, a hope
frustrated by the size and confusion of the party (66).

The professor's mistakes were emphasized once again in a passage describing his attitude toward anything which could remotely
be regarded as sacred. Waugh canceled a much revised draft—the
earlier is given here—and inserted another:

But when it came to anything religious he was suddenly transfused
with a crazy indiscriminate reverence; a kind of neurotic eagerness
to do the most that could possibly
be expected of him—an eagerness
embarrassed by a singular ignorance in one who apparently made
a close study of that subject.

But this worldly good sense was a
mere mask over the essentially
mystical nature of the professor's
mind; one touch of church furniture, and he became suddenly
transfused with reverence and an
almost neurotic eagerness to do all
that could be expected of him,
with an impulsive and demonstra-
tive devotion that added a great
deal to the glamour of our expedi-
tion together. (71)

The professor's errors give way to the fanciful effect of his behavior;
the craziness is implied rather than stated; and the eagerness becomes endearing rather than simply manic.

Throughout the rest of the trip to Debra Lebanos Waugh makes
comic use of the contrast between worldliness and reverence in the
professor's behavior and wildly mistaken judgments. The climax
of this incongruity occurs when, having feigned ill health to avoid
eating the miserable food provided by the monks, he gains privacy

for Waugh and himself, and, in first draft, continues, "'Now at last,' said the Professor, unwrapping a section of cheese, 'I feel in the heart of Ethiopia.'" Waugh had already described him to greater comic effect as he "unwrapped a little segment of cheese from its silver paper and nibbled it delicately and made a very neat job of an orange" (73). Moreover, the monastery food is so horrible that his refusal to eat it is not all that incongruous. Waugh replaces the participial phrase with one more indicative of the contradiction in the professor's attitudes: he is shown "producing a tin of Keating's [insect] powder" (83) as he exults in his contact with the unspoiled and exotic world in which he is an incongruous, over-civilized innocent.

Even more memorable, because he prefigures Mr. Youkoumian, is the Armenian proprietor of the Leon d'Or hotel in Harar, "a stout little man in a black skull-cap." In Waugh's introductory characterization one can see the outline of Youkoumian beginning to develop, and as usual Waugh refines the description:

He was an Armenian (, extremely cheerful /expansive genial/) of (very beautiful) /rare/ character; he spoke a queer kind of French with remarkable volubility /and I found great delight in all his opinions/; (he) I do not think I have ever met a more tolerant man; he (condemned no one) /had no prejudice or/ scruples of /race, creed, morals or/ of any kind whatever; (morals, religion, race /none of these [illegible]/) /there were in his mind/ none of those (sticky? lumps?) /opaque patches/ of (undigested) /inconsidered/ principle, (everything was placid [illegible]) /it was a single, translucent pool of placid doubt./ (He had the impress of no culture) /Whatever sparks of precept had/ disturbed (its surface) /it's surface/ from time to time had left no ripple; ([illegible] reflections flitted (across & left) /to & fro/ [and left] it unchanged [sic] (99)

In revision, Waugh clearly emphasized his delight in Bergebedgian and conceived the metaphor of the pool to replace the rather messy figure of digestion. Less obvious but no less important are the change from "very beautiful" to the more accurate and less contentious "rare," the distinction between "prejudice" and "scruples," and the deletion of the general terms "cheerful" and "genial."

Passages like this confuse and annoy critics who wish to label Waugh a comic or a satiric or an ironic writer because the object of

the irony or comedy or attack is never quite clear or, if clear for a
moment, stable. Ten pages further on Waugh uses the Armenians,
"A race of rare competence and the most delicate sensibility," to
deprecate himself ironically—and to deprecate directly if subtly
those qualities he envies in others. As usual, he creates his effects
with a series of small touches:

[The Armenians] seem to me the only genuine "men of the world." /I
suppose everyone at times likes to picture himself as such a person./ Sometimes, when I find that elusive ideal looming too attractively, when I envy
among my friends this one's adaptability /to (all kinds of) //diverse// com-
pany/, this one's cosmopolitan experience, /this one's (invincibility to) //
impenetrable armour against// sentimentality and humbug/ that one's
freedom from conventional prejudices, this one's astute ordering of his
finances and nicely calculated hospitality, and realize that (I shall never
really) /whatever happens to/ me /and however I deplore it/, I shall never
(really) /in actual fact/ become a /"hardboiled/ man of the world" of the
kind I read about in novels I /sometimes/ obtain at bookstalls for short
railway journeys; /that I shall always be ill at ease with nine out of every
ten people I meet; that I shall always find something startling and rather
abhorrent in the things most other people think worth doing //and something puzzling in their standards of importance//; that I shall probably be
increasingly, rather than decreasingly, vulnerable to the inevitable minor
disasters and injustices of life/—then I comfort myself a little by thinking
that, perhaps, if I were an Armenian I should find things easier. (110–111)

Particularly noteworthy are the shift from the abstract "invincibility" to the concrete "impenetrable armour"; the generalization in
the second sentence which subtly but firmly links Waugh with his
audience; the doubling of the clauses, beginning "whatever" and
"however," which express the hopelessness of his desire; and the
inspired insertion of "sometimes" which removes him from the
class of habitual consumers of trashy literature. The initial use of
"short" proves that Waugh's happiest thoughts were not always second. But the long insertion is by far the most important, for it
moves the whole passage from a casual snobbery to a moral indictment not of the Armenians, for whom Waugh has a very complicated kind of affection, but of the contemporary European world.

These passages are obviously important in helping readers of
Black Mischief to understand Waugh's attitude toward Mr. You-

koumian, but the second is even more significant for what it indicates about Waugh's sense of his persona as a writer. In *Labels* he
had referred to his own standard of judgment while undercutting
many of the forces which had shaped that judgment. In *Remote
People*, he was moving toward a common sense, toward general
principles. This shift is shown obliquely in the passage just quoted
and still more clearly in the discussion of the wildly inaccurate
newspaper accounts of the coronation. In first draft Waugh wrote
of his fellow journalists that "It seemed to me that in their zeal to
get their story in early they had not taken any trouble to see what
was going on." The reader, given the facts on the following page,
can reach this conclusion without Waugh's aid, and he revises the
sentence to read "It seemed to me that we had been witnesses of a
quite different series of events" (51) and creates the illusion that he
is letting the reader judge. In the ensuing paragraph, however,
Waugh does generalize—apparently at some remove from the subject of yellow journalism. Into the manuscript he inserted this sentence: "It seems to me that a prig is someone who judges people by
his own, rather than by their, standards; criticism only becomes
useful when it can show people where their own principles are in
conflict" (51). Perhaps he was invoking by implication the rules of
logic. In any case, this sentence is the premise on which his indictment hangs—a far cry from the sentence, exclamatory and subjective, which anticipates it in the diary: "I think I must be a prig
people do shock me so" (334).

Whether the attitude modified the style or the style created the
attitude, Waugh had found a new sense of balance. Politically he
supported white settlers in Kenya against the doctrine of native par-
amountcy and both English and Africans against the East Indians.
In first draft, he allowed local sympathies to spoil the end of a paragraph lamenting the collapse of Arab civilization in Zanzibar:

if the British had not come to East Africa the change would not have taken
place. We came to establish a Christian civilisation and we have come very
near to establishing a Hindu one. We found an existing culture which, in
spite of its narrowness and inflexibility, was essentially decent and valuable; we have destroyed that—or, at least, attended at its destruction—and

in its place fostered the growth of a mean and dirty culture. This seems to me a much graver indictment of our interference in Africa than the popular complaint about the alienation of tribal pasture in Kenya.

The content of the last sentence is irrelevant to the matter at hand; the form is loose and inconclusive. In revising, Waugh raised the content to the level of principle (neatly avoiding the possibility of a defense of the Indians) and made the form consistent with the balance of the two preceding sentences: "Perhaps it is not a matter for censure; but it is a matter for regret" (167–168).

Even more encouraging as a sign of Waugh's growth as a writer was his ability to get off a hobbyhorse. Page 168 of *Remote People* now ends, "I met at least one lady who associated [Zanzibar] with biblical time." In manuscript, he continued with a paragraph-long indictment of a target familiar in *Decline and Fall* and *Labels*: the picturesque. His descriptive definition of the term—particularly the distinction between the Swiss Guard, which is picturesque, and the Pope, who is not—is interesting but at this point irrelevant. It is not canceled in manuscript, but at some intermediate point Waugh either saw that it was irrelevant or took advice, for it does not survive in the book.

For students of Waugh's developing religious and political consciousness—one rather than divisible in many instances—the key passage in *Remote People* has always been the meditation on the contrast between the Mass at Debra Lebanos, hidden from all but priestly eyes, and the Mass on the great altars of Europe, open for all to see and hear, a triumph of Western reason over Eastern obscurantism which Waugh celebrated more extensively in *Helena*. Judging from the manuscript, Waugh intended this to be a bravura passage which he would compose on a separate occasion. He wrote two surviving drafts, both marked for insertion at the same point. The first, as one might expect, is briefer and simpler:

For anyone accustomed to the Western rite it was difficult to think of this as a Christian service and I realized the great difference that the Western Church made in its insistence on the open altar. In any controversy about Church matters one always reencounters [?] the (attitude) /view/ that the Church tends to obfuscate the simple truths of Christianity. How far away this seems from historical fact. (There are those who imagine the church of the first centuries to have) /How ill that applied [?] to first century supporters of the view/ I remember being (expla) /told how/ in that golden age a church consisted of "two or three gathered together"—simple pious men reading the gospels and expounding the lucid truths of bible Christianity. I now see the early church as something subterranean and esoteric, its doctrine confused & highly symbolized, its rites guarded & [illegible] pr ed to initiates. Muffled figures slipping away /to the Catacombs/ before dawn; locked doors in an upper room in a side street near the harbour of some mediterranean seaport; a few legionaries off duty, slinking away from their fellows. And I see the inspired reason of the West setting all this in order; the great doctors struggling with superstition & confused thinking; theology in the service of simplifying doctrine & rendering [?] it intelligible; I see the church always at war with nonsense and as the symbol of its victory, the basilica with the high altar and the sacrifice exalted (in the) /before/ the eyes of any casual tourists who happen to pass by.

The revision is not only more elaborate but more pointed and precise:

For anyone accustomed to the Western rite it was difficult to think of this as a Christian service, for it bore that secret and confused character which I had hitherto associated with the non-Christian sects of the East.

I had sometimes thought it an odd thing that Western Christianity, alone of all the religions of the world, exposes its mysteries to every observer, but I was so accustomed to this openness that I had never before questioned whether it was an essential and natural feature of the Christian system. Indeed, so saturated are we in this spirit that many people regard the growth of the Church as a process of elaboration—even of obfuscation; they visualise the Church of the first century as a little cluster of pious people reading the Gospels together, praying and admonishing each other with a simplicity to which the high ceremonies and subtle theology of later years would have been bewildering and unrecognisable. At Debra Lebanos I suddenly saw the classic basilica and open altar as a great positive achievement, a triumph of light over darkness consciously accomplished, and I saw theology as the science of simplification by which nebulous and elusive ideas are formalised and made intelligible and exact. I saw the Church of the first century as a dark and hidden thing, as dark and hidden as the seed germinating in the womb; legionaries off duty slipping furtively out of barracks, greeting each other by signs and passwords in a locked upper room in the side street of some Mediterranean seaport; slaves at dawn creeping from the grey twilight into the candle-lit, smoky chapels of the catacombs. /The priests hid their office, practising trades; their identity was known only to initiates; they were criminals against the law of their country. And the pure nucleus of the truth lay in the minds of the people, encumbered with superstitions, gross survivals of the paganism in which they had been brought up; hazy and obscene nonsense seeping through from the conquered barbarian./ And I began to see how these obscure sanctuaries had grown, with the clarity of the Western reason, into the great open altars of Catholic Europe, where mass is said in a flood of light, high in the sight of all, while tourists can clatter round with /their/Baedeckers (undisturbed) incurious of the (ceremony) mystery. (88–89)

In the second draft Waugh takes care to establish the idea of the open altar as a norm before giving the primitivist view that the earlier was the better. Furthermore, he deletes personal memories of primitivist theory in order to emphasize that the fallacy continues and flourishes; by establishing present ritual as "a great positive achievement" and theology as a "science of simplification," he negates the opposition's charges by turning their epithets to praise and adding the very important "exact" to the original "intelligible." In the following sentence he adds details about the behavior of real, as opposed to theoretical, early Christians: "furtively," "signs and passwords," "grey twilight," and "candle-lit, smoky chapels" all prepare for the contrast with "the great open altars . . . in a flood of light, high in the sight of all." The insertion within the revision is important because it shows priests forced, not choosing, to hide and because it substitutes for name-calling a description of the process by which the truth of early Christianity can be revealed and glorified. In the final sentence of the revision he contrasts place with place, church with church, rather than simple men with elaborate interiors, and emphasizes the contrast between literal and metaphorical obscurity and the light of reason and the high altar. The conclusion of the revised passage emphasizes more clearly than its predecessor the fact that the mystery is there, available and inviolable, despite the presence of the vulgar and unworthy whom, Waugh implies in context, the monks of Debra Lebanos and Eastern Christianity take such pains to exclude.

As I indicate earlier and as this passage amply demonstrates, Waugh had by the time he finished *Remote People* attained a consistently mature and serious style scarcely and intermittently observable in his first four books. There, passages like the opening paragraphs of *Decline and Fall* and some of the descriptions of the artist's paintings and behavior in *Rossetti* had about them the flavor of pastiche—very good and enjoyable pastiche, to be sure, but in a tone which might dart rapidly away from the serious to the parodic or the fanciful. Waugh never abandoned these stylistic devices, but henceforward he was able to write formal and exact prose and to create a narrative persona far different from that of the earlier books.

CHAPTER 10

Waugh Edits Waugh:
Author versus Reviser

When considering the work of any editor, there is always the distinction between what he can do well and what he should be allowed to do at all. For example, it seems to me obvious that Evelyn Waugh was a more precise and economical writer of prose than Thomas Merton. But it is less obvious that we ought to be given *Elected Silence* rather than *The Seven Storey Mountain*, and in fact the unedited version is now the only one available in England. However, when the issue is Waugh's editing of his own work, matters are somewhat more complicated, and as critics and—if the distinction can be made—as potential editors we must make textual decisions, if only by default. Particularly interesting is the text of *Brideshead Revisited* because its history of composition and revision is the most complex of any Waugh novel.

In one sense, of course, we are conducting a pseudoinvestigation of a nonproblem because in fact we do not have any choice. American readers have available only the text of the first American edition, unchanged since 1945 although Little, Brown, and Dell have issued it in coats of many colors in both cloth and paper.[1] But it is all the same text, even the one proclaiming on the cover that it is "Companion to the PBS Television Series," with Castle Howard in silhouette and oval insets of the leading actors, including Jeremy Irons, both bare-faced and moustached, and Aloysius the teddy bear. The English have no choice either, but at least their texts, Eyre

---

1. Paul A. Doyle, "Collecting Waugh—American Editions of *Brideshead Revisited*," *Evelyn Waugh Newsletter*, 12 (Spring 1978), 9.

Methuen in hard cover and Penguin in soft, incorporate Waugh's extensive revisions for the 1960 edition and are in fact the basis of the Granada television series.

Nor is there any problem—except one—about representing Waugh's final intention, for in his preface to the 1960 edition, he left no room for doubt that his critical judgment as well as his conscious authorial power were involved in the dozens of changes which he made for that edition.[2] Nor is there any transmission problem: the holograph manuscript, an uncorrected carbon typescript, proof, a private edition based on proof not corrected by Waugh, proof extensively corrected by Waugh, about three dozen authorized variants in English editions up through the first uniform edition in 1949, and the copy texts—a 1949 uniform edition with Waugh's and an editor's holograph emendations and markings—for the 1960 edition are all in public hands.[3] Further information is probably available in the files of Chapman & Hall, the original and during Waugh's lifetime the only hardcover English publisher and the only one whom Waugh took seriously in establishing his texts.

There is one crux. All versions before 1960, including the copy text, contain, as the answer to Bridey's "Do you consider . . . that there is anything vicious in my brother's connection with this German?" Charles Ryder's "No. I'm sure not." The 1960 text reads, "I'm not sure" (241). Without further evidence, according to strict constructionist bibliographers such as Ernest Sullivan, we would have no grounds for restoring, as John Mortimer did for the Granada production, "I'm sure not." Despite any arguments to the contrary, I would hesitate not even a nanosecond to adopt that reading and would add in a textual note that (1) there is no documentary evidence that this is anything but the result of a printer's and proofreader's oversight and (2) the 1960 reading makes a nonsense not only of that line but of major thematic strands in the novel.

However, not everyone would agree with me even about this, and when we come to the question of which *Brideshead* we should adopt as copy text for a scholarly edition, let alone as a text for

---

2. "Preface," *Brideshead Revisited* (London: Chapman & Hall, 1960), pp. 9–10.
3. In *Evelyn Waugh, Writer* (Norman: Pilgrim Books, 1981), I discuss these issues at some length.

interpretation, we find considerable disagreement among dedicated bibliographical theorists. James Thorpe and Tom Berger have argued, from different bases, that what may seem to be different versions are in fact "multiple versions of a work of art" if not two or more texts in fact. Thus, even if we accept Thorpe's position that "the several verbal forms in which the literary work exists while it is being written are in the private province of the writer as part of his interior dialogue with himself"[4] and thus discard everything up to the first "public version," the 1945 Chapman & Hall edition, we still have the versions, minutely altered, of the first five editions, dating from 1945 to 1947, the first uniform edition of 1949; and the 1960 edition. Which of these seven do twenty-first-century editors choose when the novel becomes public domain? Or do they regard them as separate but equal?

Hershel Parker argues that they are not at all equal and that, if separated, the protestant texts do not really exist. In fact, he is conducting the much broader argument that the study of the creation, growth, revision, and transmission of texts has not only been widely neglected but pursued with mistaken or inadequate theory.[5] Parker finds two causes for this lamentable state: first, the theory, stated most influentially by W. K. Wimsatt, that the text is all-important and that extrinsic evidence might (later critics modify this to "should") be considered irrelevant; second, the theory of W. W. Greg (this is Parker's formulation) that "an author retains, as long as he lives, complete authority over his text" (ix) and that indisputably authorial emendations should therefore be regarded as representing full and final intention.

To these widely accepted ideas Parker opposes theories about the creative process and about intention drawn from philosophers and psychologists. Most crucial is John Dewey's theory that "meaning is built into the text at the moment each part is written. The 'artist is controlled in the process of his work by his grasp of the connec-

4. James Thorpe, *Principles of Textual Criticism* (San Marino: Huntington Library, 1972), p. 41. Thomas L. Berger, "Critical Judgment, Textual Criticism, Editorial Taste, and the Text of *Othello*," delivered at a session on Critical Judgment and Textual Criticism, Modern Language Association, Los Angeles, December 1982.
5. Hershel Parker, *Flawed Texts and Verbal Icons: Literary Authority in American Fiction* (Evanston: Northwestern University Press, 1984).

tion between what he has already done and what he is to do next.'
He must 'at each point retain and sum up what has gone before as
a whole and with reference to a whole to come'" (3). This, of
course, takes the theory of organic form into the process of composition and raises some very interesting questions about "intention." Parker draws from Michael Hancher, John R. Searle, and
others to argue that there are various kinds of intention—and not
only in the composing process, for after completing a work, the
author becomes not a creator but a merchandiser, willing to com-
promise the "intention" he may have forgotten in order to get his
work published. Thus Parker dismisses changes made under editorial or censorial pressure and even changes, such as the redistri-
bution of material from the manuscript version of Chapter 8 of
The Great Gatsby, which have been generally accepted as improve-
ments.

However, Parker would go beyond R. B. McKerrow and Greg—
and well beyond Thorpe, whom he challenges directly—to use as
copy text not the first edition but the manuscript and to question
and probably reject even authorial revisions. His reason, to put it
briefly, is that extraneous meddling is likely to take place even in
the first setting of type and that thereafter the author is not likely
to be a much more effective editor than anyone else because even
he or she cannot recover the intentionality of the creative moment.
Instead—and this is perhaps the most important aspect of Parker's
book—he cites Sister Stephanie Vincec in calling for "a new kind
of literary scholarship . . . 'distinguished not only by fresh vigor
in the pursuit and analysis of historical, biographical, textual, and
bibliographical evidence but also by the alert sophistication with
which such evidence is probed for its aesthetic implications; or the
trajectory of research can go in the other direction, as when a study
begins with the recognition of an aesthetic problem which turns
out to be resolvable by external evidence'" (102).

In other words, put the scholar-bibliographer-critic at the center
of the textual and critical enterprises. He can point to enough well-
intentioned readings of faulty texts to show that the New Critics
and their retinue should be questioned if not, as he implies, dismissed as critics and demoted as academics. He is particularly harsh

about the "biographicizing"—making biographical judgments about habits of mind and character without citing or even seeking evidence outside the text—to which New Critics seem addicted. Parker is able to show in considerable detail that texts have been mucked about by authors as well as editors, so that even when the author's *words* have been retained, as in the Malcolm Cowley reordering of *Tender Is the Night*, the author's *effect* has been changed and, in Parker's view, damaged because even if the author makes and supervises the changes, he or she does not, usually, revise in the root sense and certainly does not recreate. At its most extreme, the point to which Parker takes it, this theory would regard the author's listening to any advice at all as a mistake and the New York Edition of Henry James as a disaster.

Parker is led to this extreme not so much by his theory of creativity, which seems plausible to anyone who has done extensive work with manuscripts, another's or one's own, as by his elevation of the process, indeed the physical and chronological order of composition, into a general rule for critics and textual editors. He cannot conceive, for example, that an author would introduce changes at one point and not another and still retain a sense of the relationship between new and old. He cannot conceive that, despite the literary cesarean performed on *Pudd'nhead Wilson*, the controlling vision or obsession in Twain's mind might give the book an artistic if not a textual unity and therefore that critics who praise the novel without knowing the history of its composition might be making sound aesthetic judgments. Because of his own obsession with what the author originally made of a book, he sometimes cannot see what he (or she; he cites no women writers) *has* made of the book. He condemns organicists, but he is an organicist of a far more severe type himself.

All of this raises obvious theoretical questions about the various texts of *Brideshead* and of Waugh's other novels. Many critics agree that Waugh's excisions from the three volumes of the war trilogy for the one-volume text *Sword of Honour* represented mistaken economy, and no one has lamented the restoration of manuscript readings, bowdlerized for first publication in 1928, to the 1962 edition of *Decline and Fall*. But critics have been more concerned to attack or defend the aesthetic quality of *Brideshead* than to examine its textual problems, practical or philosophical. Some critics, like those who wrote in 1964 that every word of the novel is worth study and proceeded to quote passages which Waugh cut from the 1960 edition, have no problem because they did not know that more than one text is available, and philosophically their unwitting choice of text can be defended.[6] Jeffrey Heath is considerably more sophisticated in his approach: aware that Waugh's "attitude to his work changed and developed as he matured," he argues logically that "A novel which reflected his state of mind in 1944 . . . no longer logically did so in 1959, and he made changes accordingly."[7] Both Waugh and Heath term the 1960 revisions "of minor importance." Since there are about 168 of them, it would be interesting to know what they would call significant. (Parker, of course, would answer, none of them.)

In fact, Heath thinks some of Waugh's revisions significant enough to mention in his chapter on *Brideshead*. He notes that in the fourth Chapman & Hall edition "Waugh pointed his criticism of enchanted Brideshead by making the dome a false one" (168). A few pages later, he cites a passage from the first edition on "the vital hours of a lifetime" which are akin to a historical epoch which "will, for a generation or two, stupefy the world, commit all manner of crimes, perhaps, follow the wildest chimeras, go down in the end in agony, but leave behind a record of new heights scaled and new rewards won for all mankind. . . ." Heath does not add that in the 1945 Revised Edition Waugh changed this passage to read "will, for a generation or two, stupefy the world, bring to birth and nurture a teeming brood of genius, droop soon with the weight of its grandeur, but leave behind a record of new rewards won for all mankind." Perhaps Waugh made the change because he did not want to associate the soul's "rare, classic periods" with crimes and chimeras, but Heath does not comment. However, even though we can question the consistency of his practice, we can

6. Rodney Delasanta and Mario D'Avanzo, "Truth and Beauty in *Brideshead Revisited*," *Modern Fiction Studies*, 11 (1965/66), 140–152.
7. Jeffrey Heath, *The Picturesque Prison: Evelyn Waugh and His Writing* (Kingston and Montreal: McGill-Queen's University Press, 1982), p. 276.

grant the logic of his implied argument that revisions within a year or two or three of composition come closer to representing the same artistic vision, or a clarification of it, while those made four-teen years after publication could represent a widely different vision or intention and even that "Waugh's deletions represent a serious aesthetic loss" (277).

Heath would probably have no doubt that the first—or is it the fourth? or the first uniform (which he does not mention)?—edition represents Waugh's intentions. The old conventional choice, which Thorpe scorns, would be the 1960 edition, the last published in Waugh's lifetime. Parker would insist that the manuscript—uncor-rupted by typist, typesetter, Waugh's correcting a hastily produced typescript within a week of finishing work on the manuscript (*Cat-alogue* E1102; *Diaries*, 568), Chapman & Hall editors, or Waugh's revising proofs more than five months after he finished the manu-script, in very different circumstances and in another country—embodies the real text.

But in practical terms, matters are more complicated than Parker thinks. For example, which manuscript of *Brideshead* should we choose? The "manuscript" at the Humanities Research Center, University of Texas-Austin, is bound in one volume, but that homogeneity is deceptive. As I have shown in *Evelyn Waugh, Writer* (119–120), Waugh rewrote heavily as he was composing the man-uscript, sometimes going back two weeks after he had done a first draft and totally recasting the material. And I was barely able to indicate the existence of these revisions; their nature and extent could be indicated only by a facsimile of the manuscript, and one would need a detailed guide to follow even that. And even if one could *follow* the text, one would not be able to *read* it as a novel.

While I do not want to shove Parker's argument past the point of absurdity, I do want to indicate that there are practical obstacles to putting it into effect for *Brideshead* and no doubt for other novels—and not just because of the complexity of the manuscript. Whatever Parker and his sources may say about the creative process, Waugh never regarded the manuscript as anything like a final version but regarded typescript and even proof as integral parts of the process of composition. For him, if not for Parker, the work of authorship

did not end even with publication (see Chapter 6). Taking the realities of Waugh's habits into account, a serious edition of *Brideshead*
would have to be based on one of four choices of copy text: the
privately printed edition of 1944 (with editorial emendations restored from manuscript), the first Chapman & Hall edition of 1945;
the first Uniform Edition, which incorporates Waugh's corrections
between 1945 and 1949; and the 1960 new Uniform Edition. Basing
my decision on limited experience as a printer, on more extensive
experience in using variorum texts, and on theoretical bases different from Thorpe's, I would choose the first English edition. Parker
might settle for the 1944 text, but Waugh did not see it in proof (in
most ways it *was* the proof state).

Another reason for choosing the English edition as copy text is
that real people would presumably be using the resulting book, and
it would be easier for them to comprehend successive changes if
they worked from a base. The 1949 edition has little to recommend
it: in practical terms, the notes would be working in two directions,
and in theoretical terms, when does an author's intention begin to
waver? The 1960 edition, which cuts extensively, would require a
large number of long textual notes quite distracting even to the
scholarly reader, and in theoretical terms, not even Waugh seriously
maintained that this text represented the original inspiration most
accurately.

Whichever text we choose, I think that, at least as critics and
perhaps as editors, we must reject, as based on a mere technicality,
Thorpe's distinction between draft material as "the private province
of the writer as part of his interior dialogue with himself" and the
"public version," which "has the integrity of its unique authorial
form" (42). Which of us has not seen his or her own writing in
print, been appalled at some lapse or oversight, and longed for the
chance to emend? Granted, we seldom have the opportunity, and
few would claim for these productions the integrity of a work of
art. But the dialogue with ourselves goes on. Sometimes, ad-
mittedly, that dialogue can be mere babble, or we have changed
enough, as Waugh may have done between 1944 and 1959, that we
are talking to a different self, but there is some possibility that sense

is being made. Both Thorpe and Parker would deny this, though their cutoff points are different.

Almost wholly independent of the choice of copy text, in fact, is the study of that dialogue. As authors or readers, rather than as editors, we know that it goes on all the time, and that it is always critical at bottom. Waugh, for example, clearly thought that *Brideshead* could be improved, and at times in its composition he had doubts about the whole enterprise. But he also referred to his work in progress as "M.O.,G.E.C." (*Letters*, 199), or Magnum Opus, Great English Classic—not wholly in jest. He was a bit unsettled by reports from Maurice Bowra of its reception, even before it was published, as "Cecil Beaton's favourite book. Connolly does a funny imitation of Marchmain's death-bed" (*Diaries*, 526). To have these two recurrent butts of his wit turn on him must have stung. Worse still was the response from America. When he began the novel, he told A. D. Peters that "not six Americans will understand it" (*Letters*, 177); two years later he told Robert Henriques that he "was pleased with it at the time but I have been greatly shaken by its popularity in the U.S.A.," and he wrote to another correspondent, "I thought it in good taste before and now I know it can't be" (*Letters*, 222, 223). Four years later, after—and as a result of?—publishing the Uniform Edition, he wrote Graham Greene that "I re-read *Brideshead* and was appalled. I can find many excuses—that it was the product Consule Bracken of spam, Nissen huts, blackout—but it won't do for peacetime. The plot seemed to me excellent. I am going to spend the summer rewriting it" (*Letters*, 322).

He did not do so until 1959, and in his Preface he summarized the necessity and the results:

the book is infused with a kind of gluttony, for food and wine, for the splendours of the recent past, and for rhetorical and ornamental language, which now with a full stomach I find distasteful. I have modified the grosser passages but have not obliterated them because they are an essential part of the book.

The soliloquies of Julia and Lord Marchmain he

would not now introduce . . . into a novel which elsewhere aims at verisimilitude. But I have retained them here in something near their original form because, like the Burgundy . . . and the moonlight they were essentially of the mood of writing; also because many readers liked them, though that is not a consideration of first importance.

Thorpe and Parker might agree that the "grosser passages" are as essential a part of the book as the soliloquies, the result of the mood described in Waugh's letter to Greene, and I think that any future editor and all students of the novel as a discrete artifact should regard the first English edition as definitive. But Waugh did make the changes over a period of fifteen years; we have, if we know our business at all, studied them; and we are left to assess their meaning and aesthetic (as opposed to textual) value. Both are problematic.

To give only one example, there is some controversy about Waugh's revision of Julia's and Ryder's first consummation of their love. The versions read:

> So at sunset I took formal possession of her as her lover. It was no time for the sweets of luxury; they would come, in their season, with the swallow and the lime flowers. Now on the rough water, as I was made free of her narrow loins and, it seemed now, assuaging that fierce appetite, cast a burden which I had borne all my life, toiled under, not knowing its nature—now, while the waves still broke and thundered on the prow, the act of possession was a symbol, a rite of ancient origin and solemn meaning. (Chapman & Hall, 1945, 228–229; Little, Brown, 1946, 261)

> It was no time for the sweets of luxury; they would come, in their season, with the swallow and the lime flowers. Now on the rough water there was a formality to be observed, no more. It was as though a deed of conveyance of her narrow loins had been drawn and sealed. I was making my first entry as the freeholder of a property I would enjoy and develop at leisure. (1960, 228)

Bernard Bergonzi thinks that Waugh wisely removed the implication of the first version that Ryder "is becoming carnally incorporated into the magic circle of Brideshead, a king of earthly beatitude" (which would in fact accord with Ryder's earlier feeling that at Brideshead he "believed myself very near heaven") but thinks it unfortunate (and therefore unconscious?) that "Julia could never be just a woman he was in love with. She inevitably stood for much more—for Brideshead Castle and all its treasure, both material and

spiritual."[8] The *Times Literary Supplement* (TLS) reviewer argues
that the revision contains a "horrible double meaning [that] can
hardly be unintentional. Suddenly it seems as if all the time it has
been the house, the property, that he loved" and goes on to find
"the real grossness of the novel . . . not in any details of style but
in its apparent identification of grace with property and its relega-
tion of humanity to a bad third place."[9] Bergonzi concludes that,
on examination, the revisions "have the possibly unwelcome effect
of drawing attention to the weak points in the narrative" and that
"It is . . . questionable whether the novel has gained very much
from these changes."

The *TLS* reviewer is correct, I think, in assuming that Waugh
intended the effects he perceives. Textual history provides some
evidence. In preparing the 1945 Revised Edition, Waugh anticipated the 1960 revision by changing the description of the light
"drawing out all the hidden sweetness of color and scent" to its
"spreading out all the stacked merchandise of colour and scent." In
both, the atmosphere is associated with "the head and golden
shoulders of the woman beside me." In the surrounding passages
Ryder has just asked, "Isn't this peace?" and is assured that it is not,
which seems to indicate that merely physical values—"the world
of three dimensions" perceived by the five senses that, he learns,
does not exist—are insufficient. By the end of the novel, Ryder
learns that they are not, and by the end of the novel—in this the
Epilogue differs from the Prologue—he accepts not just with resignation but with a kind of equanimity the desertion and despoiling
of the physical Brideshead.

An otherwise extremely friendly critic, Donat Gallagher, attacks
my interpretation of the specific passages, originally published in
Evelyn Waugh, Writer. He quotes the passage containing "deed of
conveyance" and "freeholder of a property" and goes on to criticize
Waugh's literary tact and what he reads as my endorsement of the

8. Bernard Bergonzi, "Evelyn Waugh's Gentleman," *Critical Quarterly*, 5 (Spring 1963), 28–30.

9. "Yet Another Visit to Brideshead," *Times Literary Supplement*, 16 September 1960, p. 194. See also Jacqueline McDonnell, *Waugh on Women* (New York: St. Martin's Press, 1985), pp. 210–211, for a comment on the passage and on the commentators.

TLS reviewer's identification of "grace with property." In some detail he points out that "Humanly attractive, 'grace' survives only because it is 'true'; what more could Waugh have done to divorce 'grace' from 'property'?"[10]

All I can say is that I wish I had the opportunity to revise and expand my discussion[11] to state more explicitly that the grossness is not Waugh's but Ryder's, that the identification of grace with property is false. But it does exist, in the mind of Charles Ryder— as character—at that point and at many earlier points in the novel. I would argue that Waugh modified the passage in an attempt to make the distinction, always difficult to do with subtlety, between the first-person narrator in his narrative present and in his preterit actions and attitudes. This distinction Gallagher fails to make sufficiently.

Jeffrey Heath, apparently untroubled by questions of revision, reaches much the same conclusion as Gallagher and I. This fact might make us question the relevance of textual criticism to the literary criticism of this or any other novel. But Heath knows more about the text than he admits. And even after textual evidence has been collected and analyzed, it is clear that the general themes are the same in all editions of the novel. As even Waugh recognized, the passages emended in 1960 were part of the fabric of the novel. But if we move beyond not only the austerities of 1944 but Waugh's mood of 1959, when he had just completed his biography of Ronald Knox, his most sober book, and when he was planning to embody a completely different version of the final years of World War II in *Unconditional Surrender*, perhaps we can regard the 1960 *Brideshead* as a critical tool rather than an authoritative text. Therefore, as I have argued and would continue to argue, major themes in the novel have been locally clarified and perhaps enriched by Waugh's revisions at all stages of composition and publication. Certainly one can understand why he made each one and is thereby led to a consideration of motives and motifs in the novel as a whole.

10. Donat Gallagher, "Industria Ditat—Mark III," *Southern Review* (Australia), 15 (November 1982), 337–339.
11. The paperback edition of *Evelyn Waugh, Writer*, published in 1986, contains a new Preface and corrections of errors in fact and grammar, but it was not possible to make more extensive changes.

Seen in this way, the textual evidence forces us to look at the whole book in a new light. Waugh's critical rereading and writing make us reread, not only textually but historically. Trying to escape the limitations of the time of composition, he permits us to see that period *as* past and therefore to see the ways in which it sustained as well as limited the artist. The best advice to all but the most rigidly formalist critic, the bugbear of Hershel Parker, who is now as rare as a grizzly in Kansas, is that given Waugh to his wife about three versions he was sending to her: "you may, must study them to see the changes" (*Letters*, 197). In the process, the critic will not only learn a good deal about the novel but be able to witness the struggle of a gifted novelist and brilliant stylist with his medium. And this is probably more important than theoretical purity in the choice of a text.

CHAPTER II

The Failure of Imagination:
Waugh's School Stories

The publication of Evelyn Waugh's biography, diaries, letters, and collected journalism over the past ten years had confirmed without much altering the suspicion of earlier readers that there is in his novels a very clear and at the same time uneasy relationship between what he lived and what he imagined. His heroes, all the way from Pennyfeather to Pinfold, obviously share some of their creator's experiences, and just as obviously Waugh isolated and inflated some of his own fears and fantasies into such diverse types as Adam Fenwick-Symes, Basil Seal, and Guy Crouchback. The conversion of fact into fiction or, more recently, the embodiment of psychic patterns in the fiction has furnished material for a kind of high-level gossip (which Waugh would by no means have deplored) or even for studies of the way in which his imagination worked. However, Waugh's efforts to escape into realism, into a more or less direct presentation of the persona of the everyday, discursive-prose-writing self, throw considerable light on his mind and method precisely because he failed to do so.

Two obvious occasions in which he flirted with self-revelation in fiction are *Work Suspended* and *The Ordeal of Gilbert Pinfold*, but in both he used techniques of displacement, first into invented circumstances, next into a split between conscious and unconscious mind, resolved only by suppression of the unconscious which Pinfold and his creator regard as victory. Less well known, but more interesting as attempts at self-presentation, are two fragments, written twenty-five years apart, in which Waugh tried and failed to make realistic fiction from biographical fact. The first is a fragmentary novel, written at the end of 1920 while he was still a schoolboy;[1] the second is "Charles Ryder's Schooldays," written about the time of his forty-second birthday in 1945.[2]

The untitled fragment—actually a fragment of a fragment, since the manuscript at the Humanities Research Center ends in midsentence—is a highly self-conscious attempt to enter "the family trade of literature." The work is dedicated "To Myself," and the dedicatory letter speaks of the difficulties faced by an author whose "surroundings . . . have been entirely literary." Willing to accept responses like "Another of these precocious Waughs. . . . one more nursery novel," he concludes that he has "not been crushed in the mill of professionalism." As evidence from the diaries and from the fragment itself indicate, Evelyn aspired to authorship in order to compete with his brother Alec, the elder by five years. In 1920, Alec was clearly dominant. His first novel, *The Loom of Youth*, portrayed school life so realistically that Evelyn could not attend his brother's—and father's—school, and Alec's war service was enviable but not emulable. On the other hand, Evelyn had a low opinion of Alec's friends and on occasion an even lower opinion of his style. During Evelyn's Lancing years, Alec's appearances frequently inspired Evelyn to turn from schoolwork to writing. In fact, his first note about the novel—assuming that the manuscript at HRC and the one mentioned in the *Diaries* are the same—calls it "the study of a man with two characters, by his brother" (*Diaries*, 107) and came about a week after Alec and his first wife—commemorated in *A Little Learning* as Evelyn's guide and playfellow—rescued him from a boring day at Lancing.

The story opens with Peter Audley's waking to a bleak March day in 1918 and follows him to his pit, or study; to breakfast; to a boring history lesson; and to preparations for Physical Training. A telegram summons him home for the visit of his brother Ralf, on

---

1. The text of the story, titled "Fragment of a Novel," is printed in *Evelyn Waugh, Apprentice*, ed. Robert Murray Davis (Norman: Pilgrim Books, 1985).
2. *Work Suspended and Other Stories, Including Charles Ryder's Schooldays* (Harmondsworth: Penguin, 1982). "Charles Ryder's Schooldays" has an introduction by Michael Sissons.

leave after three years in the trenches. Greeted by Ralf and by Moira Gage, the vicar's daughter, he is just beginning to analyze his brother when the manuscript breaks off.

As one might expect in a schoolboy's novel, the autobiographical elements are obvious. Selchurch is recognizably Lancing; Peter Audley and Ralf are, like the Waughs, five years apart; Moira Gage, as far as the story goes attached to neither brother, is modeled on Barbara Jacobs, though Moira is made Peter's contemporary rather than two or more years his senior. Waugh does relocate the family home from Hampstead to "the Hall" at Bulfrey Combe, a small rural village, and he makes Peter and Ralf three years older than the Waugh brothers.

Some Waugh critics would no doubt attribute the last two modifications of fact to Evelyn's desire to present his alter ego as more mature and more highly placed socially, but the fragment is remarkable because it is far less self-aggrandizing than exploratory. There is not much evidence from which to infer Waugh's attitude toward the setting because very little of the surviving manuscript is set in Bulfrey and the characters never reach Bulfrey Combe. Judging from the contrast between Bulfrey Combe, which "still kept most of the appearance of a country village," and Bulfrey, "a small town with two or three streets of cheap shops, a bank, and a small glass factory which formed the nucleus of a large area of slum which was gradually spreading its grimy tentacles along the roads," he was establishing the village as a refuge, already threatened, from the changes accelerated by the war. As the vicar's daughter, Moira was given a more stable background than Barbara Jacobs, whose parents battled over progressive versus traditional education as well as many other topics.

Waugh's motive for altering the ages of the chief characters was based more on social history than on personal aggrandizement. In March 1918, Evelyn was fourteen and a half; Peter is seventeen and a half for two reasons: first, to allow Waugh to place him at Selchurch in the summer term of 1914, so that he can contrast the opulence, ease, and intellectual distinction of that period with the privation, academic slackness, and war mania of 1918; second, so that Peter is faced with the immediate prospect of leaving school for the battlefront, and he knows and resents the fact that the Officer Training Corps (OTC) has not prepared him to function in that world. (One might compare Peter's reflections on the OTC exercise with Alastair Trumpington's and Cedric Lyne's experiences of maneuvers and battle in *Put Out More Flags* and Guy Crouchback's in *Sword of Honour*.) Furthermore, he is not at all sure that he can measure up to his brother's attitudes and accomplishments because "Ralf saw everything so abstractedly with such imperturbable cynicism. Peter flattered himself that he would not be able to stand it; Ralf had won the D.S.O. some months ago."

Although Peter has begun to judge Ralf's witty utterances as calculated for effect, the fragment ends before Peter can assert himself as rival in war, love (note the effect of making Peter and Moira contemporaries), or words. What does emerge is a portrait of Lancing and by extension of English society which accords very closely with much of Waugh's editorial journalism in the *Lancing College Magazine*; in "The War and the Younger Generation" in 1928; by implication in *Vile Bodies*; and finally in *A Little Learning*: his generation had been denied the pleasures promised for their youth and frustrated in the possibility of testing themselves in battle. As Peter says, in an argument over discontinuing sports prizes to divert energy and attention to the war, "Everything has been done . . . to make school life excessively unpleasant. . . . What little of the old life does remain, is what keeps it just tolerable." More seriously, Waugh, Peter, and their contemporaries, cast into a world where old values had been destroyed or corroded, were left to find their own. At no time in his life did Waugh have much confidence in the individual's ability to do so. In 1920, portraying a class of history students given no stimulation and anticipating no rewards, Waugh asserted that "Youth[,] far from being the time of burning quests and wild, gloriously vain ideals beloved of the minor poets, is essentially one of languor and repose." The language is very similar to the passage in *Brideshead Revisited* which celebrates "The Languor of Youth," "the relaxation of yet unwearied sinews, the mind sequestered and self-regarding, the sun standing still in the heavens and the earth throbbing to our own pulse."[3] However, the judgment is very different: in 1919 the languor is the result of slackness rather than the condition for spiritual fermentation. It was much easier to look back at 1922 than forward to it.

In 1920, Waugh could objectify in the war his fears of the adult world, his resentment of the system that was preparing him for it so badly, and his early, grudging respect and resentment of the elder brother who seemed to be winning the prizes—manhood, marriage, literary success—to which Evelyn aspired by means that he could not yet clearly imagine. Perhaps this is the real reason that the novel was never completed. However, Evelyn provided himself with more obvious means of escape from authorship. His first diary entries marvel at the amount of work involved—"each chapter will have to be about two sections of College bumph." When he took home the manuscript for Christmas vacation, he found

Alec apprehensive of a rival, Mother of my ruin through becoming a public figure too soon. Father likes it. Meanwhile I plot on and on at it, trying to make it take some form or shape. At present it seems a mere succession of indifferently interesting conversations. However, I believe it is fairly good and I am pretty sure to be able to get it published. It's a bloody sweat, however. (*Diaries*, 108)

Even the prospect of fame soon vanished because of "my family's disapproval and my own innate sloth," and by 10 January 1921 he had abandoned the effort. It is also possible that he could not imagine what was to happen—to him as much as to his characters—and that, having outlined his social themes but finding himself unwilling to face even an imaginative rivalry with Alec, he welcomed the return to schoolboy status.

Twenty-five years later, Waugh found a more difficult if less complex transition to a very different kind of postwar world. Although, judging from his diaries and letters, he was not dissatisfied with the kind of man he had become, he exhibited considerable doubts about the kind of writer he was to be in the future. Early in the process of writing *Brideshead* (his hero was still named Peter at this stage) he speculated that it might be the first of his novels—by

---

3. *Brideshead Revisited* (Boston: Little, Brown, 1946), p. 79.

which he apparently meant the novel in the English realistic tradition—rather than his last. Two years later, he promised his readers that future work would be concerned with style and with the presence of God in the world of the novel. In 1945, while he was letting his war experiences settle into usable form and was perhaps unwilling to test his ability to deal with the postwar world, he began research for *Helena*. But the success of *Brideshead* made it unnecessary, even unwise, for him to work very hard, and four months after he first mentioned Helena he turned to his own past, reading "my Lancing diaries through with unmixed shame" and for the next month working on "a novel of school life in 1919—as untopical a theme as could be found" (*Diaries*, 636) After the diary entry made on his forty-second birthday, we hear no more of the story "Charles Ryder's Schooldays" until my *Catalogue* of the University of Texas materials in 1981 and the independent discovery of a carbon typescript at his agent's office later in the same year.

"Charles Ryder's Schooldays" begins the day after the first entry in Waugh's Lancing diaries; like them, it deals with resentment at the new appointments by and the very existence of a new house tutor. Unlike the diaries, the story presents the tutor's appeal to Ryder for cooperation and compassion and ends with Ryder's scorning apologies and offer of compensation from the man—with very much the same words Waugh recorded in *A Little Learning*. There is little consecutive action; there is a good deal of detail about the customs by which the boys stratify themselves.

There are at least three obvious and not always discrete ways of looking at the story: in the context of *Brideshead*, to which it forms a prequel; in the context of the *Diaries*, though I am more interested in style than in content; and in the context of the earlier school story as another attempt at self-creation. In the first context, Waugh's epigraph to *Brideshead*, "I am not I" and so on, clearly does not apply to the Charles Ryder of the story or, as B. W. Handford shows,[4] to anyone else in it. First, Charles' experiences are drawn more directly from those of the youthful Waugh than at any other place in Waugh's fiction; second, because in the story there *is* no "I"

---

4. *Times Literary Supplement*, 9 April 1982, p. 412.

because Waugh tells the story in third rather than first person. The two are very closely related, I think: Waugh wanted to use the mass of material, no doubt rediscovered as he was rearranging his life and his effects at Piers Court after a six-year absence, but he also wanted to distance himself as author and person not only from his abhorred earlier self but from the character of Ryder. As he must have come to recognize, along with a number of subsequent critics, the chief problem with *Brideshead* is that many perceptive and otherwise sympathetic readers regard Ryder as a very unpleasant character. However, it is not at all clear how far the author shares this view or is even aware of the possibility that someone might conceive it. This was a problem that no amount of revision of the text of the novel could resolve. By using third person, Waugh was able to set Ryder in a physical and social context rather than let him create and dominate it. In fact, Waugh uses setting in a much different way than he had in the 1920 fragment. There all was subordinated to Peter's viewpoint. Discomforts are imposed from without by the system. In "Charles Ryder's Schooldays," the characters are dwarfed and dominated by the scene, the system is internalized, the boys oppressing each other and themselves by accepting and elaborating on a social code designed to regulate attitudes as well as behavior.

Besides third person, Waugh uses two other techniques to place and judge Ryder: in conversations among the boys, he does not include identifying tags, so that individual personality is shown to be submerged in schoolboy argot; and in diary entries by Ryder he shows the boy's immature habit of simplifying character and event into adolescent commonplaces. Compare, for example, the episode of the master—Gordon at Lancing, Graves at Spierpoint—and the printing press. In the *Diaries*, Waugh wrote:

> In the afternoon, as it was raining, Fremlin and I returned early from our walk and helped Gordon to mend his printing press. It would be priceless to have one but they are rather costly. He invited us to tea and we sat round his fire talking scandal and eating toast till chapel. Perhaps he isn't really so bad after all. (*Diaries*, 28)

In "Charles Ryder's Schooldays," the press is at first merely mentioned and provides Charles—more wistful internally and more callous externally than the Waugh of the diaries—with daydreams of "the tall folios, the wide margins, the deckle-edged mould-made paper, the engraved initials, the rubrics and colophons of his private press" (296–297). Later the master enlists Ryder and Tamplin (clearly based on Fremlin) to help him assemble it. Tamplin escapes, but Charles remains to finish the job and Graves confides in him about O'Malley's need for Ryder's support as head of the dormitory. In Charles Ryder's diary for 28 September this is reuced to

After luncheon Tamplin and I were going for a walk when Graves called us in and made us help put up his printing press. Tamplin escaped. Graves tried to get things out of me about ragging Dirty Desmond but without success.

Charles cannot admit, in writing, in his official schoolboy self, his desire for a press, and he wilfully misunderstands the tutor's motives, as Waugh did not entirely do. Elsewhere, similar incidents are treated by Ryder as diarist in a more curt and simple fashion than in Waugh's diaries, where the level of vocabulary is far higher and the complexity of sentence structure far greater than in Ryder's diary:

I don't think we shall be able to rag Woodard long, but meanwhile we are making hay. He is trying to make us use the new pronunciation in Latin, and it is an endless source for supposed misunderstanding. We have also some splendid attempts such as SOOBYOONGTEEWAY for the pronunciation of Subjunctive. He got quite bored when, on his using the new pronunciation in Greek, his pronunciation was greeted with a longdrawn wail of oooh! He threatened to send us all to our House-masters, and I believe he will carry out the threat. (*Diaries*, 20–21)

Peacock deigned to turn up for Double Greek. We mocked him somewhat. He is trying to make us use the new pronunciation; when he said oú there was a wail of "ooh" and Tamplin pronounced subjunctive soobyoongteeway—very witty. Peacock got bored and said he'd report him to Graves but relented. [Ryder's entry, 25 September 1919]

And throughout the story, the contrast between Ryder's style and that of the omniscient narrator is even greater.

Of course, the diaries do not have a plot—though, to use E. M. Forster's distinction, they do have a story—and while the story did not progress far enough for a line of action to emerge, we can discern threads which would probably have been woven into a design that was in part dictated by events already mentioned in *Brideshead*. Chief among these is the death of Ryder's mother (here and in the manuscript of *Brideshead* killed by a German shell in Bosnia; in pre–1960 *Brideshead* dying of an unspecified cause; and in 1960 dying of exhaustion, perhaps to show her self-sacrifice in a way that death as a result of combat would not). Waugh must have recognized that Charles' response, or rather his lack of response, to his mother's death in *Brideshead* was inadequate, not merely in terms of Ryder's psychology but in novelistic terms, and by emphasizing in the story Charles' memory of the news and associating it with the Spierpoint setting, he may have been preparing to link her death with Charles' rejection of Spierpoint values, his outward callousness, and his inward refusal—unlike the youthful Waugh—to analyze himself or others. A second major theme is adumbrated in the series of models for young Ryder, especially the masculine and intellectual A. A. Carmichael, contrasted with the almost maternal and emotional Frank Bates as "that one the ineffable dweller on cloud-capped Olympus, this the homely clay image, the intimate of hearth and household, the patron of threshing-floor and olive-press." Charles' worship of these deities, like the atheism or agnosticism of the Sixth Form, embodied most brilliantly in Symonds, who reads the Greek Anthology in chapel, is obviously intended to anticipate Charles' account of his irreligious background in *Brideshead*. Set between the two masters is Graves, who attempts to draw Ryder out of his contemptuous rejection of human responses. Even in the fragment he emerges not simply to illustrate a point but to stand as a complex character to set off rather than complement Charles' attitudinizing.

However, the complexity of character, especially in the conception and treatment of Charles, created what proved to be insuperable problems. For one thing, the Charles of *Brideshead* was much more reserved and sophisticated than the Waugh revealed in *A Little Learning* and other memoirs. The Ryder of the fragment, on the other hand, is far less sophisticated in style and general response and far less active intellectually and academically than the Waugh of the diaries—though, like the Ryder of *Brideshead*, he is a restaurant snob. Moreover, it does not seem possible that the rather cold and priggish Ryder of Spierpoint—however much he was beginning to reject conventional reactions—could have become the Oxonian "in search of love" who went to Sebastian's luncheon party "full of curiosity and the faint, unrecognized apprehension that here, at last, I should find that low door in the wall . . . which opened on an enclosed and enchanted garden, which was somewhere, not overlooked by any window, in the heart of that grey city" (*Brideshead*, 31). By attempting to use the harsh fact of what Waugh repeatedly felt to be caddishness, Waugh had blocked the way towards the nostalgia that is the older Ryder's most endearing quality. The "I" of Charles Ryder was not, and finally could never be, the "I" of Evelyn Waugh.

Alec Waugh believed that life could, in fact *should*, be lived in watertight compartments, and this dictum so impressed Evelyn that he used it in his diary, in both school stories, and at least by implication in *A Little Learning*. In fact, as I argued in Chapter 4, Waugh's acceptance of this belief found embodiment in the technique of his first five novels, where he used fragmentation, caricature, and discontinuity as major principles of selection and organization and distancing as a feature of characterization. If the method of the realist novel is, as various critics have argued, linked to liberal, humane values, and if Forster's "only connect" is a formal as well as a thematic principle, then Waugh was never in serious danger of becoming a realist, and the unwitting fragmentation of Charles Ryder in the story is evidence that he could not breach and perhaps not even formally recognize the gap. Various recent critics, including Ian Littlewood, have shown that he objectified conflicts rather than analyzing them.[5]

Perhaps, as is clearly the case in "Charles Ryder's Schooldays," Waugh could not bring himself to deal directly with the causes of his own coldness and misanthropy. It is certain that he did not complete any serious attempt to portray anything like his own charac-

5. Ian Littlewood, *The Writings of Evelyn Waugh* (Totowa, N.J.: Barnes & Noble, 1982). Though in no sense a work of scholarship, this book contains isolated insights about Waugh's style.

ter, either in the schoolboy fragment *Work Suspended* or in "Charles Ryder's Schooldays." Had he been able to do so, as J. B. Priestley argued in his review of *The Ordeal of Gilbert Pinfold*,[6] he might have been able to cure himself. At least he might have been able, as he never was in art or, as far as one can tell, in life, to imagine himself in a realistic mode. We cannot know, and probably he would have doubted, whether this was a Good Thing. If so, he would not have sought the methods of displacement and deflection that make him one of the most original novelists and master stylists of his generation. But then art is art, not therapy, and the fragments and failures are much less important, and finally less vital, than the completed fictions created by an incomplete man.

6. J. B. Priestley, "What Was Wrong with Pinfold," *New Statesman*, 54 (31 August 1957), 244.

Later Milieux

CHAPTER 12

The Rhetoric of Mexican Travel: Greene and Waugh

Most students of modern English literature know Graham Greene's *Another Mexico* (*The Lawless Roads* in England)[1] as a major source for setting, character, and incident in *The Power and the Glory* and, more generally, as a statement of Greene's obsessions with divided loyalty, frontiers, and the invidious distinction between spiritual enlightenment and material progress. Perhaps because Greene obviously set out to write a travel book that was as much an exploration of the self as of another country, the book has retained a vitality—and a commercial viability—shared by few of the many travel books written by his contemporaries.[2] In contrast, Evelyn Waugh's *Mexico: An Object Lesson* (*Robbery Under Law: The Mexican Object Lesson* in England)[3] is cited even by experts largely for Waugh's statement of his credo as a conservative or as evidence of his xenophobia, snobbery, and reactionary politics, and Waugh himself, choosing material from his travel books of the 1930's for a postwar anthology, was "content to leave in oblivion" a book that was more about politics than about travel.[4] However, the reputation

1. Graham Greene, *Another Mexico* (New York: Viking, 1968). References, to *AM*, are given parenthetically in the text.

2. Paul Fussell, *Abroad: British Literary Traveling Between the Wars* (New York and Oxford: Oxford University Press, 1980). This is the best and most thorough treatment of the subject.

3. Evelyn Waugh, *Mexico: An Object Lesson* (Boston: Little, Brown, 1939). References, to *M*, are given parenthetically in the text.

4. Evelyn Waugh, *When the Going Was Good* (Boston: Little, Brown, 1946), p. ix. Even in more personal travel books, Waugh took the position that "interior changes are the author's own property and not a marketable commodity." See his *Ninety Two Days* (New York: Farrar and Rinehart, 1934), p. 267.

of these books and of their authors seems to depend more on what they say than how they say it. If one examines the style and narrative strategies with which these two major novelists treat the same material, one can discover a good deal not only about technique but about the vision out of which and toward which the books were written.

Critics who examine the two books in any detail have commented on their obvious and important differences, especially in scope and purpose.[5] In quite practical terms, Greene provides a map and gives a detailed account of his movements from the Rio Grande to near the Guatemalan border during Lent and the Easter season of 1938, and the difficulties of his journey are central features of the book, as if discomfort and authenticity were, as often in Greene, indivisible. Engaged on a personal quest, Greene hopes to get to "the centre of something—if it was only of darkness and abandonment" (*AM*, 132). Although Waugh mentions some place names, it is difficult to discover from the book when he was there— August–September 1938—and where, except for the round of tourist spots near Mexico City, he actually went.[6] He is writing polemical history—political, economic, religious—not so much to prove that the oil companies were right as to prove that the Mexican government was high-handed and venal in expropriating them.

Of course, both men wrote as Catholic converts of some years' standing, but even here they illustrate the "measureless diversity" (*M*, 250) which the faith allows. As an apologist—in the strict sense of the term—for the persecuted Church in Mexico, Waugh emphasizes the order, coherence, and unity of the faith, conceding and minimizing abuses in its secular manifestation, emphasizing again and again, directly and by implication, "that it is only in material symbols that man is capable of recognizing the truth by which he lives" and that, in effect, the Incarnation redeems not only individ-

---

5. See Drewey Wayne Gunn, *American and British Writers in Mexico, 1556–1973* (Austin: University of Texas Press, 1974) and Ronald G. Walker, *Infernal Paradise: Mexico and the Modern English Novel* (Berkeley: University of California Press, 1978).
6. Waugh left no diary of the trip; only one letter from Mexico is printed in *Letters*. Christopher Sykes dates Waugh's departure from and return to England 27 July and 12 October in *Evelyn Waugh: A Biography* (Boston: Little, Brown, 1975), p. 183.

ual humans but the world they inhabit. "The world, the flesh, and the devil" do not trouble Waugh as they do Greene, whose appalled fascination with idiosyncratic definitions of all three is notorious and who, in this book as in *The Power and the Glory*, seems to believe that the only true church is, in an emphatic sense of the old term, the Church Suffering; the only true Catholic the fugitive; the only sincere Catholic in Mexico the Indian who has not been corrupted by the slackness and indifference of Spanish-Mexican civilization. The world of Waugh's faith is spacious, open, logical; Greene's is claustrophobic, decaying, full of violence, giving an occasional glimpse of a goodness that is far more inexplicable and mysterious than the evil that surrounds it. Waugh speaks of the Faith, "a habit of life and a social organization" (*M*, 293), Greene of faith which came "shapelessly, without dogma, a presence above a croquet lawn, something associated with violence, cruelty, evil across the way" (*AM*, 3).

The differences between the private and emotional Catholicism of Greene and the public and reasoned Catholicism of Waugh inform most of the comparable passages on religion in Mexico. Thus, in Greene's account of the convent in Puebla, now a Masonic museum, the description is personal, dramatic, almost cinematic. While the scene is not established dramatically, the betrayal and invasion of the convent are presented through the guide's account, with all the suspense of a mystery story, and the description of the convent's physical arrangements and furnishings is quite concrete, down to the "terribly idealized paintings of polite Carlo Dolci agonies." The guide—Greene characteristically avoids a group tour—gives him a rose "to remember those poor women by," and later Greene comes across it pressed in the pages of *Barchester Towers* (throughout his trip an emblem of soft, safe religious establishmentarianism) and reflects that the contrast between book and rose represents "all the immeasurable distance between two human minds" (*AM*, 252). Waugh treats the despoiling of the convent as an accomplished fact, calling the nuns "elderly" and "old," whereas Greene, terming them "middle-aged," emphasizes their continuing struggle to practice their vocations. The paintings, presumably those mentioned by Greene, are characterized much more generally as "a collection of very ugly paintings on velvet." Detached, though not physically, from the tour group, Waugh emphasizes the sense of the other tourists that they are committing a social gaffe because "they were prying into things with which their own lives had not contact" (*M*, 301). He is trying to influence "the general, indifferent, mildly well-intentioned, ill-informed people of America among whom public opinion is formed" (*M*, 251) in order to convince them that Catholics are not bizarre or sinister, and so he ends his argument by conceding that monastic life is suitable to very rare types while insisting that "To deny these people the right to live in the manner they require is a denial of religious liberty." His conclusion is logical; Greene's, in which the logic is implicit, is associational, subjective, and more effective.

In treating the massacre of Indians attempting to pray at the ruins of their church in Villahermosa, Greene is once again more consistently dramatic than Waugh:

They had no churches to open, but they set up a rough altar against the back wall of the one ruined church and prayed among the rubble. The soldiers came and opened fire and a few were killed—men, women, and children. (*AM*, 225)

There has lately been news of a peasants' rising in Villahermosa, the capital of Tabasco, where some peasants were murdered by troops while trying to say their prayers in the ruins of one of the churches Garrido had demolished. General Cardenas has promised redress. (*M*, 296–297)

Here the difference in context and purpose is even more instructive than in the accounts of the Puebla convent. Greene emphasizes the difference between the repressive regime in Tabasco and that in Chiapas, where a resolute priest might succeed in occupying a church and securing religious freedom for his people. Waugh exhibits no similar hope for resistance, as his final sentence demonstrates, and he contrasts this "illegal atrocity" with "illegal acts of clemency."

However, Waugh is sometimes more dramatic than Greene, as in the accounts of the popular uprising in Orizaba:

there had been no churches open in the state of Veracruz; Masses were said secretly—as in Chiapas—in private houses. Then one Sunday in Orizaba police agents followed a child who had been at Mass; she ran from them and they fired and killed her—one of those sudden inexplicable outbursts of brutality common in Mexico. Mexicans are fond of children, but some emanation from the evil Aztec soil seems suddenly to seize the brain like drunkenness, then the pistol comes out. The result of that death was an outburst of religious zeal all over Veracruz state; the peasants got into the churches in Veracruz itself and locked the doors and rang the bells; the police could do nothing, and the governor gave way—the churches were opened. The indignation was spent like an orgasm—sleep returned to Orizaba. (*AM*, 106–107)

The child had been to one of the houses in Orizaba where the police rightly believed Mass was being said; she came out alone, in the early morning, straight from her communion; she was not of those for whom the *New Statesman* would have us believe "freedom of worship continued unhampered;" the police followed her; she took fright and began to run. They shot her down in the street and returned to their quarters for their usual torpid Orizaba Sunday. But it proved different from other Sundays. News of the murder spread in the town, which was full of peasants in for the day. Suddenly they rose, broke open the doors of their church, barricaded themselves there and began ringing the bells. The C.T.M. bosses telegraphed helplessly to Mexico for advice. All over the state news spread of what had happened in Orizaba. Everywhere the churches were reoccupied. General Cardenas was just completing his plans for the confiscation of the oil properties; he dared not risk another *Cristero* uprising. The local governor was made to give way. The Bishop returned; the priests came out of hiding, and the people flocked to their churches. (*M*, 292–293)

Here Greene presents the uprising as a generalized event; Waugh has a much clearer sense of its having a beginning, development, and conclusion. Greene treats the murder as a result of topography—elsewhere he calls Mexico a place to die in, not live in (*AM*, 168)—and after finishing the tale is more impressed by the difficulty of finding an English-speaking priest to hear his own confession than in the fact that churches and priests are available. This, like Greene's consistently subjective, almost Berkeleyan view of geography, might give some pause to those who characterize him as humane. Waugh sees no hope for the Church in individual acts of heroism, which elsewhere he terms "spasmodic, spontaneous outbursts of indignation," or in the Catholic heritage of the country, termed "a wistful tenacity which, unsupported, must of its nature fail" (*M*, 305). He has a much clearer, if not more accurate, sense of the global political situation than does Greene, and considerably more hope in the political process, in which Greene has none at all.

The closest Greene and Waugh come to accord is in their descriptions of the shrine and legend of Our Lady of Guadalupe. Greene finds in the portrait of Our Lady "a grace and kindliness you will find nowhere in mortal Mexico"; Waugh finds the cathedral in which the portrait hangs "the one place in Mexico that never seemed noisy." Once again, however, the contexts differ widely: Greene places his account of the legend between a critical view of anti-Catholic superstition and a tolerant analysis of the "aristocratic skepticism" toward the shrine of an elderly Spanish lady of decayed fortune which implicitly contrasts with the simple, and pure, faith of the Indians who for Greene are the touchstones of true Christianity in Mexico and perhaps in the whole world. In contrast, Waugh uses the story as only part of an extended argument— against folklorists, scholars of comparative religion, and T. Phillip Terry, author of the travel book[7] excoriated throughout *Mexico*— in which he maintains that "the religion of the Spaniard was equally the religion of the Indian" (*M*, 272) and that this religion is true.

In general structure, the accounts are very similar: Juan Diego encounters the Virgin, who sends him to Bishop Zumarraga with a command to build a church on the spot; the bishop sends him away; the Virgin reappears and repeats the request; Zumarraga asks for a sign. The Virgin tells Diego to return the next day for his sign, but he fails to do so and avoids the site of the vision. The Virgin confronts him and tells him to pick roses in a barren place. He delivers the roses to the bishop and discovers on his serape the picture of the Virgin that now hangs at the shrine. The only major difference between these accounts and that quoted in *Terry's Guide to Mexico* is that Greene and Waugh mention Diego's request, during the second interview with the Virgin, that a more important messenger be sent.

Another superficial similarity between Waugh and Greene is the

7. T. Phillip Terry, *Terry's Guide to Mexico* (Hingham, Mass.: G. H. Ellis Co., 1940). The last copyright date in this edition is 1938.

length of the accounts: just under three pages each. This is deceptive, for Waugh's description of the shrine, account of the legend,
defense of Bishop Zumarraga against charges that he destroyed Aztec manuscripts (a charge Greene does not question), analysis of the
painting, and refutation and criticism of Terry's snobbish treatment
of the poor Indians who come to worship cover fifteen pages, while
Greene's visit to Guadalupe covers just over five. These contextual
differences account for some of the differences in narrative technique. Greene interpolates into his narrative two expository paragraphs discussing the importance of the Virgin's appearing to an
Indian and with the complexion and features of an Indian woman,
and in two other paragraphs he interpolates material identifying
Zumarraga and comparing Zumarraga's reaction with that of the
bishop of San Luis Potosí, who refused to issue the Papal Encyclical
De Rerum Novarum. Waugh presents his story with very little inter-
ruption, reserving his commentary for later.

More remarkable than these superficial differences are those in
focus, selection, emphasis, and style. Greene emphasizes certain aspects of the story, notably the Virgin's calling Diego "My son" at a
time when it was inconvenient for most Spaniards to regard the
conquered people as human.

The Bishop, of course, disbelieved Diego. Priests and Bishops are human—they share some of the prejudices of their nation and time. "My
son" may have stuck even in the Bishop's throat—however much in theory
he believed in his kinship with the Indian. . . . (*AM,* 97)

After the second request, "the Bishop demanded—with not unnatural caution—a sign." Diego's responses are given only during the
hiatus between the third and fourth apparitions; for most of
Greene's story he serves as a messenger from the Virgin to the
Bishop, who is, if not the central character, of central importance
to Greene because skeptical and aristocratic authority has been
forced to acknowledge a Virgin who "claimed a church where she
might love her Indians and guard them—from the Spanish conqueror. The legend gave the Indian self-respect; it gave him a hold
over his conqueror; it was a liberating, not an enslaving legend"
(*AM,* 97).

The contrast in focus is evident in the beginnings of the two accounts. For Greene, Diego is an actor, but not an agent:

on December 9, 1531, an Indian peasant, Juan Diego, was climbing Te-payac hill, at the foot of which the shrine now stands. The Virgin appeared to him among the rocks—there was music suddenly and light—she called him "my son" and told him to carry a message to Bishop Zumarraga that he was to build a shrine on that spot where she might watch and love the Indians. (*AM*, 96)

For Waugh, Diego's point of view is paramount, and he spends a paragraph identifying him, revealing what happened to him after the miracle, classifying him as "typical of the thousands of Indians who had accepted the conquerors' religion," and telling us where he was going on this occasion. Only then does Waugh begin the action:

Following the track across the desolate area where the town of Guadalupe now stands, passing, it is likely, the ruins where in youth he had paid homage to the native mother-goddess, he suddenly saw the place trans-fused with unfamiliar light and colour; there was the sound of music and, on a rock above him, he saw a woman, a fellow Indian in colour and type, who called him to her, addressed him as her son, told him that she was Mary and that she wished a church to be built on the spot where she was standing. He was to tell this to the Bishop. (*M*, 270)

The apparition of Waugh's Virgin is more dramatic—first light, then color, then a woman. In fact, Waugh consistently has a sense of scene, even of dialogue, far stronger than Greene's. When the Virgin finally gives Diego the sign, Greene writes, "she told him his uncle was already well and directed him to go to the top of the hill to gather roses from the rocks and take them to the Bishop" (*AM*, 99). Waugh's units of utterance are shorter, phrased like dramatic speech, with a sense of interchange even where none is marked:

He told her about his uncle being ill. She knew all about it; he would get well, she said; Diego had another duty to perform. He must take his sign to the Bishop. Above where they stood the rocks rose in a sharp, barren hill; The Lady told him to climb there and pick roses. (*M*, 271)

Throughout the rest of Waugh's account Diego's point of view dominates, and it is a very human, almost comic point of view.

Greene thinks that Diego did not return for the sign because "he forgot—or more likely the immediate *fact* of the dying man seemed more important, more true, than a vision he may himself have discounted when the Bishop talked, full of the wisdom and slowness and sane skepticism of the church authority" (*AM*, 98). Waugh assumes that "in Diego's slow, peasant mind suspicions began to arise. He was getting mixed up in affairs that were beyond his capacity. Besides, his uncle was ill" (*M*, 271). Ill—not dying—and a very convenient and human rationalization for not doing something disquieting. Later, with the roses in his serape, Waugh's Diego "trudged off again, back to the suspicious Bishop and spilt the flowers at his feet. He may have thought, on the road, that it was not much of a sign; after all, there was only his word for it that they came from the desert" (*M*, 271). This Diego is akin to Sancho Panza, a slow and earthy figure touched by a grace that is mysterious but far from solemn.

Waugh's other human character, Zumarraga, is seen far more consistently than Greene's. At first Greene appears to blame Zumarraga for his skepticism; then his request for a sign is termed natural. Waugh's Zumarraga is at first not mentioned directly, for when Diego brings his first message, "He was received with the skepticism that such tales usually arouse in the higher clergy, and sent away"—rightly, we are to assume. In describing the second visit, Waugh gives Zumarraga's response—it may be witchcraft; he has Diego followed—but Diego disappears, without knowing he has done so, from the view of the agents. Near the end of the story, in the passage already quoted, Waugh emphasizes Diego's, not the Bishop's, skepticism. Perhaps the difference in the two accounts results from Greene's desire to demonstrate that the Indian is different from and better than the Spaniards while Waugh seeks to portray the Indian as entirely human but in no way exceptional.

The concluding sentences of the two accounts imply some of this contrast:

He wrapped the roses in his serape and when he opened it to give the roses to the Bishop, the image of the Virgin was there stamped on the cloth, just as it hangs above the altar today. (*AM*, 99) he did as he was told and revealed not only the roses but a picture of his Lady, Our Lady, imprinted on the *sarape*. That is the picture which now hangs over the high altar at Guadalupe. (*M*, 271)

Greene's statement implies continuity, and he introduces Senora B. to show that Spanish skepticism has not been dispelled in four hundred years. Waugh emphasizes that it is "Our Lady," the mother of all men, and by beginning a new sentence, he gives the idea a dramatic prominence in time and setting that it does not have in Greene.

The greatest differences between *Another Mexico* and *Mexico: An Object Lesson* cannot be illustrated by short quotations or even by a discussion of differences in the motives for which they were written. It is true that Waugh was paid by an oil company to write a book defending its interests,[8] but Greene "was commissioned to write a book on the religious situation."[9] Perhaps Waugh was correct in saying of professional authors "that though most of us would not write except for money, we would not write any differently for more money,"[10] and in his case the views on religion would hardly have been of much concern to the oil company. Perhaps the distinction lies not in external motives but in the vision that informed the work. Waugh argued in his review of *Another Mexico* that "Mr. Greene is . . . an Augustinian Christian, a believer of the dark ages of Mediterranean decadence when the barbarians were pressing along the frontiers and the City of God seemed yearly more remote and unattainable. He abominates the picturesque and the eccentric . . ." (*EAR*, 249). In fact, as Waugh notes, Greene dislikes England as much as he does Mexico; at the end of *Another Mexico* he comes very near to welcoming the apocalyptic violence of a bombing raid to cleanse England of its sterile lusts and empty greed. Earlier he has condemned Taxco as "a colony for escapists with their twisted sexuality and hopeless freedom" (*AM*,

---

8. Martin Stannard, *Evelyn Waugh: The Early Years 1903–1939* (New York: W. W. Norton, 1987), pp. 478–483, gives an unsympathetic account of the trip and book. For details about the arrangements, see *Catalogue*, E240–372, passim.

9. Graham Greene, *The Lawless Roads* (London: William Heinemann & The Bodley Head, 1978), p. ix, Note to Third Edition.

10. *Ninety Two Days*, p. 5.

258), while Waugh, taking a lighter view as social historian, terms the Anglo expatriates "the last survivors of the international Bohemianism of the '20's—the army of semi-intellectual good-timers who once overran Europe . . . providing material for unnumbered light novels" (*M*, 51). Elsewhere he calls these people "nostalgic for the Classical-Christian culture from which they remotely spring, which they can find transplanted, transformed in part but still recognizable, in Mexico" (*M*, 13). To an extent, Waugh shares this view, which accounts not only for his visual pleasure in Mexican landscape and architecture but for the concept of internationalism which underlies his support of the Church as social force and the idea of international law which forms the basic premise in his argument against expropriation. His real point, however, is that civilization based on these premises is valuable and can, with effort, be preserved. For Greene, however, "the world, one begins to feel, has been used up—we can only repeat our vices and our virtues" (*AM*, 41). No wonder he has little hope and less interest in worldly processes.

Another Mexico is a better book than *Mexico*, and it is characteristic of Greene's work in ways that *Mexico* is not of Waugh's, but it is not necessarily written from a better or more generous premise, and by comparing the two we can see more clearly the limitations and strengths of each author. In these two books, Waugh is not very attractive as a special pleader for oil interests, but he does project a vision more humane and less snobbish than is generally assumed. Greene may sympathize with the dispossessed and suffering, but he is oddly indifferent or hostile to those who try to assist them. Waugh's limitations are intellectual. As Donat Gallagher observes of Waugh's nonfiction, Waugh was unable "to see beyond a clear, logical point of view once it has been conceived" and unable "to enter imaginatively into an opposing viewpoint." [11] However, this limitation does not control his way of seeing or his essential style, and his sympathies as a writer take odd and surprising turns. In contrast, Greene as a thinker seems to be on the side of the angels— or at least of the intelligentsia, opposing the things they oppose

11. Donat S. Gallagher, Preface, *EAR*, p. xix.

when they are at moral attention, and he more consistently subor-
dinates his style to his point of view, so that his narratives are more
powerful, and more narrow, than those of Waugh. Greene can impress us, but he cannot really surprise us. Waugh's opinions can
often annoy us, but his powers of style and observation sometimes
undercut those opinions to create a vision almost independent of
the autobiographical viewpoint. It may seem odd to argue that
Waugh seems fresher to some readers than does Greene because he
loves his material and sees it more humanely, but that is what the
evidence of style would seem to show.

CHAPTER 13

Recovering the Past:
Postwar First-Person Novels

Even if labels like "the Edwardian period" or "the Auden Age" are wrong—certainly they are incomplete—they give students at all levels a place to start. The difficulty of dealing with the 1940's is obvious. In the first place, it is not, except chronologically, a unit at all because the end of the war broke it in half. In the second place, no figure or school dominated the scene in England or America. Older writers such as Hemingway and Faulkner were struggling with materials and methods; younger writers did not really begin to produce significant work until late in the decade. Thematically, existential and neoorthodox writers of various persuasions seemed in conflict with each other. Technically, writers seemed content to modify or conventionalize the innovations of the great modernists. If literary historians have not been confused by this decade, it is because most have ignored even the postwar period or have presented rather flat summaries of plots and themes. However, it seems possible to discover a method by which to approach the problem, if not to solve it. Not surprisingly, that is the inductive method, and I offer not a label or an overview of the period or even a set of boundaries within which to confine a few authors but a way of clearing a little underbrush and giving us a chance to take our bearings.

The three novels I shall discuss are Evelyn Waugh's *Brideshead Revisited*, Robert Penn Warren's *All the King's Men*, and Graham Greene's *The End of the Affair*.[1] Any thread of external evidence

---

1. Editions cited are *Brideshead Revisited* (Boston: Little, Brown, 1945); *All the King's Men* (New York: Bantam Books; first edition published 1946); *The End of the*

linking them is rather tenuous. The authors were born within eighteen months of each other; all attended Oxford. Apparently neither Englishman read Warren's novel and he read neither of theirs. Waugh and Warren, who never met and whom no one has ever bothered to compare, have more in common thematically and even formally than Waugh and Greene, who used to be grouped as Leading Catholic Novelists and who were friendly enough to disagree on what some would think irrevocably divisive social and theological issues. Furthermore, the settings and subjects are quite diverse: Waugh's centering primarily in the circles of privilege in England during the 1920's and 1930's; Warren's based in a seamy and steamy political milieu based on that of Huey Long; Greene's confined to London during and just after World War II.

If we turn from surface disparity to a text, however, we can see that Waugh, at least, thought that a generalization could be made. Near the end of *Sword of Honour*, he describes Major Ludovic's preposterous novel *The Death Wish* as very much "in the movement," not so much because of its subject or even its theme but because of its congruence with the contemporary imagination:

half a dozen other English writers, averting themselves sickly from privations of war and apprehensions of the social consequences of the peace, were even then severally and secretly . . . composing books which would turn from the drab alleys of the thirties into the odorous gardens of a recent past transformed and illuminated by disordered memory and imagination.[2]

Here and elsewhere, Waugh is making very unflattering inferences about *Brideshead Revisited*, which he had come to see as deeply flawed in style and execution.[3]

But if the passage can be regarded as description rather than parody, it offers several categories in which to place the novels I have chosen. In diverse ways, all three are less concerned to resolve a plot or a problem than to show that the action is only a prelude to

---

Affair (Harmondsworth: Penguin; reproduces the text of the Viking, first U. S. edition of 1951).

2. *Sword of Honour* (London: Chapman & Hall, 1965), p. 737.

3. See *Brideshead Revisited* (London: Chapman & Hall, 1960), Preface, and Graham Greene, *Ways of Escape* (New York: Simon and Schuster, 1980), p. 118, for Waugh's letter apologizing for the excesses of the novel.

further action, unpresented and unresolved. All three turn inward rather than outward, yet all three turn away from the *Bildungsro-man's* personal focus to larger issues. And all three represent their author's first sustained attempt to write first-person narrative.

Both *Brideshead* and *All the King's Men* are retrospective accounts of the narrator's and the society's careers during the 1920's and 1930's which attempt to summarize and judge those actions in preparation for an indefinite future. Charles Ryder, Waugh's narrator, is a British army captain and former architectural painter who, from the vantage point of professional disillusionment in 1942, recounts his fascination of twenty years' standing with the aristocratic Flyte family and their country seat, Brideshead Castle; the dispersal of the family by drink, death, religious scruple, and war; and the military's desecration of the mansion and its grounds. At the end of the novel, however, the reopening of the Roman Catholic chapel, signaled by the shining of "a beaten-copper lamp of deplorable design" (351), offers Ryder hope for the future of human souls if not of man-made structures.

In *All the King's Men*, Jack Burden—déclassé southern aristocrat, former student of history, newspaperman, and researcher for un-scrupulous upcountry political boss Willie Stark—tells from the vantage point of 1939 the intricate story of the involvement of his world with Willie's, of ideals with facts, of aspirations with neces-sity, and, not at all incidentally, of the bastardies, murders, and suicides revealed or brought to pass by these complex involve-ments. At the end, Jack, reunited with his childhood love, prepares to leave the home of his aristocratic heritage and reenter politics on a higher and presumably more hopeful level.

Greene's novel is less concerned with social and political affairs than Warren's and even Waugh's. In fact, most critics read *The End of the Affair* as a complicated variety of romantic triangle. This, though limited, is accurate: Maurice Bendrix, a novelist, meets Sarah, beautiful and unsatisfied wife of Henry Miles, a bland civil servant. He has an extended affair with her; she inexplicably leaves him; and, prompted by the concern of Henry (who has known nothing of the affair), he searches for the identity of his rival. That rival, he discovers from her diary, is God: Sarah has vowed to leave

Bendrix, whom she thinks killed in a V–1 blast, if God will restore him to life. Believing that physical love can triumph over spiritual, Bendrix pursues Sarah through the rain. She sickens and dies, and inexplicable events—perhaps miracles—begin to occur. As the novel ends, Bendrix and Henry are living together, their humane peace and charity threatened only by the possibility that evidence of Sarah's heroic sanctity may erupt to destroy their uneasy secular calm and by Bendrix's reluctant acknowledgment that God's presence may demand a leap not just of faith—he has, even before the end of the novel, made that—but into a love which would shatter and transform him.

It is easier to outline the element of story (using E. M. Forster's sense of the series of events) in the first two novels because they are social and panoramic; both contain potential romans-fleuves in the context of personal narratives. The narrators must therefore be representative enough to embody the times and capable enough of reflection and change to escape from those times. As a result, these novels are also quite similar in Forster's sense of plot as explaining why and how rather than simply what happens. In both cases, the moral and to some extent the social education of the narrator is central.

Jack Burden moves downward from the idyllic and rather static world of Burden's Landing to ally himself with the new and powerful forces represented by Willie Stark. Plagued by his simultaneous attraction to and revulsion against his beautiful, hypergamous mother, who seems incapable of love, and his ineffectual and absent father, and by his unconsummated love affair with Anne Stanton (from another aristocratic family), he takes refuge in various philosophical evasions. The first, Idealism, posits that if one does not perceive an object or event, it does not exist. The second, a mechanistic philosophy which Jack labels The Great Twitch, totally negates responsibility. Finally, after experiencing the death of his real father, the resulting anguish of his mother, and the deaths of the two men closest to him, he comes to accept the moral viewpoint, learned in part from his historical research, that all actions have definite but incalculable consequences, that man can make meaningful choices.

Whereas Burden is an insider trying to get out, Charles Ryder is a member of the intellectual English middle class trying to get in. At Oxford with Sebastian Flyte he lives for a time in a pastoral world of romantic friendship in which the skull of "Et in Arcadia ego" seems for a time merely decorative. Witnessing the decay of Sebastian into alcoholism, Ryder turns to painting, thinking to live in the world of the five senses and to cultivate his art, recording by it the mansions and country houses soon to be destroyed and replaced by sordid modern buildings. This course leads him to spiritual and artistic dessication from which he is temporarily rescued by the love of Julia, Sebastian's sister, who gives him a new subject and the possibility of inheriting Brideshead Castle and living there in isolation from a crude modern world represented in part by his wife and by Julia's husband. But the Flytes are Catholics, and the deathbed repentance of her father leads Julia to renounce Charles in order to return to the Church. Separated from those he loves, Ryder at first seems arid and desolate, but the novel's epilogue reveals that he has turned from secular to divine love and has found not only a measure of peace and joy with which to face the future but a means of understanding and accepting his past.

Like Burden and Ryder, Bendrix comes to find his professional life not only unsatisfying but stultifying. He has become so hardened a novelist that he has reduced his work to a pattern and seeks acquaintance with Sarah because he is gathering material. Neither Burden nor Ryder is exactly comfortable with his life or work in the body of his story, but neither has Bendrix's sense of anguish at being forced out of old ways of working or perceives as deeply as he does change or conversion as a threat.[4]

Bendrix is more threatened by change than Ryder or Burden because he is more isolated than they, emotionally and even physically. His furnished room is superficially like Jack's hotel room, but Jack has fled from a bad marriage and from a social background to the room as welcome if empty refuge, and though the room is an

---

4. For an extended discussion of the novel as a problem of narrative technique, see my "The Struggle with Genre in *The End of the Affair*," *Genre*, 18 (Winter 1985), 397–411. The current discussion draws material from this article but does not reproduce it.

emblem of his life, it does not *contain* him as Bendrix's does. Ryder has no real home: one of the novel's most memorable episodes presents his father's attempt to dislodge him, and when, after a ten-year gap, he is shown as an adult, he has been wandering and homeless for two years. At the end of the novel, he observes that he is "homeless, childless, middle-aged, loveless" (350).

Yet these two characters have an imaginative if not a physical context which Bendrix lacks. He mentions his parents only once, as having given him a first name which no one uses (5); he has no relations, however ridiculous or embarrassing. At the end of the novel, although Bendrix has moved into Henry Miles' house and finds with him a kind of companionship, he is rather like an inverted Abou ben Adam, who loves his fellow man so that he won't have to love God. He has the possibility of community with those who have loved and been touched by Sarah, but while he can, like a jealous lover, conceive of Sarah with God in heaven, he cannot imagine a communion of saints. As Evelyn Waugh observes, "Mr. Greene's characters never know anyone. Their intense, lonely lives admit of professional acquaintances, lovers and sometimes a single child but they are never seen as having ramifications of friendship, cousinhood and purely social familiarity. Their actions are performed under the solitary eye of God."[5]

Whereas in Greene the absence of family ties reveals Bendrix's spiritual and psychological problems, for Waugh and Warren the breach of those ties, seen as normal if unattainable, is symptomatic of larger social problems. Both narrators are conscious of being emotional if not legal orphans. Ryder's mother died while serving with the Red Cross in World War I; his father, taking refuge in antiquarian collecting, isolates himself from all human contact and explicitly refuses to provide his son with moral or even social guidance. Jack Burden's legal father has abandoned his family, his antebellum house, and the values by which he had lived to hide from the "foulness" he finds in the modern world in a store-front mission, and while he offers moral advice in the most embarrassing

5. *EAR*, 550. Waugh is contrasting Greene's novels with those of Anthony Powell, which operate purely on the social plane.

kind of pamphlets, Jack is unable to connect his father's pieties to contemporary problems. His mother rejects the maternal role in favor of the illusion of youth and a series of husbands who help her to maintain it.

Because they lack a sense of family, both narrators feel, as Ryder puts it, "rather curious about people's families—you see, it's not a thing I know about" (39), and both attach themselves to substitute families. Ironically, the younger members of these surrogate groups have little more stability than the narrators. Both Friends of the Narrator's Youth (Warren's labels invite capitals) complement aspects of the narrators. Adam Stanton has a sense of direction which Burden lacks; Sebastian Flyte has an insouciance and an instinctive taste which offset Ryder's early training. But Adam and Sebastian fail because the one is too rigid, too bound by dead social codes, to live in the modern world (in this respect resembling Sebastian's elder brother, Lord Brideshead) and the other is "in love with his own childhood" (103) and in flight from adult responsibility.

Each brother figure has a sister who replaces him as focus of the narrator's love, and these women not only link the narrators imaginatively with past social and moral values (and potentially could do so through marriage), but initially fail to sustain those values. Anne Stanton and Julia Flyte enter liaisons with powerful masculine representatives of the modern world and thus abandon their respective heritages. In compensation, Burden more consciously than Ryder, both narrators marry women who are described as soulless sexual and social machines from whom their husbands retreat in disgust to the arms of the more traditionally feminine and cultured sister figures.

Apparently feminine but unsatisfactory or entirely absent are mother figures in the substitute families. In *All the King's Men*, Mrs. Stanton is dead (and Governor Stanton is a lay figure in the sentimental Electra tableau of Burden's imagining); Judge Irwin is widowed, his deceased wife present in the novel only in the few lines of a document and in an anecdote. In *Brideshead*, Lady Marchmain's whimsical charm captivates many of the minor characters, but her taste—symbolized by her sitting room, which represents "the intimate modern world" in contrast to the rest of her (absent) husband's house, which has "the august, masculine atmosphere of a better age" (138)—and the rigidity and simplicity of her moral judgments alienate or help to destroy her husband and most of her children. Both Mrs. Burden and Lady Marchmain are in a sense disruptive intruders in the worlds into which they marry: the former comes from an Arkansas sawmill to the big white house by the sea but, as far as Jack can see, possesses neither the honor demanded by the position nor the passion which would justify its breach. Lady Marchmain moves from the relatively pinched and austere world of aristocratic English Catholics to the Baroque splendors of Brideshead Castle. Neither is fulfilled by or in her new role; neither supports the male values which define it.

At the other extreme are the real maternal figures: Warren's Lucy Stark, the governor's wife, tends her husband's memory and the bastard who may not even be her dead son's; Waugh's Nanny Hawkins waits in an empty nursery for her scattered charges to return. Anything but glamorous or charming, each represents simple (some would say simpleminded) values of right belief and action. Each is initially presented in partly comic terms, Lucy presiding over a dinner table like a chief engineer aboard ship, Nanny totally miscomprehending the actual lives of her former charges. But the attitudes toward them grow more complex, and on the narrators' final visits, the simple pieties and their ends seem desirable and, with modifications for the narrator's age and life-style, attainable in contrast to the muddle of the previous action. The piety of the two women and their fidelity, Lucy's to the idea of Willie as a great man and Nanny's to the idea of the family as a functioning social (and spiritual) unit, occasion the narrator's turn toward the future with the fruits of memory and the seeds of new hope.

However, in the context of each novel these values seem for a long time unattractive because they are passive and feminine, serving to criticize or temper but not to replace masculine virtues. (These dichotomies are the authors'; their sexism is engrained, probably unconscious, and entirely symptomatic of the period.)

In the narrative present of the two novels, the best examples of these virtues exist only in documents. Ryder comprehends the qualities of Lady Marchmain's three brothers, exterminated in the war with a whole way of life, but he cannot even begin to emulate them and they are not invoked in the novel's resolution. In contrast, Jack fails to understand the meaning of Cass Mastern's acceptance of moral responsibility during most of his narrative, but at the end he is able to put it into the context of all that he has experienced.

In the foreground of the narrative, Warren's novel embodies male virtue most obviously in Judge Irwin, who, Jack says, "taught me to shoot and taught me to write and read history to me from leather-bound books in the big study in his house. After Ellis Burden went away he was more of a father to me than those men who had married my mother and come to live in Ellis Burden's house. And the Judge was a man" (40). Corresponding to the Judge in *Brideshead* is Lord Marchmain, who represents the aristocratic traditions of valor (both men served, though overage, in World War I), irony, taste, and detachment—qualities lacking in the elder Ryder, whose character and style of life are carefully juxtaposed with those of Lord Marchmain.

Jack Burden has another father figure, Willie Stark, who teaches Jack both the pleasures of and need for action in populist politics but whose pragmatic values and vulgar tastes produce on the personal level a son actuated by the basest and most selfish motives which destroy him just as surely as perverted aristocratic ideals do Adam Stanton. By the definition applied to Judge Stanton, Willie is not "a man," but he is human, and to Warren political action is meaningful. In *Brideshead*, Rex Mottram is Willie's counterpart: he seduces the traditional, idealized female without understanding her qualities, and he is involved in politics. But whereas Willie is human, Rex "wasn't a complete human being at all. . . . he was something absolutely modern and up-to-date that only this ghastly age could produce. A tiny bit of a man pretending he was the whole" (200). Rex has no issue, physically or politically: his daughter is stillborn and his politics (and all politics, Waugh implies) are barren maneuverings for advantage.

For both Waugh and Warren, the deaths of the father figures carry major symbolic weight, and in each case, the dying man embodies a partial or incomplete good reaching toward the good itself. Judge Irwin's death is almost Roman: he shoots himself in the heart (not the head—considerable point is made of this) rather than reveal that he is Jack's natural father and rather than have his long-forgotten corruption by bribery revealed. News of his death causes Jack's mother to exhibit genuine feeling for the first time in Jack's experience. Her emotion leads to her eventual recognition of her true self and to her reconciliation with Jack. The knowledge of his paternity sustains Jack, for he has "swapped the good, weak father for the evil, strong one" (354) who could take action and live in the world. The other father figure, Willie, teaches Jack not about hunting, ancient weapons, and history but about the nature of man as a political animal. Yet as he is dying Willie repents of his success as a mere politician and reiterates the dream that "It might have been all different" (400)—that is, that he might have been Willie Stark the statesman and visionary instead of becoming defined by his title, Boss. This vision, which Lucy Stark reiterates, sustains Jack on the political level as his knowledge about the Judge and his mother and his new understanding of his legal father sustain him on the personal level. In the end, Jack attempts to blend the moral legacies of his three fathers—action, thought, and belief—in political activity.

Because Charles Ryder must make an act of faith rather than attempt external action, the death of Lord Marchmain, though elaborately described, is dramatically simpler than anything in Warren. Just before he dies, Lord Marchmain acknowledges and accepts the grace of God and returns to the Roman Catholic faith he had first embraced for his wife's sake. But he does not capitulate to the feminine and fanciful. His act of acceptance, the sign of the cross, undercuts the frilly pieties of his wife, the icy theology of his eldest son, and his own elaborate irony. It gives, though Waugh does not emphasize the fact, Ryder a pattern of masculine response to religious faith.

In fact, this episode functions much as the judge's death does in Warren's novel. Women may be sources of moral teaching or romantic aspiration or temptation, but they cannot serve as useful examples because they are not in the world. The heroines of these novels are essentially passive, apparently incapable of fulfillment without a man. The same thing is basically true of the false mother figures. That is, both act, but their actions produce disastrous results because their mates have not been satisfactory; because they must therefore attempt to act independently; and because their sons, without a domestic male model, are warped by the excess or dislocation of maternal attention. Lucy Stark and Nanny Hawkins serve by waiting and by reducing the complexity of mature experience literally to the nursery level. Feminine values are enduring but unavailing; male action is necessary but willful and potentially destructive. Both novelists search for ways in which to salvage masculine values rooted in the immediate secular past and to refurbish them by drawing on enduring values associated with women.

In *The End of the Affair*, Sarah Miles has a much more active role. Waugh noted in his review of the novel that Greene's earlier heroines had been "subhuman" but that Sarah was "consistently lovable" (*Month*, 6 September 1951; *EAR* 404, 405). More important, she tries and expects to find meaning in a relationship with a man. Like the other heroines, she fails to do so, but her struggle is more sustained and more wrenching than Julia's rather matter-of-fact return to her faith and Anne's moral collapse into the affair with Willie and physical collapse at the deaths of her lover and brother. It is also more convincing and more interesting.

At the end of the novel, Ryder has attained not a family but a community or, in theological terms, the Communion of Saints, and he is reconciled to the loss of Brideshead as literal and symbolic home by the relighting of the sanctuary lamp, the sign that God's purpose is continually being fulfilled through human struggle.[6] Jack Burden is able to leave Burden's Landing, though not the values it has come to represent, married to Anne and ready to join a new political organization.

For Waugh and Warren, though the struggle to attain justice or

6. Waugh originally titled the novel, or perhaps its first section, "A Household of the Faith" in the manuscript version, now at the Humanities Research Center, University of Texas-Austin. Though he abandoned the title, he kept the theme, though in practice he may have restricted the term too narrowly to Brideshead and its inhabitants.

sanctity will continue, the major action is resolved. As in the *Bil-dungsroman*, the central character discovers a mode of thinking and behaving in which his true self can be realized and in which he can rest. There is a real sense of resolution of plot and of emotional release at the end of both novels. In Greene's ending, however, the terms of the struggle have just been defined clearly, and while it is possible to imagine Bendrix's ultimate surrender of his old self, the ending is not positive but negative, not reconciliatory but defiant.

Roland Barthes asks, "If there is no longer a Father, why tell stories? . . . Isn't storytelling always a way of searching for one's origin, speaking one's conflicts with the Law, entering into the dialectic of tenderness and hatred?"[7] Like Barthes, Graham Greene passes beyond literal or symbolic fathers to *the* Father, and his novel seems to us more modern, or postmodern, because it presents overtly the struggle between the storyteller and the form as well as the struggle between lower- and uppercase creators—and refuses to resolve either.

Yet in one way the novels have the same resolution: having submitted to or recognized the authority of tradition or of God, the characters are effectively neutered. Bendrix and Sarah are unable to enjoy physical love, and Bendrix turns to Henry for platonic companionship. Although there is no reason why Ryder and Julia might not eventually be married even under the stricter Canon Law of 1944—her previous marriage is not recognized by the Church; no information is given about the validity of his—Waugh did not raise the possibility and in fact explicitly forbade this kind of resolution in any movie of the film. Perhaps, in making the pair spiritual brother and sister, Waugh was forestalling the possibility of a kind of incest. And while Jack and Anne do marry, the impression given in the novel is that the union is due more to inertia than to passion, and Jack's mother must realize that she is old and therefore sexless in order to be forgiven. The Catholic novelists seem to insist on thoroughly conventional marriage or none at all, and though Warren allows his erring characters to wed, he does so rather per-

7. *The Pleasure of the Text*, trans. Richard Miller (New York: Hill and Wang, 1975), p. 47.

functorily. While it would be ridiculous to generalize from only three instances, social historians and feminist critics might be able to expand on this very tentative generalization.

The more interesting literary issue is the formal solution which all three writers chose: retrospective first-person narrative. To the student of literary history, especially the history of literary form, the most interesting question is why these writers chose to use for the first time this particular form, and why they chose it not just in their personal and professional lives but in this literary situation.

Warren's account is superficially the clearest. His story began as a verse drama "in 1938, in the shade of an olive tree by a wheat field near Perugia" and consequently was "concerned more with the myth than with the fact, more with the symbolic than with the actual."[8] In the process of changing the story from myth to mimesis and from drama to fiction,

Burden got there by accident. He was only a sentence or two in the first version—the verse play from which the novel developed. . . . It turned out, in a way, that what he thought about the story was more important than the story itself. I suppose he became the narrator because he gave me the kind of interest I needed to write the novel. He made it possible for me to control it. He is an observer, but he is involved. . . .[9]

Greene apparently made his decision a priori: he felt sterile as a writer and chose to write this novel in first person as "an escape from the pattern" of his earlier fiction because it was "a method I had not tried."[10]

Waugh did not explain why he changed his mind and chose first-person narration either in *Work Suspended*, permanently interrupted by the outbreak of World War II, or in *Brideshead*, but it is clear that in both novels he was attempting to render a more complex re-

8. Robert Penn Warren, "*All the King's Men*: The Matrix of Experience," *Yale Review*, 533 (December 1963), 161–167; reprinted many times. The text cited is *Robert Penn Warren's* All the King's Men: *A Critical Handbook*, ed. Maurice Beebe and Leslie A. Field (Belmont: Wadsworth Publishing Company, 1966), p. 27.

9. Ralph Ellison and Eugene Walter, "The Art of Fiction XVIII: Robert Penn Warren," *Paris Review*, no. 16 (Spring–Summer 1957), 113–140; quoted from Beebe and Field, *Robert Penn Warren's* All the King's Men, p. 65.

10. *Ways of Escape* (New York: Simon and Schuster, 1980), pp. 141–143.

sponse to experience than in his earlier, more objective fiction. When he reviewed *The Heart of the Matter* he found that

the great change in this new adventure is the method of telling. For the first time there is a narrator; everything is seen through his eyes and with his limitations. Instead of an omniscient and impersonal recorder we have the chief character giving his distorted version; a narrator who is himself in course of evolution, whose real story is only beginning at the conclusion of the book, who is himself unaware of the fate we can dimly foresee for him. (*EAR*, 404–405)

Perhaps Waugh had been influenced in this criticism by his reading of Henry James; perhaps he thought it a more realistic way of rendering complexity, of man in relation to God, than his old objective method.

There seems to be no other external evidence, but it is possible to speculate about their motives. Both Greene and Waugh had earlier thought Somerset Maugham's use of first person too easy, "a contemptible practice," in Maugham's paraphrase of Waugh.[11] Maugham's narrator responded that "as we grow older we become more conscious of the complexity, incoherence, and unreasonableness of human beings," adding that "I should not be surprised to learn that with advancing years the novelist grows less and less inclined to describe more than his own experience has given him. The first person singular is a very useful device for that purpose."

Waugh and Warren were both forty-one when their first first-person novels were published; Greene was forty-seven when *The End of the Affair* appeared. To that extent, Maugham was accurate, though perhaps, as is not uncommon, matters were more complex than he realized. Conversely, matters may sometimes be less complex than Roland Barthes imagined, but his view of third-versus first-person narration offers a more intriguing perspective than Maugham's:

The "he" is a typical novelistic convention; like the narrative tense [preterit] it signifies and carries through the action of the novel; if the third

11. Maugham cites the source of Waugh's remark as the *Evening Standard*, but no bibliographer of Waugh has been able to find the source. Maugham's remarks are in fact an aside of the first person narrator in *Cakes and Ale* (Garden City: Doubleday, Doran, 1930), pp. 215–217.

person is absent, the novel is powerless to come into being, and even wills its own destruction.

In sophisticated work, however, "the 'I' takes its place beyond convention and attempts to destroy it. . . ."[12]

Barthes' third-person narration sounds remarkably like the work of "Bendrix the scribbler": "it attracts the conformist and the least dissatisfied" (as well as those who use convention for novelty's sake); "In any case, it is the sign of an intelligible pact between society and the author; but it is also, for the latter, the most important means he has of building the world as he chooses" (35–36).

Warren and Greene might agree with the concept, though Waugh would reject a Frenchman as quickly as he would a theorist, but in fact all three novelists turned to the first person in novels very similar in direction to, if for very different particular purposes than, those which Barthes describes. Warren discovered Burden as narrator because he needed him to make the narrative work. Both Greene and Waugh had grown weary of a fixed method; both had considerable reverence for the great novelists of the nineteenth century; both were by or near the end of the World War II in the process of rejecting the uncritical secular realism of their contemporaries. And both desired to break with a form which, in leaving out God, gave only a flattened and incomplete picture of the individual (*EAR*, 302). They chose first-person narration not just for its Jamesian-impressionist questioning of the classical novel's conception of reality but for the way in which it allowed them to break through the social veil, to allow for uncertainty, mystery, and the breaking of "the chain of cause and effect" (*EAR*, 57) which that form of the novel had imposed both by its plot and by its pragmatic ontology. At the same time, both writers—Waugh, as always, the more aggressively—resisted attempts to turn their novels into Catholic tracts in which the godly were always happy. They might adapt the structure and even the language of the hagiography, but they refused to abandon the texture and many of the techniques of the novel. In writing for a secular audience, they seemed to feel that

12. Roland Barthes, *Writing Degree Zero*, trans. Annette Lavers and Colin Smith (New York: Hill and Wang, 1968), p. 35.

both literary and apologetic strategy were best served by a skeptical narrator's struggling with material beyond the scope of his secular, modern techniques.

Ultimately, this fusion of genres proved unstable for both Waugh and Greene, while only specialists in southern American literature know what happened to Warren as a novelist. Waugh turned against *Brideshead Revisited*, parodying it in the feverishly romantic theme and lush language of Ludovic's preposterous *The Death Wish* (*Unconditional Surrender*, 1961). Never again did he use first person in his novels—one, *Helena* (1950), an overt hagiography. Greene continues to publish novels in first person, but the Catholic theme has become more and more attenuated.

However, a particular kind of literary experiment does not have the same kind of authority as a scientific one—even when it is successful. In fact, generic or cross-generic experiments are irreproducible. So are themes: the attempt to recover past values as a way of preparing for the future is obviously more important to Waugh and to Warren than it is to Greene, but Greene is really focusing more tightly on the same general situation. The attempt to judge the past and integrate it with a possible and valuable future was precisely the task undertaken not only by these novelists but by Arthur Miller in *All My Sons*, by Henry Green in *Back*, by the producers of scores of home-from-the-war Hollywood movies, and at least implicitly by most of the war novelists.

If the decade seems drab, sepia-toned rather than mauve, yellow, or red, it does so because the alternatives were retreat into nostalgia or fantasy or both—or acceptance of the rather grim orthodoxies of Roman Catholic moral theology or of existentialism. If the characteristic solutions of postwar, 1940's work are personal and provisional rather than social and determinative, readers as well as writers had learned to distrust wholistic solutions, to regard society and its institutions as mechanical and alterable frameworks within which they must move rather than as organic structures within which to live, and to attempt to preserve the personal past and to find redeeming value in its complexity (note the spider webs of motive and action in Warren's novel, the fishing thread by which God draws man to Him in Waugh's, and the sordid searching for sordid actions in Greene's), accepting, if at all, the cultural inheritance as part of a process rather than as a sacred object.

Out of seeming chaos, coherence; out of a muddled past, a possible though not necessarily lovely future; out of sin and violence, hope; out of destruction and despair, purpose. However conservative and even orthodox these patterns may seem to us, privileged by hindsight, they were not conventionally imposed in these novels, and in the first five years after the war, the tracing of the patterns filled a need for readers on several levels of sophistication.

CHAPTER 14

Love Among the Ruins: Text and Contexts

After the success of *Brideshead Revisited* and especially after Waugh's assertion in "Fan-Fare" that in the future his novels would "represent man more fully . . . in his relation to God" (*EAR*, 302), Waugh spent considerable energy for almost a decade in writing novellas (*Scott-King's Modern Europe*, *The Loved One*, and *Love Among the Ruins*) which ran directly counter to that promise. In doing so, he was not just reverting to what some critics thought of as his anarchic early manner. Instead, he was, consciously or not, working out a philosophical and ethical context less strictly doctrinal and more flexible in accounting for human conduct than that of *Brideshead* and thereby establishing a basis for his war trilogy. The case of *Love Among the Ruins* is particularly interesting because of its long gestation period, because of the care Waugh took to make it more than a mere joke at the expense of the Welfare State, and because of its generic and thematic relationship to the dystopias of two contemporaries whose work he knew and respected.

I

Like many novels set in the future, *Love Among the Ruins* is really about contemporary society, in this case Welfare State England, bleak and unlovely under the postwar austerity program instituted by Attlee's Labour government. The Festival of Britain in 1951 was intended to announce to the world that England had recovered in finances and morale, and a central feature of the exposition was the Dome of Discovery—which Waugh converts into the Dome of Security. After he finished the story, he took pains to have it published the day before the coronation of Queen Elizabeth II as a coronation present from a loyal though mischievous subject. This, he implied, was what Elizabeth was inheriting and promising to cherish and defend.

However, Waugh had a purpose underlying the tease, and, though disguised, that purpose is moral. More than a hint about its nature can be found in a controversy in 1943 with Dr. Marie Stopes over "Religion in State Schools." Dr. Stopes pointed to the higher percentage of juvenile delinquency among products of Roman Catholic schools than among those of other schools and deplored the use of tax money to subsidize institutions which produce social deviants. Waugh replied that he

was not brought up to regard the evasion of the police as the prime aim of education, nor has my subsequent observation of the world given me any reason to think that either the wickedest men or even the worst citizens are to be found in prison. The real enemies of society are sitting snug behind typewriters and microphones, pursuing their work of destruction amid popular applause. . . . No doubt by bringing my children up Catholics I am putting them in appreciable danger of imprisonment, but they must not reproach me with it. They belong to a church whose most illustrious figures in any age and country have suffered the extremities of the law. Moreover, sir, a regular perusal of your own pages gives me the impression that, if things go as you wish, by the time they are hardened in crime, gaols will have grown so congenial and the rest of the country so heavy with restraints, that they will have the laugh on their innocent old father whom a Protestant education keeps on the right side of the law.[1]

In 1953, the conceit of prisons more pleasant than the outside world flowered in *Love Among the Ruins*, but of course in a deeper sense the story grew out of Waugh's entire intellectual history. Inversion, he implies and had for twenty-five years implied in his fiction and stated in his nonfiction, is perversion, and its end is madness, destruction, death—or, what he feared far more than any of these, boredom. Boredom is largely an aesthetic rather than a moral consideration, but Waugh had read enough theology to know that, besides *accidia*, which is defined as "sadness in the face of spiritual good" and is allied to despair, there is a similar condi-

1. "Religion in State Schools," *New Statesman and Nation*, 26 (2 October 1943), 217, and (16 October 1943), 251. Stopes' letters appeared (25 September 1943), 202, and (9 October 1943), 233.

tion, common among people ignorant of the very existence of spiritual good and therefore outside the economy of salvation and damnation: "*pigritia*, plain slackness, which is a deflexion from, if not an outrage against, the divine order." Idleness and boredom led, he argued, to apathy, resentment, and "a sense of abandonment" (*EAR*, 573, 575).

Waugh's belief that Western civilization was in an advanced state of decay provided an ordering principle for his work and for his view of the world. His early experience with the change, privation, and decay brought to his own private universe by World War I was reinforced not only by ensuing events but by the cyclic theories of history he read at Lancing and Oxford. Like many of his immediate predecessors—James Joyce, William Butler Yeats, and F. Scott Fitzgerald among the best known—he had no difficulty in bringing his experience and theory to bear on the modern world. Sometimes the theme is mentioned overtly, as in the title of *Decline and Fall* or in the short story "Out of Depth," which dramatizes the English decline into barbarism and the rise to dominance of the black races. Sometimes it is less obvious, but like atmospheric pressure it is always present, a condition of the world in which his characters live and move.

Waugh and his characters found two ways of dealing with change and decay: counterattack and acceptance. The first method involves a political and ethical approach to modern ills. "The spirit of the age," he once wrote, "is the spirits of those who compose it and the stronger the expressions of discontent from prevailing fashion, the higher the possibility of diverting it from its ruinous course" (*EAR*, 583). For this purpose he wrote *Mexico: An Object Lesson* and other pronouncements which affirmed civilization as a difficult achievement "under constant assault" which "takes most of the energies of civilized man to keep going at all."[2] Acceptance of the modern world, on the other hand, involves what ultimately are spiritual values, not simply the long view of history but man and society considered under the aspect of eternity. Critics who accuse Waugh of cruelty and, more frequently, of nostalgic snobbery for

2. *Mexico: An Object Lesson* (Boston: Little, Brown, 1939), p. 337.

an aristocratic society, missed the importance of this distinction. Waugh might seem to long for the stable and ordered world of the past, but he knew that the society he desired "never existed in history nor ever will" (*EAR*, 583) and that "man is, by nature, an exile and will never be self-sufficient or complete on this earth" (*Mexico*, 21).

Tony Last's fate in *A Handful of Dust* demonstrated Waugh's awareness that attempts to preserve an old way of life for its own sake were futile, foolish, and sentimental, however touching they might be: hoping to find the embodiment of his Victorian Gothic dream, Tony stumbles into a microcosm of feudal society without God, based on force, slavery, and ties of blood. This basically spiritual theme is stated even more clearly in *Sword of Honour*, in which Guy Crouchback learns that "quantitative judgments don't apply"[3] and that, in his modest way, he must return good for evil. This is another way of saying that Waugh differed from other cyclical theorists because he was a Christian, specifically a Catholic: St. Augustine's "Here we have no continuing city" echoes through all of his novels, in which he admits and almost rejoices in secular disasters and defeats. Something of this spirit lies behind his denial that he was a satirist: satire, he said, depends on accepted social norms to induce shame in those who violate them. Amid the shameless chaos of the modern world, he maintained, the artist could only attempt "to create little independent systems of order of his own" and imitate the monks who preserved through the barbarian invasions the spark of learning (*EAR*, 304).

Belief in a divine order does not necessarily mean a solemn approach to experience. Waugh could see the contemporary world outside the confines of theological and moral perspectives as amusing in its aberrancy, and his lack of hope for the modern world made him less censorious than those who believed improvement possible. Like G. K. Chesterton, Joseph Conrad, Rudyard Kipling, and others, he did not assume that not to be good was automatically to be evil. Besides heaven and hell, Catholic theology pro-

---

3. *Sword of Honour* (London: Chapman & Hall, 1965), p. 546 and passim. The sentence is a refrain marking the stages of Guy Crouchback's movement toward charity.

vided limbo for those invincibly ignorant of the truth. Waugh's limbo could be a lively place, inhabited by characters like Captain Grimes, Basil Seal, Mr. Youkoumian, and Mr. Baldwin—so lively that Edmund Wilson argued convincingly that Waugh loved anarchic energy for its own sake and somewhat less persuasively that his attempts to subdue it to theological orthodoxy led to his decline as a novelist.[4]

Yet the early novels are filled with characters who fear that there will be nothing for them to do. John Beaver, the spiritless demivillain of *A Handful of Dust*, has no function in society, and neither does any of the other male characters. Beaver has no talents, but there are no meaningful careers open even to men like Basil Seal who have both talent and energy. In fact, much of the energy exhibited in Waugh's early novels is motion for its own sake or for the sake of destruction. Without vital connections to the society they inhabit, the characters must be wild particles like Basil or, like Adam Fenwick-Symes, suffer entropic loss of energy to their environment.

One significant exception to these generalizations can be found in *Black Mischief*, which demonstrates and in part celebrates the vitality of natives who live in a savage but coherent and traditional society. The Emperor Seth, wishing to modernize his empire, can only destroy; energetic, almost prelapsarian barbarism, like that of the Earl of Ngumo, seems far more vital and attractive. He also exhibits a lively sense of survival and even helps to mount a successful coup in defense of traditional values and his own prerogatives. But his candidate is hopelessly gaga and dies when the crown is placed on his head, and the resulting European occupation is dull and uniform. In *Love Among the Ruins*, the process has gone twenty-one years further. Programmed Dulness has reduced politics, art, private life, even dress, to gray and spiritless flatness. The slogan of Liberty, Equality, Fraternity had, in Waugh's view, been a will-o'-the-wisp which led to a slough of despond. For this slo-

4. Edmund Wilson, "Splendors and Miseries of Evelyn Waugh," *Classics and Commercials* (New York: Vintage, 1962), pp. 298–305. The essay, primarily a review of *Brideshead Revisited*, was first published in 1945.

gan he proposed to substitute "Liberty, Diversity, Privacy" in order
to foster the spirit as well as the body.

Confronted with a dull and mechanical world, some of Waugh's
heroes, such as Paul Pennyfeather and William Boot (both, like
Miles, victims of women), find in privacy their greatest good. Less
passive characters like Basil and Dennis Barlow seek diversity in
odd corners of the world and in even odder pursuits: revolutions, a
cannibal feast with one's mistress the main course, a job in a pet's
cemetery, and the impromptu cremation of the loved one. Basil and
Dennis both combat the modern world, but the women they deal
with are different: Basil's Prudence is silly, and Basil is attracted to
silly women because he can dominate them; Dennis is attracted to
Aimée Thanatogenos because, "sole Eve in a bustling hygienic
Eden, this girl was a decadent" with "a rich glint of lunacy" in her
eyes.[5] In fact, most of Waugh's heroes, active or passive, seek escape
or consolation in women. All, like Miles Plastic, are disappointed.

Denied any outlet, formed on no idea, given no goal, Miles Plastic becomes a pyromaniac, a scourge of the packing-case, sterile
world which shaped him. Like Aimée, only in destruction can he
assert and assuage the demands of his spirit. Like Waugh, he both
loves the past and hates it for what it has allowed the present to
become; like Waugh, he denies Browning's assertion in the nine-
teenth-century version of "Love Among the Ruins" and the implications of other romantic poetry that love can survive the ruins of
the civilization which fostered the very idea of romance.[6]

II

Waugh no doubt had a fairly clear idea of his general theme and
even of setting and situation when he began to write *Love Among
the Ruins*, but he had a good deal of trouble finding a way to embody them. In fact, though it would not be quite accurate to label

5. *The Loved One* (London: Chapman & Hall, 1958), p. 46. This, the Uniform
Edition, seems to be identical with the first English edition of 1948. The American
edition has significant variants from this text.

6. For a study of allusions and parody in the story, see Peter Miles, "Improving
Culture: The Politics of Illustration in Evelyn Waugh's 'Love Among the Ruins,'"
Trivium, 18 (May 1983), 7–38.

his postwar literary career as desultory, it is true that between 1946 and 1952 he tended to work far more tentatively and slowly than at any time since writing *Scoop*. *Helena* was in the works for almost four years, and though *Scott-King's Modern Europe*, *The Loved One*, and *Men at Arms* went fairly quickly, it took him just under three years to complete *Love Among the Ruins*.

Initially titled "A Pilgrim's Progress: A tale of the near future," the first draft of the story was finished by 3 October 1950 (*Catalogue*, E688). If the manuscript at the University of Texas represents this first draft,[7] it is obvious that Waugh retained the method he used for *The Loved One* and for his early novels: push through a first draft quickly and revise at leisure (*Diaries*, 680). It also seems obvious that he pushed more rapidly than he should have, for in the eleven pages and a fragment he introduces three major settings, two professions, a brief history of the future, and a shift to another country.

Waugh found the last part of the story much less satisfactory than the first (*Catalogue*, E689), and subsequent revisions confirmed his judgment: the first four manuscript pages are a very fair approximation of the final version's first chapter, but the rest was heavily revised and in some cases altered radically in plot. Even so, the manuscript embodies the essential satiric point of the story: the future, secularized and leveled according to socialist platforms of the 1930's and practices of the 1940's, will be sterile and boring beyond sane endurance.

To emphasize what had been destroyed, Waugh sets the opening scenes at a handsome country estate, first calling it Malfrey, then, rejecting the impulse to link his new story with *Put Out More Flags* (where Malfrey is the home of Barbara Seal Sothill and her aptly named husband) and altering the name to Mountjoy. Ironically, the mansion and its grounds, planned decades earlier, come to fruition for the benefit of prisoners. As he predicted in 1943, life in prison has been made far more comfortable than life outside. Miles Plastic, sent to Mountjoy for arson with the first group of prisoners, is

---

7. This manuscript, identified as A hereafter (and as A24a in the *Catalogue*), consists of eleven heavily corrected pages of legal-size paper.

about to be released as cured, much to his own discontent and that of Mr. Sweat, an old lag who has adjusted to the new penology but laments the insecurity of a system in which anyone can be discharged without warning. Miles' contribution to this and all dialogues is almost monosyllabic, for he is presented throughout as semiliterate, spiritually stunted, and capable only of vestigially human sentiment. The next morning, the Governor and the Minister of Welfare congratulate him as the first successful product of Mountjoy, inform him of his new job in the Euthanasia Service, and pose for publicity stills.

In this initial version, Miles spends a month at the Health Centre, whose activities are sketchily described; meets a girl whose beard is the result of Voluntary Sterilization; and, rendered completely inactive by a strike, walks to Mountjoy, burns it to the ground, and returns refreshed to the Centre. An emotional hangover follows, and his despondency attracts the bearded Pamela's sympathy. Their love flourishes, partly because her red beard reminds him of flames, but almost immediately Miles is summoned to the Ministry. Because he carries a picture of Pamela and promises to take it with him, the Regional Director, guilty of dereliction of duty in her case, assumes that Miles has been sent to inspect him and applies for Euthanasia as the second chapter ends.

The third chapter is a single scene in which the Minister of Welfare, his public relations staff, and the gruesome Miss Flower tell Miles of the plan to have him lecture throughout the country as evidence that the new penology is successful and to display the model of the new Mountjoy. Going beyond the recent Festival of Britain's architectural form, an Egg in a Box, this is a Box in an Egg. The staff rejects Miles' plan to marry Pamela, he their plan to marry him to Miss Flower, in a paired series of No's which conclude the chapter.

This is almost the last verbal wit attempted in the first draft. Chapter 4 summarizes Miles' lecture tour; reproduces his orthographically heterodox letter to Pamela, whose beard again reminds him of flame; and recounts the incineration, under a full moon, of the Bevan City Hostel, Miss Flower, and the model. The scene shifts to the Ministry, where officials are attempting to deal with the loss of Miss Flower, the more serious question of replacing the model, and the still more detrimental association in the public mind of Mountjoy and fire. Their solution to the last problem (a foreshadowing of Trimmer's fate in *Sword of Honour*) is to ship Miles to America, where he is last seen entrained in the Midwest, passing numerous wooden houses, awaiting a full moon, and bearing a box of matches.

Waugh's recognition that the second half of the story was unsatisfactory soon triumphed over his hope of a quick sale. By 17 October, writing to his agent, A. D. Peters, from New York, he proposed to double the length for any prospective buyer, and on 25 November, back in England, he had withdrawn the first version and was considerably expanding it (*Catalogue*, E690, 692).

Here the story's textual history becomes obscure. At least one typescript of the first version had been circulated, and one page of some typescript was included in another fragmentary manuscript, offshoot of and supplement to the first and filed with it at the University of Texas (*Catalogue*, A24b). Between this second manuscript, whatever its date, and the first printed version, no tangible evidence seems to have surfaced. External evidence, however, shows that Waugh soon abandoned his revision and expansion, first for a trip to Israel to write an article on the Holy Places for *Life*, then, after a brief resumption of the story, to go to France to write the first draft of *Men at Arms*. By early 1952, Waugh had almost completed this novel, but he was further distracted from the story by a proposal that he work on a film script with Sir Carol Reed, which he did from May to July 1952. At some unspecified point between between then and November 1952, he completed the story and sent it to be typed. At least, he completed nine thousand words according to his count (*Catalogue*, E768), and he was seldom far off. The final published version is roughly eleven thousand words long, and since the story was not published in any form until well into 1953,[8] he would have had time to add to it.

The fragmentary secondary draft manuscript shows Waugh's

---

8. *Love Among the Ruins: A Romance of the Near Future* (London: Chapman & Hall, 1953). This edition is cited parenthetically in the text. Another version with minor variants, the most important of which is the omission of Miles' wedding, was pub-

changing conception of his plot and characters. The manuscript is almost as long as the first draft and covers far less action in much greater detail. This tendency is discernible in a comparison of the opening paragraph of the second draft with its counterpart in the first. For one thing, Waugh made the farewell scene of A into two scenes in B. In A, the Minister and the Governor send Miles on his way. In B, the official and public ceremony is followed by a scene with the Deputy Chief in which Miles is informed of his new duties. The two versions do not overlap conveniently, but the following passages give a good idea of Waugh's practice in revising.

"A position has been found for you in our neighboring town. You will be janitor at the Euthanasia Ward."

"You are now an integral part of Welfare", said the Minister. "We have put your foot on the bottom rung of the ladder. It is there for you to climb, not competitively of course but by natural (Service) stages. In a year or two you may move up to Voluntary Sterilization, perhaps even to Compulsory Sterilization, a department which demands the highest qualities of Service. Who knows one day you may become Minister. Ha, ha."

"Ha, ha, ha, ha", said the Governor.

"Wherever you go you will take the Message of Mountjoy: 'There is no such thing as a criminal. There are only the victims of inadequate social services.' Are the photographers ready?"

"They are just outside, Minister."

"Bring them in. We will now shake hands. That's right, turn towards the camera but look at me. Try and smile. State be with you my dear boy."

Flash.

"Well of [*sic*] you go, Miles," said the Governor. "Your dossier has gone in advance. All you need are your personal (documents) /papers/." He handed Miles a sheaf of forms.

At length Miles spoke: "*Must* I go? How long for? What do I have to do to get back."

"Come, come, you're rehabilitated now, remember. It's your turn now to give back to the State the service the State has given you. Be careful, you've dropped your Certificate of Personality. That is a *vital* document." (A, p. 4)

"Well, Miles, from now on I must call you Mr. PLASTIC" said the Deputy Chief. "In less than a minute you become a citizen. This little pile of

lished in *Lilliput*, 32 (May–June 1953), 73–96. Versions very close to the volume form were published in *Commonweal*, 58 (31 July 1953), 410–422, and in *Tactical Exercise* (Boston: Little, Brown, 1954).

papers is *You*. When I stamp them Miles the Problem ceased to exist and
Mr. Plastic the Man is born. We are sending you to Satellite City, the
nearest Population Centre where you will be attached to the Ministry of
Progress as a sub-official. In view of your special training you are not
being classified as a Worker. The immediate material rewards, of course,
are not as great. That, some of us think, is one of the features of the New
Britain which still requires enlightened reconsideration. But you are defi-
nitely in the Service. We have set your foot on the bottom rung of the non-
competitive ladder. From our secluded spot we shall watch your progress
in Progress.

The Deputy Chief Guide picked up the rubber stamp and proceeded to
his work of creation. Flip-thump, flip-thumb the papers were turned &
stained.

"There you are, Mr. Plastic", said the Deputy-Chief handing Miles, as
it were, the baby. At last Miles spoke: "What must I do to get back here?"
he asked.

"Come, come, you're rehabilitated now, remember. It is your turn to
give back to the State some of the service the State has given you. You will
report this morning to the Area Progressive. Transport has been laid on.
State be with you, Mr. Plastic. Be careful, that's your Certificate of Human
Personality you've dropped—a *vital* document." (B, p. [1])

Much more than expansion is involved, of course. In fact, details
about levels of the Service in A have been deleted in B. More important to Waugh's satiric purpose is the distinction between
Worker and subofficial, to be developed in Chapter 2 and here fore-
shadowed. In cutting Miles' three sentences to one Waugh makes
Miles seem laconic rather than cretinous and the question, fore-
shadowed by Soapy and Sweat's slaughter of the peacocks, more
ominous. Furthermore, in expanding B, Waugh has emphasized
the society's worship of forms and their processing, and at the end
of the scene has revised two sentences into one, eliminating a feeble
verb and isolating emphatically the final phrase.

While Chapter 1 of A is a recognizable outline for the fragmentary revision, the two versions of Chapter 2 diverge widely. In A,
the town to which Miles is sent is not even named; in B, the Satellite City of the final version is clearly recognizable, and the isolated workers of A are merged in B into "a silent, shabby, shadowy
procession," trudging up and down in endless circles like Eliot's
London crowds. The bored desperation and alienation specifically

named in A are rendered specifically in B and provide a motive for
the demand for Euthanasia, here traced through various stages.
Waugh's expansion extended to character as well as setting: the
nameless and faceless Higher Official of A becomes in B the ironically named Dr. Beamish, survivor and symbol of the leftist thirties
who has been disillusioned by "the fulfilment of his early hopes."
He serves not only to allow Waugh to aim more surely his satiric
thrusts but also to give a human reason for the inefficiency of the
Euthanasia Service. In A, the service is merely overburdened; in B,
the fact that many clients die natural deaths while waiting is a result
of Dr. Beamish's personal style and reversed political opinions, for
he considers imposing a fee for the service and laments the loss of
initiative which causes modern people to ignore opportunities for
self-destruction.

Even more important than the clearer characterization of Dr.
Beamish is the evolution of Pamela, the fellow worker with her
flame-red beard, into the nameless ballet dancer whose beard becomes—in a revision from "strong, ginger"—"silken, corn-gold."
Instead of a companion and equal, she is made into a fascinating
and beautiful woman whose final speech in the chapter, "What a lot
you don't know. . . ." [Waugh's ellipsis] implies a secret knowledge
and promise of further revelation.[9] In B, that revelation is the experience of their love, which—unlike the brief and commonplace
flirtation of the first version—is a profound spiritual experience for
Miles. The affair is contrasted with Miles' sex education courses,
compared in detail first with his ancestors' training in cricket or in
Greek paradigms. Miles' love is more like "the splendours of the
Iliad," and Waugh devotes several lines to the meaning of that love:
a search for total loss of self in fusion with the other. In B, however,
the affair is short and its effects unsatisfactory. After a night of love
beneath the moon, Miles still feels restless, takes a walk, and, on
the final page (a carbon typescript identical to its manuscript counterpart in A) burns Mountjoy and sets out for home, "walking for
pleasure."

9. Waugh's connection of love with art is even more obvious in *The Loved One*.
For a discussion of that theme, and its introduction at a late stage of composition,
see my *Evelyn Waugh, Writer* (Norman: Pilgrim Books, 1981), pp. 210–211.

In shaping the final version of *Love Among the Ruins*, Waugh had moved through at least one manuscript and typescript and possibly several between B and the published version. In the process, he had come to a much clearer understanding of his central theme: the impotence of bureaucracy finally to subdue and regulate human nature, shown as unregenerate by any secular economy. To this end, Waugh began his final story not with the string quartet of A (the first sentence of which it preserves as the opening of paragraph three[10]) but with the dry observation that "Despite their promises at the last Election, the politicians had not yet changed the climate. . . . The weather varied from day to day and from county to county as it had done of old, most anomalously" (1). Further support for the theme is provided in the introductory characterization of Mr. Sweat, unnamed and merely labeled as a burglar and member, with Miles, of the first batch of prisoners at Mountjoy in A. By the completion of the final version, Waugh had expanded the hint about "the old Scrubs" in Sweat's dialogue into a clear identification of Sweat and Soapy as "survivals from another age," professional criminals with an appreciation of various types of custody and treatment. In another passage added by the published version, Sweat scornfully contrasts his first and his most recent sentencing: threats of hellfire with labeling as an "anti-social phenomenon." Though the Christian attitude toward sin is introduced, it is not enforced: Sweat has been reformed by neither system, but like the prisoners in *Decline and Fall* he finds more security in condemnation and rigid rules than in the modern, impersonal jargon of the penologists.

The contrast between old and new systems is still more heavily underlined by the major expansion for the final version of the account of Miles' arson trial. In A, the matter is summarized in a few sentences, moving casually from Miles' training in an Air Force station to the crime:

Here he tended a dish-washing machine until after a few weeks, he moodily burned the place to the ground. He found the blaze exhilarating, a

---

10. Waugh apparently acquired the formulas of music appreciation from John Donaldson. See *The Letters of Evelyn Waugh*, ed. Mark Amory (New Haven and New York: Ticknor & Fields, 1980), p. 337. The letter is dated 28 September 1950.

notable experience in a life sadly lacking in such spectacles, and when taxed with the matter, proudly avowed its authorship. Eminent authorities testified at his trial. The charges of multiple manslaughter were reduced to plain arson and he was committed to the new experimental prison which was just opening at Mountjoy Castle, the ancestral home of a one legged V.C. who was evicted to receive him. (A, p. 3)

In the final version, Waugh moved more subtly from training to trial without transition so that the nature of Miles' act emerges gradually. Furthermore, Waugh orders the account to emphasize the legal system's and the Air Force's sympathetic treatment of Miles. First his adjutant testifies that he did good work; then the charges, ranging from Arson to Treason, are reduced to Antisocial Activity; then the psychologist defends Miles' act as normal and cleverly executed. Protesting widows and orphans are cited for contempt, and the prosecution is silenced.

This contrast between old and new continues in Waugh's handling of the character of the Minister of Welfare. In A, he is a man "not much like anyone Miles had seen before in orphanage, Air Force, or prison. He was perhaps a little like the sexual offenders on the first floor but he seemed less jolly" (A, p. 4). He is not further described or characterized. By the final version, this character has fissiparated into the Minister of Welfare, a conventional politician with enough wit to recognize the Chief Guide's fallacies, and the Minister of Rest and Culture, an earthy, old-fashioned type whose colloquial dialogue, here as in the final chapter, sets off the pomposities of his colleague's speech.

Both a reminder of the past and added satiric thrust against the emotional and intellectual sources of the Welfare State are provided by Waugh's resurrection of the demipoets Parsnip and Pimpernell from *Put Out More Flags* to serve as pathetic foils to the ironic Dr. Beamish who pronounces their epitaph: "*New Writing*, the Left Book Club, they were all the rage. Pimpernell was one of my first patients" (44). Parsnip is a comic figure at the Euthanasia Service because of his recurrent failures of nerve; this time it holds and he goes to extinction. So much for the gang of poets which dominated public attention in the 1930's.

A final instance of Waugh's sense of satiric detail and timing is provided by the variant accounts of Miles' trip to the Ministry. In A, the narrative gap between summons and appearance is filled by the Regional Director's reaching for a Euthanasia application; Miles immediately reappears in the Minister's office. In the final version Waugh eliminates the incidental comedy and focuses on Miles in Whitehall, identifiable as "at the very heart of things" by the fact that the elevators work "very very often." And as Miles looks out the window at "a strange purposeless object of stone," "A very old man, walking by, removed his hat as though saluting an acquaintance. Why? Miles wondered" (48). And so might American readers: the object is the Cenotaph, a memorial to the dead of World War I, dedicated in 1920 in the mute presence of England's Unknown Warrior. This figure, called by the *Times* "an emblem of 'the plain man,'"[11] recalls at the end of the story the other types— "complete man of the renaissance," "gentle knight," "dutiful pagan," and "noble savage"—against whom Miles, "the Modern Man," is defined at the beginning. Waugh further implies that the England of Welfare is worth neither dying nor living for.

As might be expected, the differences between the B fragment and the published versions are more subtle than those between first and final attempts. During the course of final revision, Waugh obviously noted that the extended comparison involving sex education was not especially appropriate to Miles' experience. At any rate, it was eliminated. The figures in B about salaries, taxes, and expenses, obviously intended to show the plight of the officials in contrast to the relative opulence of the Workers, must have seemed on reconsideration overly specific, for he had shown far more effectively, in concrete detail, the drabness of the officials' lives. *Love Among the Ruins* was not an economic treatise nor even a diatribe against leveling Socialist policies but a satiric parable about the spirit-numbing effects of those policies. Envy or hatred of the workers, however tangentially implied, would be inappropriate to the story's tone because the officialdom has brought these ills upon itself.

11. "Armistice Day," *Times*, 11 November 1920, p. 15.

The most significant change from B to published version, the development of Clara as a symbol not only of beauty but of the past, goes beyond isolated character or incident to the working out of the plot and Waugh's full realization of his theme. In A, Waugh implied that Miles would go on to set fire after fire whenever boredom overlapped a full moon. His condition was pathological, the effects of the arson on him brief, his condition perhaps curable by the presence of Pamela, whose flamelike beard provides an adequate substitute as long as they are together. But most of these points are merely implied in A. The unnamed dancer of B is a much more complex character and symbol. However, Waugh rushed the story toward its end, implying that earthly love, even at its most intense, is insufficient to satisfy Miles' longings, for Miles burns Mountjoy after what seems to be a satisfactory night of love, and the story ends, if the termination of B is an ending, with many issues unresolved.

In the final version, of course, Waugh makes Clara's beard not a mere occasion for her meeting Miles but, like the "rich glint of lunacy" which sets Aimée Thanatogenos apart from other American girls in *The Loved One*, the source of her attraction for Miles as symbol of her difference from the world of Welfare. Her room, moreover, is furnished with pictures and other objects from the past. As Miles says, "It reminds me of Prison," and Waugh adds, "It was the highest praise he knew" (30). When Clara becomes pregnant, Miles is given a link to the future to complement his tenuous link with a past whose ease and grandeur are symbolized by Mountjoy and reflected in Clara's possessions. When, in order to return to dancing, she chooses to have an abortion and an operation which replaces the beard with "something quite inhuman, a tight, slippery mask, salmon pink" (40), Miles is cut off from a human future. In burning Mountjoy, he cuts himself off from the inaccessible human past:

The scorched-earth policy had succeeded. He had made a desert in his imagination which he might call peace. Once before he had burned his childhood. Now his brief adult life lay in ashes; the enchantments that surrounded Clara were one with the splendours of Mountjoy; her great golden beard, one with the tongues of flame that had leaped and expired among the stars; her fans and pictures and scraps of old embroidery, one with the gilded cornices and silk hangings, black, cold and sodden. (43)

Thus, when he is summoned to Whitehall, he leaves with a clear mind, unlike the lovesick and quasi-literate Miles of A. Shown the model of the new Mountjoy, not a Box in an Egg but "a familiar, standard packing-case, set on end," Miles has apparently reached the end of his spiritual odyssey:

It fell into place precisely in the void of his mind, satisfying all the needs for which his education had prepared him. The conditioned personality recognized its proper pre-ordained environment. All else was insubstantial; the gardens of Mountjoy, Clara's cracked Crown Derby and her enveloping beard were trophies of a fading dream.

The Modern Man was home. (50)

His equanimity is so great that he can accept Miss Flower as his bride. Only the disquieting question "When can we get divorced?"—reminiscent of his earlier "What must I do to get back here?" almost forty pages earlier—indicates that he retains any individual standards. It also foreshadows his shift of mood during the marriage ceremony when, fidgeting, he finds his lighter, "a most uncertain apparatus. He pressed the catch and instantly, surprisingly there burst out a tiny flame—gemlike, hymeneal, auspicious" (51). Without hope or memory, Waugh strongly implies, Miles can find pleasure only in destruction.

III

Some critics find the story's conclusion depressing: Frederick J. Stopp, contrasting it with Dennis Barlow's burning of "his immediate past," finds Miles' pressing of the lighter "no liberating action," [12] and James F. Carens assumes that Waugh is predicting "a civilization in which rebellion itself can only be futile and destructive." [13] Another and perhaps better way of saying it is that, given

12. Frederick J. Stopp, *Evelyn Waugh: Portrait of an Artist* (Boston: Little, Brown, 1958), pp. 153. Stopp also draws the parallel between Aimée's "rich glint of lunacy" and Miles' pyromania.

13. James F. Carens, *The Satiric Art of Evelyn Waugh* (Seattle: University of Washington Press, 1966), p. 156.

the society, destruction is itself a creative and laudable act. For one thing, it is an act of will, and Waugh's successive revisions not only make Miles less cretinous but more of a free agent. In his rejection of his conditioning he is, as Carens notes, a precursor of Alex in Anthony Burgess' *A Clockwork Orange*—a far more hopeful book in both the English and American versions[14] than Carens realizes, precisely because Alex regains freedom of choice. For Burgess, like Waugh well versed in Catholic theology, free choice of a lesser good (since we cannot choose evil per se) is better than no choice at all. Perhaps an equally suitable analogy is the Misfit in Flannery O'Connor's "A Good Man Is Hard to Find." O'Connor maintained that this multiple homicide had the greatest capacity for spiritual growth of any character in the story[15]—not that this is necessarily a great deal. Like the Misfit, Miles at the end of his story is aware of his situation and prepared and able to alter it. The fact that he is the direct product of the modern world—Alex and the Misfit are less clearly so—is Waugh's crowning irony and his final word on bland sociologized secularism.

However, *A Clockwork Orange* is based not on Welfare State but cold war England and not on privation but relative opulence. More useful in establishing an immediate thematic context for *Love Among the Ruins* are books by almost exact contemporaries, George Orwell and Henry Green, which also extrapolated from conditions in England in the mid- and late 1940's. Green had known Orwell at Eton and Waugh at Oxford and later. Waugh became acquainted with Orwell not long before Orwell's death and wrote that he found *Animal Farm* an "ingenious and delightful allegory" (*Letters*, 211), reviewed Orwell's essays respectfully, and wrote to Orwell a perceptive if partisan criticism of *Nineteen Eighty-Four*. Early in their careers, Waugh had reviewed Green's *Living* in glowing terms, though later he objected privately to certain features of Green's novels.

More important than these biographical links, of course, are the

---

14. See my "On Editing Modern Texts: Who Should Do What and to Whom?" *Journal of Modern Literature*, 3 (April 1974), 1012–1013.

15. Flannery O'Connor, "On Her Own Work," in *Mystery and Manners*, ed. Sally and Robert Fitzgerald (New York: Farrar, Straus & Giroux, 1969), p. 111.

comparisons possible not only among the visions of the future contained in *Nineteen Eighty-Four, Concluding,*[16] and *Love Among the Ruins* but among the techniques by which they are rendered. Orwell's novel is well enough known to use as a point of reference. This book is of course the most fully rendered antiutopia and is in places—especially in the long quotations from Emmanuel Goldstein's book and in the appendix on Newspeak—not anything like a novel. Furthermore, Orwell is far more pessimistic than either Waugh or Green. As a socialist, he was perhaps more worried about the betrayal of socialist ideals and programs than were people who never expected anything concrete of socialism or, in Waugh's case, anything at all of politics. Thus, while Orwell posits a sharp change in national and international politics, makes his chief representative of government an expert torturer, and establishes a political teleology of power for its own sake, both Green and Waugh assume, at least for the purposes of their narratives, that life will go on very much as it has and that the kind of English gentleness and inefficiency praised by Orwell in "England Your England" will continue.

Whereas Orwell takes considerable pains to explain the transition from present to posited future, Waugh mentions a Bevan-Eden Coalition and assumes that buying votes with Welfare State programs will continue. Green does not bother to explain the transition at all, though he obviously deplores it. Waugh's chief agents of government are not omniscient and omnipotent ideologues but bureaucrats trying to cover their own backsides when programs fail; Green's are mistresses of a girls' school, worried about the charges under their pseudoparental care and about the Reports which they may have to file if things go too badly wrong.

The narrowing of focus is also observable in the narrative technique of the three books. Although Winston Smith is the observer and chief actor of *Nineteen Eighty-Four*, Orwell is interested in him as the last man in Europe, with attitudes surviving from a past age, and the interest is placed on the mechanism more than on Winston's personal response to it. Waugh presents Miles Plastic's private, in-

16. *Concluding* (London: Hogarth Press, 1948).

deed psychotic, response to the conditions which the state has created. In *Concluding*, Green focuses so intensely on the characters' private concerns that he uses only one setting and seems to regard political conditions precisely as conditional rather than causative.

In fact, Green and Waugh resist the idea that the individual can be controlled by the state. Even more than Aldous Huxley's characters in *Brave New World*, Orwell's are subject to psychological engineering; there is only the Party; there are no Islands to which creative dissidents can be sent. At first glance, Waugh's Miles Plastic is the complete embodiment of the Modern Man as a result of an education which featured "halls adorned with Picassos and Legers [where] he yawned through long periods of Constructive Play. He never lacked the requisite cubic feet of air. His diet was balanced and on the first Friday of every month he was psychoanalyzed" (6). But the conditioning fails.

Green's plot is more complex and less conclusive than either Orwell's or Waugh's. It focuses on the attempt of Mr. Rock, an aged and honored scientist, to retain the cottage in which he and his granddaughter live in the face of the machinations of Miss Edge, the more ambitious of the coheads of the school, which comes to represent the State in miniature. But no serious threat is mounted; there are only speculation and gossip amid the preparations for the annual Founders Day Dance and the very poorly suppressed scandal of the disappearance of two of the girls. By the end of the novel, one of the girls is still missing, the granddaughter has announced her engagement, and Rock's female goose (named Ted) has for the first time taken flight. Nothing really has happened; the vague threats have been fended off for another day; Mr. Rock goes to bed and, "On the whole he was well satisfied with his day" (254).

Although they differ in the finality of their closure and in their explanation of the process by which the present becomes the future, all three authors establish a link between the two times for the obvious reason that this kind of story is really about contemporary society. There are, however, considerable differences in the ways in which the links and contrasts are established. As various critics have observed, Orwell's London is essentially the London of the end of World War II in its shabbiness and deprivation of what we in the

West like to think of as normal comforts. As in many modern dystopias, the setting is urban, the characters enclosed, "the place where there is no darkness" a model for the society as a whole. The past is represented only by the false refuge of the room which Winston and Julia share, the book in which Winston keeps his subversive diary, the fragmentary memories of the old Prole whom Winston seeks out in the pub, and the paperweight which, like the room, is a false refuge from the power of Big Brother.

In contrast, both Green and Waugh use as setting a Stately Home, a country house preserved more or less intact, though converted respectively to girls' school and prison, which the characters regard as an imaginative oasis in the desert of the Welfare State. More important, these homes do not simply *imply* value; they embody it, so that even Miss Edge, the fluttery bureaucrat of *Concluding*, loves the house and grounds which she has helped to desecrate. Despite the edict from on high to begin raising pigs, there is no question that the house will in some sense endure even the stupidities of officialdom. In fact, the connection with the vital and organic, if smelly, will tie the house more closely to its origins than to the paper-shuffling modern world. Moreover, the characters can actually *hide* from authority and from each other in grounds which seem almost wild.

In *Love Among the Ruins*, the country house is used more ambiguously. Mountjoy was

planned and planted in the years of which [Miles] knew nothing; generations of skilled and patient husbandmen had weeded and dunged and pruned; generations of dilettanti had watered it with cascades and jets; generations of collectors had lugged statuary here; all, it seemed, for his enjoyment this very night under this huge moon. Miles knew nothing of such periods and processes, but he felt an incomprehensible tidal pull towards the circumjacent splendours. (2)

Contrasted not only with the shabbiness of Satellite City and the model of the new Mountjoy, a packing case set on end, but with the human beings who inhabit and manage it, Mountjoy *is* the past. Green's characters dwell in their house and its grounds and are enough at home to be able, occasionally, to ignore it. Waugh's characters are less than their setting; Mountjoy is a set piece, not a place to live and grow. In fact, the very point of Mountjoy as prison, as far as Waugh is concerned, is that the inhabitants *not* change. When Miles sets fire to Mountjoy, he cuts himself off from a fragment of the past which cannot be translated into the contemporary world. But while Mountjoy exists, Waugh is more interested in the house than he is in the people.

Another major difference is in the attitudes toward language. As the appendix on Newspeak indicates, Orwell is primarily interested in language as technology; even his relatively brief description of the natural world is spare and merely functional because he does not want to limit the amount and kind of reference to the past. Waugh is interested in language as artifact, while Green is interested in the creative powers of language. This contrast, less obvious and more striking than any comparison with Orwell, can be seen in the descriptions of nature in the two novels. Waugh writes of "a rich, old-fashioned Tennysonian night" but goes on to note that "No gold fin winked in the porphyry font and any peacock which seemed to be milkily drooping in the moon-shadows was indeed a ghost, for the whole flock of them had been found mysteriously and rudely slaughtered a day or two ago in the first disturbing flush of this sudden summer" (1).[17] Thereafter, and of course in the title itself, Waugh employs allusion in order to measure the fall from grace in the language and spirit of the future and is interested in the natural world only insofar as it can be described in rich, traditional language.

For example, moonlight is for Waugh evocative of romantic situations, as in his allusion to *The Merchant of Venice* in Miles' post-coital speech, "On such a night as this I burned an Air Force Station and half its occupants" (30). For Green, the moon, at least as it appears to the characters,

was still enormous up above on a couch of velvet, blatant, a huge female disc of chalk on deep blue with holes around that, winking, squandered in the void a small light as of latrines. The moon was now all powerful, it covered everything with salt, and bewigged distant trees; it coldly flicked

17. Professor Rowland Smith points out that Waugh probably borrowed the slaughtered peacocks from Green's *Loving*. Green, of course, had adapted the lingering death of Lord Tangent for his novel *Nothing*. See *Letters*, 328.

the dark to an instantaneous view of what this held, it stunned the eye by stone, was all-powerful, and made each of these three related people into someone alien, glistening, frozen eyed, alone. (189)

Like Waugh, Green is foregrounding language, especially its sounds and rhythms, but he is not alluding but emphasizing the uniqueness and power of the moon through the language and showing, in a much more powerful manner than would be appropriate to Waugh, the way in which his characters participate in and are dominated by nature.

And while Waugh's birds, the peacocks, are slaughtered—by two canny convicts who save the evidence to prove, if necessary, that they are not rehabilitated—Green's birds are inviolate and independent. The flight of Mr. Rock's goose may be intended to parallel the flight of one of the school's inmates and the anticipated flight of Elizabeth Rock into marriage. Certainly the goose's flight conveys surprise and delight in the unexpected, a freedom from the rules anticipated at the beginning of the novel when Mr. Rock, though bound by the fog, knows that somewhere above it must be "a flight of birds fast winging,—Ted knows where, he thought." And Green uses figurative language and even epic simile, not in allusion but in direct celebration of the surprise and richness of the world. As Eric Auerbach has demonstrated, this style suspends time and offers possibilities of extension in space so as to run counter to the basic tendency of the novel of the future, which is by definition about time and change.[18]

Rather than change, *Concluding* offers process, the implied passage of the seasons and the toppling of huge trees by the weather and clouds of starlings that in the morning "ascended in a spiral into blue sky; a thousand dots revolving on a wave, the shape of a vast seashell pointed to the morning . . ." (19). Though this vision is dissipated by the sound of the dormitory bell calling the girls to rise to their unnatural and asexual environment, at evening the starlings return "suddenly by legion . . . in one broad spiral . . . and so, as they descended through falling dusk in a soft roar, they

18. Erich Auerbach, *Mimesis* (Garden City: Doubleday Anchor, 1957), Chapter 1.

made, as they had at dawn, a huge sea shell that stood proud to a moon which, flat sovereign red gold, was already posed full faced to a dying world" (177). But the world will rise again; the missing girl is probably not dead, and it does not seem to matter much anyway; the headmistresses, despite their mild and nervous repression of the girls being trained (even less effectively than Miles) as servants of the State, will "never learn what happens here" as the girls' natural vitality escapes their control. And even the headmistresses, tired at the end of the day, know that they can use the power of the bureaucracy against it, like judo experts, and preserve their place and their uneasy peace, which is no more than they deserve, but, in Green's mild vision, not very much less.

In one respect, Waugh resembled Orwell in having a polemic purpose, however indirect and teasing his warning against the tendencies of modern government may have been. As a result, characters and situations have a tendentious purpose: Winston must be crushed and Miles driven to pyromania in order to illustrate the diminishing possibilities of the human spirit and the extremes to which it can be driven. There is, Orwell's O'Brien implies, no such thing as nature, especially human nature, only what the Party dictates. For Waugh, the irreducible, vital quality of humanity is destructive. In contrast, Green seems to be a sort of vitalist, opposing natural process to bureaucratic regulation, implying that the two opposing elements can endure even in a single person, and celebrating human desire and what is usually called human weakness. Both Orwell and Waugh believed that human beings could successfully be manipulated (see Waugh's *Letters*, 302), but Green seems to be saying that humanity is strong enough to leave room for the individual, the idiosyncratic, no matter what the pressure. Personal desires lead to inefficiency; inefficiency allows room for life; life allows for inefficiency. So it goes, in a cycle much more optimistic than that posited in the same words by Kurt Vonnegut. Perhaps this vision demonstrates once again that humanism, in the modern sense, has no place even in a dystopia. Orwell implies that nothing could be done; Waugh implies that only negative assertion of the will can be implemented on the secular plane; Green implies that nothing *has* to be done; his characters need only *be*.

In effect, therefore, Orwell solved best the problem of combining antiutopia and novel not because he was the best novelist but because he was the best essayist. Green solved the problem by more or less ignoring it. Waugh, never an especially effective controversialist in discursive prose and more comfortable as a novelist with outward speech and events than with ideas, wrote what he later called "a brief, very prettily produced fantasy about life in the near future with certain obvious defects," made into a short work because of "the realization that the characters lacked substance for more than a short story" (*EAR*, 441). It did not seem to occur to him that anything but character could sustain a longer work, and he seemed content in this instance "purely to amuse."

However, Waugh was not merely wasting or even marking time in spending this effort on *Love Among the Ruins*. By the time that he completed it, Orwell was dead and Green was, in Waugh's view, declining as a novelist. It seems probable that Waugh's attempt to complete his own dystopia led him to become more clearly aware than he had ever been of the stylistic and philosophical differences between his métier and that of Green, whose early work he had championed. More important, *Love Among the Ruins* led Waugh to define clearly if not subtly his response to postwar England, a necessary stage in working out major themes in *Sword of Honour*.

Conclusion: Waugh and the Generation of Decline

If we are to see Waugh and his contemporaries as more than failed modernists or ur-black humorists, we need to establish a clear context in which to see their work. The preceding chapters obviously represent very tentative steps toward creating one, and at this point I can only suggest some of the terms in which further discussion can be made more precise.

Even before we begin, however, the period in which Waugh, Graham Greene, George Orwell, Christopher Isherwood, Henry Green, and Anthony Powell flourished needs a name. "The Age of Auden" is a label which skews the discussion toward poetry—and toward a narrow range of poetry—at the expense of the most talented novelists of the period. Furthermore, the label embodies a political bias which even Orwell rejected. "The Nineteen Thirties" seems unduly limiting, for major writers of the period developed their sensibilities and in many cases their methods in the years before and continued to develop both in the years thereafter—in the cases of Greene and Powell, to the point at which I write.

Similar objections can be raised to most other chronological, biographical, and ideological labels. If, however, we look at the most basic fact, when the major novelists were born rather than when they finished or flourished, we can see that they are very closely grouped:

1903 Orwell, Waugh
1904 Greene, Isherwood
1905 Green, Powell

English literary history provides no ready-made label, and though the Conservative party lost the election of 1903, it seems unduly tendentious to call them the post-Conservative generation. However, in 1905 Elliott Mills published *The Decline and Fall of the British Empire*, which Samuel Hynes perceptively links with Baden-Powell's Boy Scout movement and other responses to England's entry into the twentieth century.[1] While not everything in Mills' book or Hynes' chapter can be applied to the six novelists I have listed, their responses to contemporary society in their fiction make "Generation of Decline" seem appropriate as a working label.

The oldest of these novelists was eleven, the youngest eight, when England declared war on Germany. All went to public schools—Orwell, Green, and Powell to Eton; Waugh to Lancing; Greene to Berkhamsted; Isherwood to Repton. Though like their elders they came to expect that the war would last long enough for them to join the fighting, none was old enough to see action. All but Orwell passed through Oxbridge between 1922 and 1926. None had left his twenties when the Depression began. All were just young enough, given the will and some ingenuity, for active service in World War II.

As this sketch indicates, these writers were a far more homogeneous literary generation than their modernist predecessors in class and education. In fact, all but Green belonged to "the moneyless, landless, educated gentry who managed the country. . . ."[2] They had grown up expecting to have, or to be able to reject, jobs in the family firm, whether it was the Yorkes' factory or the Blairs' colonial service (these two, who actually followed the family trade, felt it necessary to write pseudonomously), and all were given the traditional, which in most cases meant classical, middle-class education.

That education may have been narrow, but it was thorough, and it provided this generation with opportunities to sharpen wits and

---

1. Samuel Hynes, *The Edwardian Turn of Mind* (Princeton: Princeton University Press, 1968), Chapter 2.
2. Evelyn Waugh, *Work Suspended*, Part I, Chapter 2. This fragment was first published in 1942; the most recent publication is in *Work Suspended and Other Stories, Including Charles Ryder's Schooldays* (Hammondsworth: Penguin, 1982).

style in debate and writing, official and otherwise. Waugh characterized that education most memorably as "the preparation for one trade only; that of an English prose writer."[3]

At the same time, this generation was exposed to what we now call popular culture, mass-produced social comedies set in schools, like those dissected in Orwell's "Boys' Weeklies"; tales of exploration upon which Waugh based his early "In Search of Thomas Lee" and the last third of A Handful of Dust; exotic tales of adventure in the Rider Haggard vein which Scobie adapts for his dreams and for the tale which distracts the dying boy in The Heart of the Matter.

This unofficial education may have had even more effect on this generation than on its predecessors, in part because, like other forms of mass journalism, it was becoming more widely available, but in even larger measure because this generation could see that traditional forms were breaking down. Waugh knew as early as 1921 that his generation—and he thought of it in chronopolitical terms—was very different from its predecessors, even from immediate predecessors who had, like his brother Alec, fought in the trenches. His diaries, his editorials for the Lancing College Magazine, his early professional journalism, and Vile Bodies reiterate in various ways the same points: the older generation was politically and morally bankrupt; the middle generation was reduced in numbers and psychologically stunted by the war; the younger generation was left without guidance except what they could find in artistic, intellectual, and (after 1930) religious traditions which had no widespread currency in the postwar world and therefore had aesthetic rather than moral or social authority over those who elected to live by them.

Those who went on to university found it no less difficult to share the experience of those who had come before. The Cambridge of the Bloomsbury Group and the Oxford of Ronald Knox—at least that described in Waugh's biography as a place of intellectual excitement, warm friendship, and reverence for at least selected elders—had given way, at least for Waugh and his friends, to a very different kind of university.

3. Evelyn Waugh, A Little Learning (Boston: Little, Brown, 1964), p. 140.

The major difference, occasioned and in part caused by the war, was the loss for the Generation of Decline of something like *pietas* toward their elders, toward their universities, and toward each other. The Bloomsbury Group may have rejected many conventional views, but their attitudes toward people and social institutions were in some ways reassuringly familiar. G. E. Moore, their favorite don, was central, perhaps crucial, to the development of Bloomsbury: more than thirty years after studying with him, Maynard Keynes felt compelled to reexamine and question Moore's ideas in an essay for the Bloomsbury Memoir Club. Ronald Knox exerted a different kind of influence on the slightly younger Oxford generation virtually destroyed by war. Oxford in the 1920's seems to have had no comparable figure. "Sligger" Urquhart probably desired similar influence, but Waugh's generation seems to have regarded him as a figure of fun left over from a previous generation when they thought of him at all, and in any case he seemed more interested in religion and social standing than in ideas. Waugh retained an interest in C. R. M. F. Cruttwell, his tutor, but it was wholly antipathetic and derisive. Perhaps Maurice Bowra, Dean of Wadham (or, as he was termed in undergraduate journalism, the Queen of Podham), was the prototype of the popular Oxford don in the 1920's: witty, graceful, "light" in several senses. At Cambridge, Isherwood paid too little attention to the dons to be able to dislike, or even identify, any of them very clearly as individuals.

The university as an institution failed to capture the loyalty or even the interest of this generation. Its members did not seem to see it as preparation *for* anything. In part, this attitude arose from the fecklessness of young men, observable in other times and territories, but it may also have been derived from the view that the university did not arise from or lead to the kind of cohesive society that Bloomsbury grew out of and into. Of the five who went to university, only Powell took a degree, and a Third at that. Learning of the Bloomsbury or Knox sort may have seemed irrelevant to the social and economic realities that confronted them outside the university.

Nor did the young of 1920's Oxbridge reverence themselves and each other as had earlier generations. Isherwood at Cambridge sounds like a preliminary sketch of Charles Ryder at Oxford in *Brideshead Revisited*—isolated in a private world with a single friend. Waugh's Oxford set was fragmented by rivalries and snobberies. Bloomsbury intellectuals believed that they could overturn received ideas and replace them with more progressive theories and methods, that society could be reformed and ultimately transformed, and that the group of the elite and elect—of which they saw themselves and each other as the core—could be gradually but almost infinitely expanded. They were, to extend Camus' term slightly, revolutionaries. The Oxford of Ronald Knox, less interested in secular reform, provided the dramatic struggle of the individual soul toward the true church and toward spiritual authenticity. So in a way they too were revolutionaries. The Generation of Decline were, in contrast, rebels. Having experienced but not really earned the disillusions of the war, they did not trust anyone over thirty, but, unlike the American young of the 1960's, they did not have much more confidence in anyone younger. They seemed to be more interested in amusing and scoring off each other.

However, they could not for long be indifferent to the necessity of earning a living, and the difference between their situations and Virginia Woolf's ideal of five hundred pounds a year and a room of one's own indicates how drastically English society had changed. However much Woolf excoriated the materialism in the novelistic methods of Arnold Bennett, H. G. Wells, and John Galsworthy, in her own novels written through the end of the 1920's it is difficult to find any evidence that she regarded the social and economic fabric as significantly changed from December 1910, when she supposed that human character had changed. Moreover, even *A Room of One's Own* is as firmly grounded in physical reality as any Bennett novel, though of course in a different way, and she believed, or said, that a fixed income was really fixed. She could maintain this attitude because the immediate world of her experience was not all that different from what it had been in 1910.

But most of the young men who went down from university lacked independent income and could not depend on continued support from their families. They had to, and did, find jobs: Powell with the Duckworth publishing house; Greene with a provincial newspaper and then with the letters department of the *Times*; Green and Orwell with the family firms. Isherwood (supported by his family) and Waugh resisted, and Waugh, fired as a schoolmaster and unsuccessful as an applicant for a job selling shoe polish, reluctantly entered the family trade of literature. All except Green finally managed to escape honest work for varying periods, but all sporadically worked in the various jobs, vaguely in the arts, among which Englishmen seem to move so easily in ways bewildering to Americans.

But when they escaped, these writers did not tend to become declassé or deracinated in quite the same ways as Conrad, Joyce, Lawrence, Eliot, Pound, and Hemingway. Orwell tried to become proletarian or countryman at various periods; Greene, like Lord Marchmain in *Brideshead Revisited*, chose to live abroad after the war; and Isherwood spent over half of his life in California; but even they for the most part retained class and national traits in ways that the modernists had not. In their prime, the Generation of Decline traveled widely and wrote extensively about their journeys, but unlike Lawrence, whose so-called travel books were the result of settling into a place, the writers of this generation always seemed to be passing through on a circuit which led back to England.

Once there, they did not gather in groups. In part, this was due to temperament and upbringing. Using the persona of John Plant to reflect on his own previous career as he prepared for middle age and a new kind of literary achievement, Waugh asserted that

There was little love and no trust at all between any of my friends. . . . each knew the other so well that it was only by making our relationship into a kind of competitive parlour game that we kept it alive at all. We had all from time to time cut out divergent trails and camped on new ground, but we always, as it were, returned to the same base for supplies, and swapped yarns of our exploration. (*Work Suspended*, Part II, Chapter 2)

The failure of this group to look like a group was also due to their strong tendency toward heterosexuality and conventionality. All except Isherwood married; all who married had families. Most, with varying degrees of standing and ambition, preferred the country, and a very private home, to a flat in London, though all (with the exception of Green) did business as thoroughly professional men of letters. Some even wrote letters to the *Times*, though Greene was no longer there to receive them.

This necessarily generalized outline of the lives of this literary generation hardly fits the pattern for the Romantic artist embodied in Stephen Dedalus's "silence, exile, and cunning." Though most of these writers created public personae, the extremes represented by Waugh's country squire and Orwell's working man, they tended to see the artist as participating in humanity rather than standing outside and legislating for it. Their values came not so much from the imagination as from political and religious structures—though as Catholics discovered of Greene and Waugh and socialists of Orwell, they could prove idiosyncratic and uncertain allies.

Like their styles of living, the writers of whom they approved were very different from those canonized by the high modernists. And it was a different kind of enthusiasm. It is difficult to imagine any of these writers' learning another language in order to read in the original the work of a revered writer, as Joyce learned Norwegian to read Ibsen; displaying Eliot's enthusiasm for the symbolists; or, like Pound, searching the literatures of the past in order to create a new canon. In fact, none did any significant translating.

As schoolboys and university students, however, they reflected rather than created taste. Most of them were at least one literary generation behind. In his late twenties, Waugh argued that only the middle-aged could be truly modern because it took that long to catch up. Waugh's youthful reading is at this point the most thoroughly documented. It included Shaw (he thought his mother a Candida, his father a Morrell), Samuel Butler, and other late Victorians and early Edwardians, and by his last year at Lancing he had read, if not understood, some of Katherine Mansfield's stories. Their own juvenile efforts were, as Waugh said of his, "imitative of the worst of my reading," patriotic, religious, and hair-raising in turn. And, except for Henry Green's *Blindness*, they showed evidence of competence rather than precocity.

By the late 1920's, when the Generation of Decline began to work toward voices and methods of their own, the high modernists had become thoroughly established, if not Establishment, and the younger novelists seem to have decided quite consciously not to emulate them. By this time, they certainly knew the modernist canon, and Waugh ("The Balance"), Greene ("The Bear Fell Free"), and Orwell (parts of *A Clergyman's Daughter*) put that knowledge, however briefly, to work.

But though they learned from the modernists (Waugh was especially struck by Eliot's use of leitmotif), their scale of literary values was quite different. They did not bother to attack Bennett, Wells, and Galsworthy as Virginia Woolf had. On the other hand, though she honored E. M. Forster personally, she did not emulate him, while Isherwood and Waugh thought very highly of his novels and Waugh had several Forster pamphlets in his library. Powell persuaded Duckworth to publish the collected edition of Ronald Firbank's novels, and Waugh praised them in his first extended piece of literary criticism. Orwell claimed that Somerset Maugham was the most important influence on his fiction, and Waugh regarded him as a masterly technician and showed, in "Tactical Exercise," that he could write in Maugham's flat, realistic/ironic vein. Orwell and Waugh praised and defended P. G. Wodehouse in much the same terms, and Orwell and Greene praised and emulated, without conspicuous success, the novels of Joseph Conrad.

In fact, these novelists were more likely to admit to a taste for popular culture than for high art. Particularly important for them in technical terms was the fact that they were part of the first generation to grow up watching films. In their youth, movies were enough of a novelty to command their fascinated attention, though the youthful Evelyn Waugh was so sure that they were not art that he rarely bothered to record titles in his diaries. At Oxford, he reviewed and helped to make movies; Green saw two films a day during term; and Greene later became a major reviewer of film. Of the six major novelists of this generation, only Green and Orwell never worked for a movie studio. This immersion in film strongly influenced their techniques, as evidenced by "I am a camera" near the beginning of Isherwood's *Goodbye to Berlin*; Waugh's use of film conventions in "The Balance"; and his and Greene's use of techniques analogous to camera movement and montage throughout their careers.

The interest in film was more than technical; by concentrating on surface behavior, the novelists of this generation avoided not only the Bennett equation of character with material culture but the Woolf equation of sensibility and value. The texture of fictional worlds in Waugh and his contemporaries is thinner than those of the realists and postimpressionists because they see the world in a different way.

This summary of the lives and literary careers of a half-dozen prolific writers is obviously the sketchiest of preliminary maps to a rich, complex, and virtually unexplored period in the development of the English novel. The formal and historical elements which set the Generation of Decline apart from their predecessors and successors must obviously be described and analyzed in much greater detail. Some of that detail is now available in the autobiographies of Waugh, Greene, Green, Isherwood, and Powell; in the collected essays, letters, or journalism of Orwell, Waugh, Greene, and Isherwood; and in the mass of fugitive work by and about the individual members of the generation. Whatever they are called, and I do not insist on the label I have devised, our understanding of both the context and of the individual works of these novelists depends on our seeing them as a distinct generation responding in original fashion to a world very different from that of writers by whose standards they have been judged in the past.

Works Cited

PRIMARY

A Bachelor Abroad. New York: J. Cape/H. Smith, 1930.
Black Mischief. London: Chapman & Hall, 1962. Uniform Edition, with a Preface by Waugh.
"Blinding the Middle-Brow." *Tablet*, 168 (18 July 1936), 84.
"Bonhomie in the Saloon Bar." *Night and Day*, 1 (22 July 1937), 24–25.
"The Books You Read." *Graphic*, 5 July 1930, p. 33.
"The Books You Read." *Graphic*, 27 September 1930, p. 509.
"The Books You Read." *Graphic*, 25 October 1930, p. 174.
Brideshead Revisited. Boston: Little, Brown, 1946. Uniform Edition, with a Preface by Waugh. London: Chapman & Hall, 1960.
"British Policy in Aden; A Conference of Tribal Chiefs." *Times*, 17 March 1931, p. 13.
Decline and Fall. Boston: Little, Brown, [1928]. New Uniform Edition, with a Preface by Waugh. London: Chapman & Hall, 1962.
The Diaries of Evelyn Waugh. Ed. Michael Davie. Boston: Little, Brown, 1976.
"An English Humourist." *Tablet*, 168 (17 October 1936), 532–533.
The Essays, Articles and Reviews of Evelyn Waugh. Ed. Donat Gallagher. Boston: Little, Brown, 1984.
Evelyn Waugh, Apprentice: The Early Writings, 1910–1927. Ed. Robert Murray Davis. Norman: Pilgrim Books, 1985.
A Handful of Dust. London: Chapman & Hall, 1964. Uniform Edition, with a Preface by Waugh.
Helena. London: Chapman & Hall, 1950.
"International List." *Night and Day*, 1 (11 November 1937), 23.
"A Journey to Abyssinia." *Graphic*, 22 November 1930, p. 350.
"A Journey to Abyssinia—Alarums and Excursions." *Graphic*, 13 December 1930, p. 504.
"A Journey to Abyssinia—Champagne for Breakfast." *Graphic*, 20 December 1930, p. 544.
The Letters of Evelyn Waugh. Ed. Mark Amory. New Haven and New York: Ticknor & Fields, 1980.
A Little Learning. Boston: Little, Brown, 1964.

Love Among the Ruins: A Romance of the Near Future. London: Chapman &
Hall, 1953.
"Love Among the Underdogs." *Night and Day,* 1 (7 October 1937), 29.
The Loved One. London: Chapman & Hall, 1958. Uniform Edition. Lon-
don: Chapman & Hall, 1965. Uniform Edition, with a Preface by
Waugh.
Mexico: An Object Lesson. Boston: Little, Brown, 1939.
Monsignor Ronald Knox. Boston: Little, Brown, 1959.
Ninety Two Days. New York: Farrar and Rinehart, 1934.
The Ordeal of Gilbert Pinfold. London: Chapman & Hall, 1957. Boston:
Little, Brown, 1957.
Put Out More Flags. Boston: Little, Brown, 1942. Uniform Edition. Lon-
don: Chapman & Hall, 1967.
"Religion in State Schools." *New Statesman and Nation,* 26 (2 October
1943), 217.
"Religion in State Schools." *New Statesman and Nation,* 26 (16 October
1943), 251.
Remote People. London: Duckworth, 1931. The manuscript, also cited in
the text, is in the Berg Collection of the New York Public Library.
Robbery Under Law. London: Chapman & Hall, 1939.
Rossetti: His Life and Works. London: Duckworth, 1928.
Scoop. London: Chapman & Hall, 1964. Uniform Edition, with a Preface
by Waugh.
Sword of Honour. London: Chapman & Hall, 1965.
Tactical Exercise. Boston: Little, Brown, 1954.
"'Tess'—As a 'Modern' Sees It." *Evening Standard,* 17 January 1930, p. 7.
Tourist in Africa. Boston: Little, Brown, 1960.
Vile Bodies. New York: J. Cape/H. Smith, 1930. This text preserved in
editions published by Little, Brown. London: Chapman & Hall, 1947.
Uniform Edition. With a Preface by Waugh, in the Uniform Edition.
London: Chapman & Hall, 1965.
When the Going Was Good. Boston: Little, Brown, 1946.
The World of Evelyn Waugh. Ed. Charles J. Rolo. Boston: Little, Brown,
1958.
Work Suspended. London: Chapman & Hall, 1942.
Work Suspended and Other Stories Written before the Second World War. Lon-
don: Chapman & Hall, 1949.
Work Suspended and Other Stories, Including Charles Ryder's Schooldays. Har-
mondsworth: Penguin, 1982.

SECONDARY

Note: References to society columns cited in Chapter 8 have not been
included in this list.
Arlen, Michael. *The Green Hat.* New York: George H. Doran, 1924.
"Armistice Day." *Times,* 11 November 1920, p. 15.
Auerbach, Erich. *Mimesis.* Garden City: Doubleday Anchor, 1957.
Balfour, Patrick. *Society Racket.* London: John Long, 1932.

Barthes, Roland. *The Pleasure of the Text.* Trans. Richard Miller. New York: Hill and Wang, 1975.
——. *Writing Degree Zero.* Trans. Annette Lavers and Colin Smith. New York: Hill and Wang, 1968.
Beaton, Cecil. *The Wandering Years: Diaries: 1922–1939.* London: Weidenfeld and Nicolson, 1961.
Beebe, Maurice, and Leslie A. Field, eds. *Robert Penn Warren's All the King's Men: A Critical Handbook.* Belmont: Wadsworth Publishing Company, 1966.
Benedict, Steward H. "The Candide Figure in the Novels of Evelyn Waugh." *Papers of the Michigan Academy of Science, Arts, and Letters,* 48 (1963), 685–690.
Berger, Thomas L. "Critical Judgment, Textual Criticism, Editorial Taste, and the Text of *Othello.*" Unpublished paper, delivered at the session "Critical Judgment and Textual Criticism," Modern Language Association, Los Angeles, December 1982.
Bergonzi, Bernard. "Evelyn Waugh's Gentleman." *Critical Quarterly,* 5 (Spring 1963), 23–36.
Blayac, Alain. "Evelyn Waugh's Drawings." *Library Chronicle of the University of Texas,* n.s. 7 (1974), 42–57.
Bowen, Elizabeth. *Collected Impressions.* New York: Alfred A. Knopf, 1950.
Burns, Thomas F. Unpublished letter to Robert Murray Davis, 26 November 1982.
Carens, James F. *The Satiric Art of Evelyn Waugh.* Seattle: University of Washington Press, 1966.
Carew, Dudley. *A Fragment of Friendship: A Memory of Evelyn Waugh when Young.* London: Everest Books, 1964.
Cohen, Nathan. "A Profile of Evelyn Waugh." Unpublished transcript of broadcast on CBC Radio, 28 October 1969.
Davis, Robert Murray. *A Catalogue of the Evelyn Waugh Collection at the Humanities Research Center, The University of Texas at Austin.* Troy: Whitston, 1981.
——. "On Editing Modern Texts: Who Should Do What and to Whom." *Journal of Modern Literature,* 3 (April 1974), 1012–1020.
——. *Evelyn Waugh, Writer.* Norman: Pilgrim Books, 1981.
——. "The Struggle with Genre in *The End of the Affair.*" *Genre,* 18 (Winter 1985), 397–411.
——. "Title, Theme, and Structure in *Vile Bodies.*" *Southern Humanities Review,* 11 (Winter 1977), 21–27.
——. "*Vile Bodies* in Typescript." *Evelyn Waugh Newsletter,* 11 (Winter 1977), 7–8.
Davis, Robert Murray, Paul A. Doyle, Donat Gallagher, Charles E. Linck, and Winnifred M. Bogaards. *A Bibliography of Evelyn Waugh.* Troy: Whitston, 1986.
Delasanta, Rodney, and Mario D'Avanzo. "Truth and Beauty in *Brideshead Revisited.*" *Modern Fiction Studies,* 11 (1965/66), 140–152.

Doyle, Paul A. "Collecting Evelyn Waugh—American Editions of *Brideshead Revisited*." *Evelyn Waugh Newsletter*, 12 (Spring 1978), 9.

Dyson, A. E. *The Crazy Fabric*. New York: St. Martin's Press, 1965.

Evelyn Waugh: The Critical Heritage. Ed. Martin Stannard. London: Routledge & Kegan Paul, 1984.

Ford, Ford Madox. *The Good Soldier*. New York: Vintage, 1958.

Forms of Modern Fiction. Ed. William Van O'Connor. Bloomington: Indiana University Press, 1959.

Friedman, Alan. *The Turn of the Novel*. New York: Oxford University Press, 1966.

Frye, Northrop. *Anatomy of Criticism*. Princeton: Princeton University Press, 1957.

Fussell, Paul. *Abroad: British Literary Traveling between the Wars*. New York: Oxford University Press, 1980.

Gallagher, Donat S. "Black Majesty and Press Mischief." *London Magazine*, 22 (October 1982), 25–38.

———. "Industria Ditat—Mark III." *Southern Review* (Australia), 15 (November 1982), 334–343.

Graves, Robert, and Alan Hodge. *The Long Weekend: A Social History of Great Britain, 1918–1939*. London: Faber and Faber, 1949.

Green, Henry. *Concluding*. London: Hogarth Press, 1948.

Greene, Graham. *Another Mexico*. New York: Viking, 1968.

———. *The End of the Affair*. Hammondsworth: Penguin; reproduces text of the Viking, U.S. first edition, 1951.

———. *The Lawless Roads*. London: William Heinemann & The Bodley Head, 1978.

———. *Ways of Escape*. New York: Simon and Schuster, 1980.

Gunn, Drewey Wayne. *American and British Writers in Mexico, 1556–1973*. Austin: University of Texas Press, 1974.

Hall, James. *The Tragic Comedians: Seven Modern British Novelists*. Bloomington: Indiana University Press, 1963.

Hamnett, Nina. *Is She a Lady? A Problem in Autobiography*. London: Allan Wingate, 1955.

Handford, B. W. "Charles Ryder's Schooldays." *Times Literary Supplement*, 9 April 1982, p. 412.

Harvey, W. J. *Character and the Novel*. Ithaca: Cornell University Press, 1965.

Heath, Jeffrey. *The Picturesque Prison: Evelyn Waugh and His Writing*. Kingston and Montreal: McGill-Queen's University Press, 1982.

Heller, Joseph. Review of *The End of the Battle*. *Nation*, 194 (20 January 1962), 62–63. Reprinted in *Evelyn Waugh: The Critical Heritage*.

Hemingway, Ernest. *Death in the Afternoon*. New York: Charles Scribner's Sons, 1932.

———. *The Sun Also Rises*. New York: Charles Scribner's Sons, 1926. Scribner Library Contemporary Classics Edition.

Huxley, Aldous. *Antic Hay*. London: Panther, 1984.

Hynes, Samuel. *The Edwardian Turn of Mind*. Princeton: Princeton University Press, 1968.

Isaacs, Neil D. "Evelyn Waugh's Restoration Jesuit." *Satire Newsletter*, 2 (1965), 91–94.

Jebb, Julian. "The Art of Fiction XXX: Evelyn Waugh." *Paris Review*, 8 (Summer–Fall 1963), 72–85.

Jervis, Steven A. "Evelyn Waugh, *Vile Bodies*, and the Younger Generation." *South Atlantic Quarterly*, 66 (Summer 1967), 440–448.

Kellner, Bruce. *Carl Van Vechten and the Irreverent Decades*. Norman: University of Oklahoma Press, 1968.

LaFrance, Marston. "Context and Structure of Evelyn Waugh's *Brideshead Revisited*." *Twentieth Century Literature*, 10 (April 1964), 12–18.

Lentfoehr, Sister Thérèse. "My Meeting with Evelyn Waugh." *Evelyn Waugh Newsletter*, 11 (Spring 1977), 3–4.

Linck, Charles E., Jr., and Robert Murray Davis. "The Bright Young People in *Vile Bodies*." *Papers on Language and Literature*, 5 (1969), 80–90.

Little Innocents: Childhood Reminiscences. Ed. Alan Pryce-Jones. London: Cobden-Sanderson, 1932.

Littlewood, Ian. *The Writings of Evelyn Waugh*. Totowa, N.J.: Barnes & Noble, 1982.

Macaulay, Rose. "Evelyn Waugh." *Horizon*, 14 (December 1946), 370–376.

McDonnell, Jacqueline A. *Waugh on Women*. New York: St. Martin's Press, 1985.

Marcus, Steven. "Evelyn Waugh and the Art of Entertainment." *Partisan Review*, 23 (Summer 1956), 348–357. Reprinted in *Representations: Essays on Literature and Society*. New York: Random House, 1975. Pp. 88–101.

Maugham, W. Somerset. *Cakes and Ale*. Garden City: Doubleday, Doran, 1930.

Merton, Thomas. *Elected Silence*. London: Hollis and Carter, 1949.

———. *The Seven Storey Mountain*. New York: Harcourt, Brace and Company, 1948.

———. *Waters of Silence*. London: Hollis and Carter, 1950. London: Theodore Brun Ltd. [Limited Edition].

———. *The Waters of Siloe*. New York: Harcourt, Brace and Company, 1949.

Miles, Peter. "Improving Culture: The Politics of Illustration in Evelyn Waugh's 'Love Among the Ruins.'" *Trivium*, 18 (May 1983), 7–38.

Mitford, Jessica. *Daughters and Rebels*. Boston: Houghton Mifflin, 1960.

Nichols, Beverly. *Crazy Pavements*. London: Jonathan Cape, 1927.

O'Connor, Flannery. *Mystery and Manners*. Ed. Sally and Robert Fitzgerald. New York: Farrar, Straus & Giroux, 1969.

Pakenham, Frank. *Five Lives*. London: Hutchinson, 1964.

Parker, Hershel. *Flawed Texts and Verbal Icons: Literary Authority in American Fiction*. Evanston: Northwestern University Press, 1984.

Powell, Anthony. *Messengers of Day*. New York: Holt, Rinehart and Winston, 1978.

Priestley, J. B. "What Was Wrong with Pinfold." *New Statesman*, 54 (31 August 1957), 244.

Richards, Grant. *Author Hunting*. 2d ed. London: Unicorn, 1960.

Savage, D. S. "The Innocence of Evelyn Waugh." *Western Review*, 14 (Spring 1950), 197–206.

Shroder, Maurice Z. "The Novel as a Genre." *Massachusetts Review*, 4 (Winter 1963), 291–308.

Stannard, Martin. *Evelyn Waugh: The Early Years 1903–1939*. London: Dent, 1986. New York: W. W. Norton, 1987.

———. "The Mystery of the Missing Manuscript." *Times Higher Education Supplement*, 1 June 1984, p. 13.

Stopes, Marie. "Religion in State Schools." *New Statesman and Nation*, 26 (25 September 1943), 202.

———. "Religion in State Schools." *New Statesman and Nation*, 26 (9 October 1943), 233.

Stopp, Frederick J. *Evelyn Waugh: Portrait of an Artist*. Boston: Little, Brown, 1958.

Sykes, Christopher. *Evelyn Waugh: A Biography*. Boston: Little, Brown, 1975.

Taylor, A. J. P. *English History 1914–1945*. Vol. 9 of The Oxford History of England. New York: Oxford University Press, 1965.

Terry, T. Phillip. *Terry's Guide to Mexico*. Hingham, Mass.: G. H. Ellis Co., 1940.

Thérèse, Sister M. "Waugh's Letters to Thomas Merton." *Evelyn Waugh Newsletter*, 3 (Spring 1969), 1–4.

Thorpe, James. *Principles of Textual Criticism*. San Marino: Huntington Library, 1972.

Trilling, Lionel. *The Liberal Imagination*. New York: Viking, 1950.

Van Vechten, Carl. *The Blind Bow-Boy*. Pocket Book Edition. New York: Alfred A. Knopf, 1925.

———. *Firecrackers*. New York: Alfred A. Knopf, 1926.

———. *Parties*. New York: Alfred A. Knopf, 1930.

Walker, Ronald G. *Infernal Paradise: Mexico and the Modern English Novel*. Berkeley: University of California Press, 1978.

Warren, Robert Penn. *All the King's Men*. New York: Bantam Books, 1946.

Wasson, Richard. "*A Handful of Dust*: Critique of Victorianism." *Modern Fiction Studies*, 7 (1961/62), 327–337.

Watt, Ian. *The Rise of the Novel*. Berkeley: University of California Press, 1957.

Waugh, Alec. *My Brother Evelyn and Other Portraits*. New York: Farrar, Straus & Giroux, 1967.

Wilson, Angus. "The House Party Novels." *London Magazine*, 2 (August 1955), 53–55.

Wilson, Edmund. *Classics and Commercials*. New York: Vintage, 1962.

"Yet Another Visit to Brideshead." *Times Literary Supplement*, 16 September 1960, p. 594.

Index

Acton, Harold, 31n, 128, 131
Allott, Kenneth, *The Rhubarb Tree*, 44
Amis, Kingsley, 27
Amory, Mark (see *Letters*)
"Antony, Who Sought Things That Were Lost," 126
Aquinas, St. Thomas, 97
Arlen, Michael, 30–48 passim; *The Green Hat*, 5, 31–48 passim, 256
"Armistice Day," 234n, 256
Asquith, Katherine, 60, 106, 108
Asquith, Lord and Lady, 132
Attlee, Clement, 220
Auden, W. H., 203; *Journey to a War* (with Isherwood), 11n
Auerback, Erich, 242; *Mimesis*, 242n, 256
Augustine, St., 223
Ava, Lord, 131

Bachelor Abroad, A (see also *Labels*), 51 76n, 145n, 255
Baden-Powell, Robert, 246
Bakhtin, M. M., 89
"Balance, The," 122, 126, 127, 127n, 138, 252
Balfour, Patrick, 131; *Society Racket*, 134n, 256
Bankhead, Tallulah, 130
Barchester Towers, 193
Barth, John, x
Barthes, Roland, 214, 216–217; *The Pleasure of the Text*, 214n, 257; *Writing Degree Zero*, 217n, 257
Basil Seal Rides Again, 122
Beardsley, Aubrey, 21
Beaton, Cecil, 132, 173; *The Wandering Years*, 130n, 257

Beebe, Maurice, 215n, 257
Beerbohm, Max, 80
Bell, Clive, 32
Bellamy, Edward, *Looking Backward*, 27
Benedict, Stewart H., "The Candide Figure in the Novels of Evelyn Waugh," 30n, 257
Bennett, Arnold, 249, 252, 253
Bergebedgian, Mr., 158–159
Berger, Tom, 167; "Critical Judgment, Textual Criticism, Editorial Taste, and the Text of *Othello*," 167n, 257
Bergonzi, Bernard, "Evelyn Waugh's Gentleman," 174–175, 175n, 257; *Reading the Thirties*, 3n
Bevan, Aneurin, 238
Bible, 139, 141–142
Black Mischief, 9, 48, 55, 61, 65, 66n, 87n, 151, 152, 159, 224, 255
Blake, William, 95
Blayac, Alain, "Evelyn Waugh's Drawings," 116n, 257
"Blinding the Middle-Brow," 74, 255
Bogaards, Winnifred M., xi
"Bonhomie in the Saloon Bar," 44n, 255
"Books You Read, The," 255
Booth, Wayne C., x
Borotra, Jean, 133
Bosardi, "Babe," 137
Bosardi, Tony, 136
Boucher, François, 39
Bowen, Elizabeth, 5, 11; *Collected Impressions*, 10n, 257; *The Demon Lover*, 10
Bowra, Maurice, 173, 248
Bracken, Brendan, 173
Bradbury, Malcolm, 27

Brideshead Revisited, xiii, 10, 26, 52, 57, 58, 60, 61, 78, 81, 84, 85, 87, 87n, 122, 165–167, 169–177, 181–182, 183–184, 186–187, 203–219, 220, 250, 255
"British Policy in Aden," 150n, 255
Bronte, Emily, *Wuthering Heights,* 5
Browning, Robert, "Love Among the Ruins," 225
Brownlow, Lord, 131
Burgess, Anthony, *A Clockwork Orange,* 27, 237
Burne-Jones, Edward, 54
Burnett, W. R., 72, 80
Burns, Thomas F., 93, 107n, 257
Burton, Sir Richard, *First Steps in Africa,* 154
Butler, Samuel, 251
Byron, Robert, 130

Cabell, James Branch, *Jurgen,* 126
Calder-Marshall, Arthur, 79
Campbell, "Archie," 135
Camus, Albert, 249
Canova, Antonino, 115
Carens, James F., 236–237, *The Satiric Art of Evelyn Waugh,* 236n, 257
Carew, Dudley, 71n, 90; *A Fragment of Friendship,* 90n, 121n, 257
Carroll, Lewis, 59; *Alice Through the Looking-Glass,* 25, 142
Cecil, Lord David, 81
Chamberlain, Peter, *Sing Holiday,* 44
Chaplin, Charles, 81n, 143
"Charles Ryder's Schooldays," 179, 179n, 183–188
Chesterton, G. K., 223
Chirico, De, Giorgio, 132
Cohen, Nathan, "A Profile of Evelyn Waugh," 28n, 257
"Come to the Coach House Door, Boys," 118
Comfort, Alex, 91
Compton-Burnett, Ivy, 80, 82
Connolly, Cyril, 44n, 53–54, 74, 173, *Enemies of Promise,* 76, 80
Conrad, Joseph, 3, 5, 223, 250, 252; *Heart of Darkness,* 6, 7; *Nostromo,* 7
"Conversion," 123–125
Cooper, Gladys, 130
Cowley, Malcolm, 169
Cruttwell, C. R. M. F., 248

"Curse of the Horse Race, The," 118
Cynic, The, 119–120, 121

D'Arcy, Martin, S. J., 52
D'Avanzo (see Delasanta)
Davie, Michael (see *Diaries*)
Davis, Barbara Hillyer, xi
Davis, Robert Murray (see also Linck), *A Catalogue of the Evelyn Waugh Collection . . . ,* 77, 81n, 84n, 116, 128n, 129, 152, 183, 226, 226n, 228, 257; *Evelyn Waugh, Apprentice,* 115n, 138n, 255; *Evelyn Waugh, Writer,* ix, 47n, 63n, 127n, 171, 176n, 231, 257; "On Editing Modern Texts," 27n, 237n, 257; "The Struggle with Genre in *The End of the Affair,*" 207, 257; "Title, Theme, and Structure in *Vile Bodies,*" 140n, 257; "*Vile Bodies* in Typescript," 128n, 257
Davis, Robert Murray, et al., *A Bibliography of Evelyn Waugh,* 150n, 257
De Rerum Novarum, 197
"Death in Hollywood," 62
Decline and Fall, 6, 22, 30–32, 44n, 45–47, 55–56, 56n, 59–61, 65–66, 70, 87n 122, 126, 128, 134, 146, 161, 164, 169, 222, 232, 255
Delasanta, Rodney, "Truth and Beauty in *Brideshead Revisited,*" 170n, 257
Dewey, John, 167
Diaghileff, Sergey, 75
Diaries, ix, 54, 78n, 86, 90, 93, 119, 122, 127, 138n, 148, 173, 179, 182, 183–185, 226, 255
Dickens, Charles, 78
Donaldson, John, 232n
Donegall, Lord, 131
Dos Passos, John, 80; *The Forty Second Parallel,* 73
Douglas, Norman, x, 16–20, 29; *South Wind,* 14, 17–18, 23, 83
Dowson, Ernest, 124
Doyle, Paul A., xii; "Collecting Evelyn Waugh," 165n, 258; *A Reader's Companion to . . . Waugh,* 137n
Dyson, A. E., *The Crazy Fabric,* 89n, 258

Eden, Anthony, 238
"Edward of Unique Achievement," 126

Eliot, T. S., 74, 230, 250, 251, 252; *Fragments of an Agon*, 72; *The Waste Land*, 72

Elizabeth II, Queen, 220–221

Ellison, Ralph, "The Art of Fiction XVIII: Robert Penn Warren," 215n

End of the Battle, The, see *Unconditional Surrender*

"English Humorist, An," 75n, 255

"Essay," 121–122

Essays, Articles and Reviews of Evelyn Waugh, 11n, 19, 21–23, 27, 30n, 31n, 35, 44, 58, 62, 67–69, 75, 76, 78–80, 82–85, 87, 88, 88n, 98, 137, 138, 151, 200, 208n, 216, 217, 220, 222, 223, 244, 255

"Ethiopia Today," 151

Evelyn Waugh, Apprentice, xiii, 115n, 117n, 138n, 255

"Fan-Fare," 80, 220

Farr, D. Paul, xi

Faulkner, William, 203

"Fidon's Confetion," 118–119

Field, Leslie A., 215, 257

Fielding, Henry, *Joseph Andrews*, 6, 14; *Tom Jones*, 14

Firbank, Ronald, x, 5, 8, 11, 17, 20–25, 29, 31, 70–72, 75, 78, 83, 88, 252; *Caprice*, 22; *Concerning the Eccentricities of Cardinal Pirelli*, 23–24; *The Flower Beneath the Foot*, 22; *Vainglory*, 21

Fitzgerald, F. Scott, 41, 65, 222; *The Great Gatsby*, 168; *Tender Is the Night*, 169

Fitzgerald, Zelda, 41

Fleming family, 117

Ford, Ford Madox, 12n; *The Good Soldier*, 11–12, 258

Forster, E. M., 8, 87, 185, 187, 252; *Pharos and Pharillon*, 80; *A Passage to India*, 18

Fowler, H. W., *Modern English Usage*, 103

Fowles, John, *The French Lieutenant's Woman*, 6

"Fragment of a Novel," 179–182, 188

Fragonard, Jean Honoré, 39

Frank, Waldo, 32

Frankau, Gilbert, 69

Fremlin, Rupert, 184, 185

Friedman, Alan, *The Turn of the Novel*, 9n, 258

Frye, Northrop, x, 16; *Anatomy of Criticism*, 14n, 258

Fuad, King, 133

Fussell, Paul, *Abroad*, 147n, 191n, 258

Gallagher, Donat S., xi, 11n, 69, 150n, 201, 201n; "Black Majesty and Press Mischief," 147n, 258; "Industrial Ditat—Mark III," 175–176, 176n, 258

Galsworthy, John, 8, 249, 252; *The Forsyte Saga*, 46

Gardner, Evelyn, 128, 145, 145n

Gathorne-Hardy, Edward, 136, 137, 137n

Gaudi, Antoni, 76

Gerhardi, William, 31n

Gibbon, Edward, 81n

Gibbs, Sir Philip, 69

Gordon, E. B., 184

Graves, Robert, *The Long Weekend*, 130n, 258; *The Reader Over Your Shoulder*, 78, 80, 81n,

Green, Henry, 72, 80, 82, 83, 128, 245–253; *Back*, 218; *Blindness*, 251; *Concluding*, 237–244, 258; *Living*, 71–73, 237; *Loving*, 241n; *Nothing*, 83, 241n

Greene, Graham, x, xi, 80, 86, 173, 174, 245–253; *Another Mexico (The Lawless Roads)*, 191–202, 200n, 258; "The Bear Fell Free," 252; *British Dramatists*, 83; *A Burnt-Out Case*, 86–87; *The End of the Affair*, xiv, 85, 203–208, 213–219, 258; *The Heart of the Matter*, 83–85, 88, 216, 247; *In Search of a Character*, 87; *The Name of Action*, 73, 83; *Our Man in Havana*, 28; *The Power and the Glory*, 191, 193; *The Quiet American*, 85–86; *Ways of Escape*, 86n, 204n, 215n, 258

Greenidge, Terence, 126

Greg, W. W., 167, 168

Guinness, Bryan, 128, 131, 134

Guinness, Diana, 128, 135

Guinness sisters, 130

Gunn, Drewey Wayne, *American and British Writers in Mexico, 1556–1973*, 192n, 258

Haggard, H. Rider, 247

"Half in Love with Easeful Death," 62

Hall, James, *The Tragic Comedians,* ix, 3n, 13n, 130n, 258
Hall, Mr., 156
Hamnett, Nina, 132, 135–136; *Is She a Lady?* 136n, 258
Hancher, Michael, 168
Handford, B. W., 183, 255
Handful of Dust, A, 9, 22–23, 60, 61, 65–67, 71, 87n, 116, 145, 223, 247, 255
Hardy, Barbara, "Towards a Poetics of Fiction," 4n
Hardy, Thomas, *The Mayor of Caster-bridge,* 5; *Tess of the D'Urbervilles,* 70
Harris, Jeanette Gregory, xi
Hartnell, Norman, 135
Harvey, W. J., 5; *Character and the Novel,* 5n, 258
Heath, Jeffrey, xi, 170, 176; *The Pictur-esque Prison,* 170n, 258
Heath Mount Magazine, 120
Helena, 52n, 61, 64, 84, 161, 183, 218, 226, 255
Heller, Joseph, x, 29; *Catch-22,* 28; *God Knows,* 29; Review of *The End of the Battle,* 29, 258
Hemingway, Ernest, 30–48 passim, 51, 55, 203, 250; *Death in the Afternoon,* 71n, 258; *The Sun Also Rises,* 31–38, 43, 258
Henderson, Gavin, 137n
Henriques, Robert, 173
Heygate, John, 129
Hiawatha, 120
Higdon, David Leon, *Shadows of the Past in Contemporary British Fiction,* 3n
Hodge, Alan (see Graves, Robert)
Hoffman, Frederick J., "Aldous Huxley and the Novel of Ideas," 17n
Hopkins, Gerard Manley, 95
"House: An Anti-Climax, The," 121, 122
"Household of the Faith, A," 213n
Howard, Brian, 131, 132, 135–137, 144n
Howard, Mrs. Francis, 132
Hudson, W. H., *The Purple Land,* 33
Hugel, Baron Freidrich von, 46
Hutchinson (singer), 132
Huxley, Aldous, ix, x, 8, 14–21, 29, 30–48 passim, 51; *After Many a Sum-mer Dies the Swan,* 10; *Antic Hay,* 5, 8, 16, 19, 21, 30–48 passim, 258; *Brave New World,* 19, 27, 239; *Crome Yellow,* 17–19, 32–33; *Eyeless in Gaza,* 74; *Island,* 19; *Point Counter Point,* 20; *Those Barren Leaves,* 8, 18–19, 22; *Time Must Have a Stop,* 19
Hynes, Samuel, 246; *The Auden Gener-ation,* 3n; *The Edwardian Turn of Mind,* 246n, 258

Ibsen, Henrik, 251
Ignatius Loyola, St., 99; *Spiritual Exer-cises,* 100
Iliad, The, 231
"In Search of Thomas Lee," 247
"International List," 255
Inge, Dean, 133
Irons, Jeremy, 165
Isaacs, Neil D., "Evelyn Waugh's Res-toration Jesuit," 140n, 259
Isherwood, Christopher, 11, 245–253; *Goodbye to Berlin,* 252; *Journey to a War,* 11n; *Lions and Shadows,* 248; *Mr. Norris Changes Trains,* 9

Jacobs, Barbara, 180
James, Henry, x, 19, 216; "The Art of Fiction," 6n
Jebb, Julian, "The Art of Fiction XXX: Evelyn Waugh," 7on, 83, 87–88, 259
Jervis, Steven A., "Evelyn Waugh, *Vile Bodies,* and the Younger Generation," 130n, 259
Johnson, Bryan, 3n
Johnson, Samuel, *Rasselas,* 14
Joost, Nicholas, xi
"A Journey to Abyssinia," 146n, 255
"A Journey to Abyssinia—Alarums and Excursions," 146n, 255
"A Journey to Abyssinia—Champagne for Breakfast," 146n, 255
Joyce, James, 3, 5, 74, 222, 250, 251; *A Portrait of the Artist as a Young Man,* 251; *Work in Progress,* 73, 80
Jungmann sisters, 130

Kellner, Bruce, *Carl Van Vechten and the Irreverent Decades,* 38n, 48, 259
Keynes, John Maynard, 248
Kindersley-Guinness wedding, 133
Kinlock, Kitty, 131
Kinross, Lord (See Balfour, Patrick)

Kipling, Rudyard, 7, 68, 82, 223
Knox, Ronald, 80, 176, 247–249
Kolek, Leszek, xi
Kylsant-Henderson wedding, 131

Labels (see also *A Bachelor Abroad*),
    5in, 72, 131, 146, 161
Lactantius, 52
LaFrance, Marston, xi, 26; "Context
    and Structure of Evelyn Waugh's
    Brideshead Revisited," 26n, 259
Lawrence, D. H., 3, 5; *The Man Who
    Died*, 8
Lear, Edward, 137
"Let the Marriage Ceremony Mean
    Something," 129
Leavis, F. R., 88
Léger, Fernand, 39
Lentfoeher, Sister Thérèse, "My Meet-
    ing with Evelyn Waugh," 106n, 259
Letters, ix, 12, 22, 48, 54, 60, 64, 68,
    71, 81, 83, 85, 86n, 90–93, 105–108,
    110, 128, 129, 145n, 173, 177, 192n,
    232n, 237, 241n, 243, 255
Lewis, Wyndham, *Satire and Fiction*,
    70n
Linck, Charles E., Jr., xi, xii, 145n;
    "The Bright Young People in *Vile
    Bodies*, 128n, 130n, 259
"Literary Style in England and Amer-
    ica," 80
Little Learning, A, 54, 58, 117, 118n,
    119–121, 125, 126, 138n, 145n, 179,
    181, 183, 187, 247n, 255
Littlewood, Ian, 187; *The Writings of
    Evelyn Waugh*, 187, 259
Lodge, David, 27
Long, Huey, 204
Love Among the Ruins, xiv, 6, 27, 115,
    220–244, 256
"Love Among the Underdogs," 44n,
    256
Loved One, The, 27, 61–63, 82, 84n,
    87n, 220, 225n, 226, 231n, 235, 256

Macaulay, Rose, "Evelyn Waugh," 57n,
    259
Malaher family, 118
"Man Hollywood Hates, The," 81n
"Manager of 'The Kremlin,' The," 126
Mansfield, Katherine, 251
Marcus, Steven, "Evelyn Waugh and

the Art of Entertainment," 4n, 89n,
    259
Maria Pasqua, 91
Marjoribanks, Edward, 131
Maugham, W. Somerset, 216, 252;
    Cakes and Ale, 73, 77, 216n, 259;
    Christmas Holiday, 77
Maugham, Mrs. W. Somerset, 131, 135
McDonnell, Jacqueline, 44n; *Waugh on
    Women*, 36n, 175n, 259
McEachern, Neil, 132, 138
McHale, Brian, 3n; "Why Is the En-
    glish Novel So Boring?" 3
McKerrow, R. B., 168
Meckier, Jerome, xi
Men at Arms, 226, 228
Merchant of Venice, The, 241
Merton, Thomas, xiii; *Elected Silence*,
    93–105, 93n, 107, 108, 165, 259; *The
    Seven Storey Mountain*, 92–105, 92n,
    107, 108, 165, 259; *The Waters of Si-
    lence*, 107–111, 107n, 259; *The Waters
    of Siloe*, 105–110, 107n, 259
Messel, Oliver, 133
Mexico: An Object Lesson, 79n, 191–202,
    222–223, 256
Miles, Peter, "Improving Culture,"
    215n, 259
Miller, Arthur, *All My Sons*, 218
Mills, Elliott, *The Decline and Fall of the
    British Empire*, 246
"Mr. Isherwood and Friend," 11n
Mitford, Diana, 131n
Mitford, Jessica, *Daughters and Rebels*,
    134n, 259
Mitford, Nancy, 12n, 26n, 30n, 91–92,
    133; *The Blessing*, 92; *Love in a Cold
    Climate*, 92; *The Pursuit of Love*, 91
Monsignor Ronald Knox, 25n, 56n, 176,
    256
Moore, G. E., 248
Morgan, Mrs. Evan, 135
Morris, William, 54; *News from No-
    where*, 27
Mortimer, John, 81; Television version
    of *Brideshead Revisited*, 166
Mortimer, Raymond, 80
Moses, Henry, 115
"Multa Pecunia," 119

"Neglected Masterpiece, A," 72
Nichols, Beverley, 30–48 passim;
    Crazy Pavements, 31–48 passim, 259

Ninety-Two Days, 51, 81n, 123n, 191n, 200, 256

O'Brien, Kate, *Pray for the Wanderer,* 71n
O'Connor, Flannery, "A Good Man Is Hard to Find," 237; "On Her Own Work," 237n, 259
O'Connor, William Van, *Forms of Modern Fiction,* 17n, 258
Oke, Richard, *Frolic Wind,* 69n
Ordeal of Gilbert Pinfold, The, 4n, 53, 56n, 61, 82, 89n, 100–101, 101n, 178, 188, 256
Orwell, George, 245–253; *Animal Farm,* 237; "Boys' Weeklies," 247; *A Clergyman's Daughter,* 252; *Coming Up for Air,* 10n; "England Your England," 238; *Nineteen Eighty-Four,* 237, 241, 243, 244
"Out of Depth," 222

Pakenham, Frank, 90, 131; *Born to Believe,* 90n; *Five Lives,* 90n, 259
Pares, Richard, 137n
Parker, Hershel, 167; *Flawed Texts and Verbal Icons,* xiii, 167n, 167–177, 259
Peacock, Thomas Love, 14
Pelly, Denis, 135, 136, 145n
Pelly, Mrs. Denis (Elizabeth Ponsonby), 135, 137
Peters, A. D., 77, 128, 152, 173, 228
Philippians, Epistle to, 139
Picasso, Pablo, 134, 239
"Pilgrim's Progress: A tale of the near future," 226
Pistol Troop Magazine, 117
Plunkett-Greene, "Babe," 136, 145n
Plunkett-Greene, David, 132, 145n
Ponsonby, Baron, 145n
Ponsonby, Elizabeth, 133, 135, 136, 145n
Pope, Alexander, 15; *Dunciad,* 14; *The Rape of the Lock,* 21
Pound, Ezra, 250, 251
Poussin, Nicholas, 32
Powell, Anthony, 12n, 26n, 64, 80, 81, 88n, 245–253; *Afternoon Men,* 9; *A Dance to the Music of Time,* 82; *Messengers of Day,* 53n, 259
Powers, J. F., 80
Priestley, J. B., 188; "What Was Wrong with Pinfold," 188n, 259

Proust, Marcel, 46
Pryce-Jones, Alan, *Little Innocents,* 118n, 259
Put Out More Flags, 9, 10, 25, 61, 64–65, 79, 87n, 181, 233, 256
Pynchon, Thomas, x

Reed, Sir Carol, 228
"Religion in State Schools," 221n, 256
Remote People, xiii, 53n, 57, 69n, 146–163, 256
"Return of Lancelot, The," 125
Richards, Grant, *Author Hunting,* 21n, 260
Richardson, Samuel, 16
Robbery Under Law (see *Mexico: An Object Lesson*), 256
Rolo, Charles J., *The World of Evelyn Waugh,* 118n
"Ronald Firbank," 70, 126
Rossetti, Dante Gabriel, 57, 146
Rossetti: His Life and Works, 54, 57, 164, 256
Rosten, Leo, 75
Ruskin, John, 54

Safire, William, 72
Saki (H. H. Munro), *The Unbearable Bassington,* 7–8
Savage, D. S., "The Innocence of Evelyn Waugh," 89n, 260
"Scenes of Clerical Life," 80
Scoop, 9, 51, 59–61, 64–65, 76, 77, 87n, 145, 226, 256
Scott-King's Modern Europe, 220, 226
Searle, John R., 168
Selassie, Haile, 146
Shaw, George Bernard, 8, 251
"Sheriff's Daughter, The," 118
Shroder, Maurice Z., "The Novel as a Genre," 4n, 260
Siddal, Elizabeth, 54
Sillitoe, Alan, 10
Sims, George, F., 152n
Sissons, Michael, 179n
Sitwell, Osbert, 31n
Smith, Lady Eleanor, 130–132, 134–136
Smith, Rowland, 241n
Spark, Muriel, 68; *The Comforters,* 82
Spengler, Oswald, 8
Stanley, Dean, *Eastern Church,* 46
Stannard, Martin, xi; *Evelyn Waugh: The Critical Heritage,* 29n, 258; *Eve-*

lyn Waugh: The Early Years 1903–1939,
129, 134, 143n, 200n, 260; "The
Mystery of the Missing Manuscript,"
131n, 139n, 260
Stopes, Marie, 221; "Religion in State
Schools," 221n, 260
Stopp, Frederick J., 66, 103, 236; *Eve-
lyn Waugh: Portrait of an Artist,* 66n,
103n, 236n, 260
Sutherland, J. A., *Fiction and the Fictio
Industry,* 3n
Sutro, John, 130, 154
Swift, Jonathan, 146
Swinburne, Algernon Charles, "Ata-
lanta,"124
Sword of Honour, 10n, 26, 44n, 52, 59,
61, 63–64, 87n, 116, 169, 181, 204,
223, 223n, 228, 244, 256
Sykes, Christopher, *Evelyn Waugh: A
Biography,* 77n–78n, 192n, 260
"Sympathetic Passenger, The," 126
Synge, John Millington, 71

Tactical Exercise, 5n, 229n, 256
Tait, Stephen, *The Rhubarb Tree,* 44
Taylor, A. J. P., *English History 1914–
1945,* 8n, 260
"Technician, The," 77
"Temple at Thatch, The," 126
Tennyson, Alfred Lord, 241; *Idylls of the
King,* 63
Terry, T. Philip, *Terry's Guide to Mex-
ico,* 196–197, 197n, 260
"'Tess'—As a 'Modern' Sees It," 71,
256
Thackeray, William Makepeace, *Vanity
Fair,* 6
Thérèse, Sister M., 106, 107; "Waugh's
Letters to Thomas Merton," 97,
111n, 260
They Were Still Dancing (see also *Remote
People*), 53
Thorpe, James, 167, 168, 174; *Principles
of Textual Criticism,* 167n, 260
Tourist in Africa, 52n, 56, 57, 111n, 151,
256
Tree, Iris, 133
Tree, Viola, 136, 144
Trilling, Lionel, x, 5, 88; *The Liberal
Imagination* 5n, 260
Trollope, Anthony, *Barchester Towers,*
193

Turgenev, Ivan, *A Sportsman's Sketches,*
33
"Turning Over New Leaves," 72, 83
"Tutor's Tale, The," 127, 127n
Twain, Mark, *Pudd'nhead Wilson,* 169
"Twilight of Language, The," 125, 126

Unconditional Surrender, 12, 28–29, 44,
57, 115, 145, 176, 218
Urquhart, F. F. ("Sligger"), 248

Van Doren, Mark, 93
Van Vechten, Carl, 30–48 passim; *Blind
Bow-Boy, The,* 31–42 passim, 260;
Firecrackers, 31–41 passim, 260; *Par-
ties,* 31, 41–43, 260; *Spider Boy,* 31
Vico, Giambattista, 8
Vile Bodies, xiii, 15, 20, 22, 25, 31, 47–
48, 55, 59–63, 70–72, 87, 87n, 126,
128–146, 181, 247, 256
Vincec, Sister Stephanie, 168
Voltaire, 81; *Candide,* 14, 15, 257
Vonnegut, Kurt, 243

Walker, Ronald G., *Infernal Paradise:
Mexico and the Modern English Novel,*
192n, 260
Walter, Eugene (see Ellison, Ralph)
"War and the Younger Generation,
The," 138, 181
Warren, Robert Penn, *All the King's
Men,* xiii, 203–219, 257, 260; "*All the
King's Men:* The Matrix of Experi-
ence," 215n
Wasson, Richard, 67; "*A Handful of
Dust:* Critique of Victorianism," 67n,
260
Watkin, Fr. Aelred, 91
Watt, Ian, 16; *The Rise of the Novel,* 4n,
260
Watteau, Jean Antoine, 133
Waugh in Abyssinia, 57
Waugh, Alec, 69, 117, 123, 179, 180,
182, 247; *The Loom of Youth,* 123–
134, 179; *My Brother Evelyn and Other
Portraits,* 117n
Waugh, Arthur, 117
Waugh, Mrs. Evelyn (Gardner), 133,
134
Wells, H. G., 249, 252
Wesley, John, 141
When the Going Was Good, 191n, 256

White, Martin, 132
Whittemore, Thomas, 156–158
Wilson, Angus, "The House Party
  Novels," 20n, 260
Wilson, Edmund, 260; "Splendors and
  Miseries of Evelyn Waugh," 224n
Wimsatt, W. K., 167
Wodehouse, P. G., 128, 140, 252;
  Laughing Gas, 74–75; *The Week-End
  Wodehouse*, 77
"Woman's Curse, A," 117–118
Woodard, F. A., 185
Woolf, Virginia, 3, 249, 252, 253; *Or-

lando*, 46; *A Room of One's Own*,
  249
Work Suspended, 5n, 52, 54–55, 55n, 60,
  61, 75n, 76–78, 78n, 179, 188, 215,
  246n, 250, 256
World of Evelyn Waugh, The, 118, 256
World to Come, The, 120–121, 126
Wren, Christopher, 8

Yeats, William Butler, 8, 222
"Yet Another Visit to Brideshead,"
  175n, 260
Yorke, Henry (see Henry Green)